Teaching Children as the Spirit Leads

by K.J. Allison

WITH A
RESOURCE HANDBOOK
FOR RUNNING YOUR
PRESCHOOL PROGRAM

LOGOS INTERNATIONAL Plainfield, New Jersey

Teaching Children as the Spirit Leads
© 1977 by Logos International
All Rights Reserved
Printed in the United States of America
International Standard Book Number: 0-88270-192-4
Library of Congress Catalog Card Number: 77-81946
Published by Logos International, Plainfield, New Jersey 07061

Teaching
Children
as the
Spirit Leads

To God our Father
To Jesus my Savior who loves little children
To the Holy Spirit who patiently teaches me
and
To those who care about children and who have encouraged
me
my parents
my husband
my brothers and sisters in Christ
Marge
Paul
Merrily
Francois
Saunny
Jim
Azra
Barbara
and
To all the children I have had the privilege of knowing

In memory of Dr. Sarah Gudschinsky, my teacher, sister in the Lord, and International Literacy Coordinator for Wycliffe Bible Translators and Summer Institute of Linguistics.

A special thanks to my husband, without whose patient editorial work and suggestions this book would not have been published. Thanks also to Carey Moore, former editor of Wycliffe's *In Other Words*, for his encouragement and editorial assistance and to Rev. Paul Morell for his valuable suggestions and corrections. Thanks also to Saralee Debley for the preliminary typing of the manuscript, suggestions, and correspondence with me and the publisher. Lastly, I wish to thank Liz Voth, Fe Alberstine, and Alison Bari for the typing of the final manuscript after revision.

CONTENTS

PART ONE:

TEACHING CHILDREN AS THE SPIRIT LEADS

PART TWO:

RESOURCE HANDBOOK
FOR RUNNING YOUR OWN
PRESCHOOL PROGRAM

PREFACE

Through prayer, perseverance, study, and experimentation, I found an approach to teaching which worked for me in widely varying situations: a public school in inner-city Los Angeles, a Christian day-care center in Norman, Oklahoma, a church nursery in Dallas, a Tzeltal Indian village in southern Mexico and a missionary station in the Philippines. Central to this personal teaching approach are these important tenets:

1. Do not do for a child what he can do for himself.
2. A carefully preplanned environment brings order to the classroom and calmness to the children. It also permits child management of the environment.
3. Each child has abundant resources already stored within him; find out what these are and build on them.
4. There is no such thing as religious training and secular training—Jesus is all day long.
5. If it isn't fun, don't teach it!
6. In every situation, be open to the leading of the Holy Spirit.
7. Rely on the Holy Spirit to select and guide your Bible lessons.

In the following discussion I cite examples from my own experience to help illustrate methods and situations. They are not held up as examples to be emulated, but are given as a testimony of God's dynamic development program at work in His imperfect people. In other words, if I can follow the Holy Spirit to successful teaching, so can you.

The picture-stories in chapter eleven were originally done at the Free Methodist Day-Care Center in Norman, Oklahoma. The stories are the actual words dictated by the children of that center. Photos were taken by Len Whalley, Bruce Humphrey, and my husband Joe. All Scripture quoted is from the New American Standard Version, unless otherwise noted. Final editing was done by Claire Rundle.

This book is written from a classroom perspective. It is obviously directed toward preschool teachers, the parent-surrogates of our day. But it is also written for parents, to whom the God-given responsibility of training their children rightfully belongs. It is my hope that the information given in this volume will help parents both at home and in choosing a preschool or day-care center program, should they find it necessary. Finally, this book is written to program directors who have the opportunity of shaping programs which will glorify God, inspire teachers, and properly guide little children.

Teaching Children as the Spirit Leads

1

SET FREE

You shall know the truth, and the truth shall make you free.

John 8:32

I stood before the straight lines of highly disciplined young girls. At my word, they sprang into action: "Attennn-tion!" Instantly twenty-four shiny batons flashed into the sun. As they moved through their snappy routines, not an eyelash nor a wiggle was out of place. They were champion baton twirlers; they were my pride and joy.

"Teaching is your thing! Why don't you become a schoolteacher?" mother suggested.

"*School* teacher?" I replied with disdain.

"Why not? You're a natural—just look at your students—"

"But that's not *school* teaching."

"I thought you liked teaching—"

"Not *school* teaching. I'll never become a *school* teacher."

My seemingly contradictory attitude was confusing to my mother. If one likes teaching, obviously one should be a schoolteacher. And what's wrong with being a schoolteacher? Nothing, of course, except that I was not free to choose that option. My thinking was distorted by certain false values and irrational attitudes.

"Everybody is a schoolteacher" I thought. "It's so common—so predictable. If you're a female college

1

graduate, you're likely to be either a nurse or a teacher. Not me! Absolutely no status in that!" I was bound by this kind of thinking. I needed to be set free.

Within two months after graduation from college, I was set free. It happened like this: For about six weeks I had been longing to make things right between me and God, longing for a fresh start in life. Then I heard that Jesus died in my place. Since He was the one who paid my sin debt to God, He was the one I had to go through to be reconciled to God.

With awe, I placed my trust in Jesus Christ as my personal Savior. From that moment to this very day, I began to be set free from false values. But I was not just freed *from* something. Once I saw myself as God's new creation, I was also freed to *become* something—to become the real person God intended. I found myself free to develop the natural gifts He had placed within me and, at the same time, free to tap God's own resources. Now I could be useful.

Three years after this freeing process began, it was to be tested. I amazed myself by joyfully beginning a teacher-training program for the Los Angeles inner-city schools. Armed with Proverbs 31:26 ". . . And the teaching of kindness is on her tongue," I began my internship as a kindergarten teacher in the Watts district of Los Angeles.

When I taught baton twirling, my students were eager and receptive. They wanted to please me. But I found that public school teaching was very different. Many of the kindergarteners were suspicious and resentful, not only of school but also of white teachers. Suddenly it hit me! All the time I had been teaching baton twirling, my ego was being enlarged. My students had fed my ego, and that was my chief reward. But now my ego was being starved!

My first few wrenching weeks in Watts revealed how radically my values had changed. I found that I really did want to teach, whether or not it fed my ego. My reward, I saw, would come from a child's excitement over learning. I plunged even more resolutely into teaching, but I soon

2

encountered new difficulties. It wasn't long before I realized that I needed answers I hadn't found in college courses. Problem after problem served to keep me in a constant state of frustration.

The school system called for the use of many workbooks, which I felt were largely too advanced and too abstract for many of my students. I could see that the children needed direct access to their environment more than "seat work." Yet, for fear of the system, which demanded finished workbooks as proof of "learning," I passed out the books and tried to guide the children through the two-dimensional exercises. The class, made up of energetic children on different levels of development, was difficult to control. Thoroughly exasperated, one day I "blew my cool"!

"I am sick and tired of *standing* here trying to get you to listen to these workbook directions—"

I was interrupted by a boy sincerely trying to be helpful.

"Then why don't you *sit down*, Miz Allis?"

The suggestion made sense. I did sit down, and began to reevaluate my methods, philosophy, and motives. I began to seek God's help and wisdom in all aspects of teaching.

The Lord brought to mind an incident which at the time had seemed insignificant. A few years earlier I had accompanied a friend to a nursery school. There the teacher showed me beads that formed a square. That was a revelation to me: square numbers could be physically handled; they were tangible! In all my own schooling things were learned by rote, and as such were really never grasped experientially. Concepts were seldom relevant. School was something to be endured because our cultural system demanded it.

From my own experience, I knew that learning in an abstract and superficial way never brought me in touch with the beauty and excitement of really understanding a part of God's creation. It seemed a shame that anyone should miss such an adventure. As I continued teaching kindergarten, I saw that I was largely armed with the same methods that

3

had impoverished my own education, and I also saw that a great many new teachers today have the same problem—despite the lip service paid to the term "discovery method." I knew I had to find a better way!

Finding this better way took me searching through various philosophies, methods, and educational theories; it took me through lectures, classes, and books. It drove me to observe and participate in various programs and schools. It forced me to experiment and evaluate. Sometimes it led me to dead ends, contradictions and confusion. But through all this, I continued to seek God's help to sift the worthwhile from the worthless, and He was faithful to lead me. Without the guidance of His Holy Spirit, I never would have made it through the quagmire of conflicting ideas, nor would I have had the courage to apply Christian premises to every teaching situation that I encountered, with the purpose of leading children to Christ.

I have spoken to many Christian parents and teachers in the course of my quest, and I know that untold numbers face the same problems and frustrations that I faced in trying to teach their children adequately, while still maintaining a fully integrated Christian approach to life. Perhaps you are among this number. If so, I invite you to come along with me and share my adventure in learning.

2

THE TEACHER OR "THE METHOD"?

But if any of you lacks wisdom, let him ask God, who gives to all men generously and without reproach, and it will be given to him.

James 1:5

Seeing a little child's face light up with the thrill of discovery is to the teacher what applause is to the performer. But how do you bring about that thrill? What teaching method productively guides a child's mind? I've come to think that it's whatever method you believe in.

The reason I can make such a statement is this: Just as it is true for the learner that he hasn't learned until he has "discovered" a bit of knowledge for himself, so also it is true for the teacher. A teacher can never teach by a method until she has "discovered" it for herself. Whether it be her own method or a modification of someone else's, she has to feel it's hers and be sold on its effectiveness.

Every great teacher has believed passionately in his own method. Laubach, Dewey, Montessori, and others, Christian and non-Christian—each believed that he had found the way. Yet their ways were vastly different from each other. One insisted on order and precision; another believed "tidiness" was futile. One believed in phonics, another in sight reading. One stressed materials; another felt materials were unnecessary. Some were disciplinarian, others extremely permissive. Yet, all these approaches worked!

5

When a method is proven to work, people want to mass produce it, and sell it "in cans." But many methods that are successful with their authors fall apart when other teachers try to copy them. Why? Because success depends not upon the method, but upon the teacher. A good teacher is something like an artist. Her work must be fresh and original to be really good. A warmed-over method doesn't have the needed spontaneity. It must be an intensely personal approach capable of meeting the needs of particular children in a particular setting. Furthermore, the teacher must feel comfortable with it.

Does this mean good teachers just grope around until they hit on success? Some do just that; but the Spirit-led teacher can go directly to God for help in analyzing the problem, defining the goals, and working out a solution. To know whether you're a successful teacher, you need to know the instructional goals you plan to attain. The Christian teacher must dig into the Scriptures to determine what teaching goals and methods are in harmony with God's goals. A method may be successful in the eyes of the world, but if it's based on values that poison a student's mind it can hardly be called successful by Christian standards.

Part of the secret in being a good teacher is tapping one's own God-given creativity. What keeps most teachers from finding their own personal approach is fear—fear of failure, fear of losing control of the class, fear of what the principal will think, fear of not using the provided materials in the prescribed way.

In most schools, teachers are provided kits and workbooks designed by experts. Who dares not follow the advice of an expert? So, unfortunately, the teachers try to push the children through the materials like so many cogs on an assembly line.

Not that these materials should not be used. The problem is that most teachers do not realize what the materials can and cannot do, so they don't understand how to use them most effectively. Materials are tools; they are not teachers,

6

nor do they necessarily teach. The implanting of knowledge in the mind cannot come alone from sequence charts, curriculum guides, workbooks, etc. It must also come from the real world, firsthand, in a way that stimulates the inner mind. Real things, real events, real interpersonal relationships—only after such exposure can a young child truly appreciate the contents of a workbook. Workbooks, primers, and the like are fun and stimulate new ideas, only after a volume of firsthand experiences has been stored within.

In my first kindergarten, we were obliged to use preaddition workbooks. Generally, these were a credit to their expert authors. They were a valuable tool in their place. But their place was not, in my opinion, to be used en masse: "Now we will all turn the page and do thus and so. . . ."

Here's how I settled on using them. I presented the major concepts to be taught to the children both individually and in short group demonstrations throughout the days prior to the introduction of the workbooks. Then during the math period I would review a concept, reduce it to a two-dimensional level, and show the children how to proceed with their workbooks on their own.

After the very first day, everyone was on a different level. A few children finished their workbooks in three days, while others spent the entire school year on them. Then what happened to the review of concepts during the math period? I dropped it!

Those who were finished with their workbooks worked with concrete items to develop other math concepts. For instance, I gave them counting cubes, which I had glued together to represent number concepts. The children were able to work out their own .addition and subtraction problems until these operations became clear and automatic. For example, after taking an "8 block" and lining it up with a "3 block," the child would have to experiment with other blocks until he found the "5 block" which, when placed on top of the "3 block," matched the height of the "8 block." Then the child would write down his findings. Thus "8=3+5" was made concrete. The children's math papers were products of their own experiments—nothing rote about those papers!

Meanwhile, the children who were still working on their preaddition workbooks were free to consult with me, and indeed, were required to do so before proceeding on to new sections. As each child completed his entire workbook, he was allowed to take it home and keep it. This proved to be a great incentive. Some children chose to work on their workbooks even during their free-time activities!

Thus, after daring to try a different way of using workbooks, I found an approach which worked for me. I no longer dreaded math sessions, but instead, I found myself looking forward to them. And the workbooks, which triggered my breaking away from stereotyped performances, became a profitable tool for me and an enjoyable exercise for the children.

What are some of the qualities that most successful teachers have in common? I have observed that among the most prominent are:

> humility
> courage
> resourcefulness
> passion
> tenderness
> perseverance

A teacher must be humble to admit she needs help. If she's humble, she can learn from her students. If she isn't, she won't learn from anyone. If she's humble, she isn't likely to become rigid in her ways.

She has to have courage to break with old systems if she sees they aren't reaching her students. She has to have courage to experiment, to try different techniques, and to risk failure.

She must be resourceful, not stumbling over deficiencies in equipment or programs, but seeking to find new outlets, new ways and new ideas even when the old way still seems sufficient—and especially when it doesn't.

She must teach with a passion, throwing herself into it as if her life depended on it. She must care enough never to be satisfied with halfway jobs or canned answers. Her slogan should be Colossians 3:23: "Whatever you do, do your work heartily, as for the Lord rather than for men. . . ."

She must realize her responsibility towards the young, impressionable lives she influences, and must tread softly. Tenderness must be her companion, lest her insensitivity crush her students.

And she must not give up. Some teachers never reach their potential because they just give up. She has to want to be successful.

So it's not the method, it's the teacher. A Christian teacher needs, above all, a vital, growing walk with the Lord. We are ambassadors for Christ; we must faithfully represent Him. And if the kingdom of God and His righteousness are first in our lives, we can know that God will guide us to bless the little children.

Climbing, jumping, swinging, pumping. . . . Active play develops coordination and socialization.

Little children like to use muscles.

3

GUIDELINES FROM GOD

To know wisdom and instruction . . .
To receive instruction in wise behavior . . .
To give . . . to the youth knowledge and discretion . . .
A wise man will hear and increase in learning. . . .

Proverbs 1:2-5

To be successful, the teacher must be in touch with how children learn. We must work with, not against, the inherent plan of growth and development that is placed within every child by the Creator. In order to work in harmony with God's creation, let's take our guidelines from the very principles that He, himself, uses in teaching His children.

This is the way God teaches:	**Therefore:**
1. God uses "life" as lesson material.	1. We also should use "life" as our lesson material.
2. He teaches by concrete examples—not abstractions.	2. We also should teach by concrete examples.
3. He presents concepts in order, carrying each new revelation on the shoulders of what we already know.	3. We should present concepts in order, carrying the unknown on the shoulders of the known.
4. He gives us just the amount of knowledge we can assimilate at the time.	4. We should follow the natural learning pattern of children.

12

5. God's ways are reflected in the natural order of the universe.	5. We should prepare the physical environment of our classrooms to reflect His order.
6. His Word is the ultimate authority.	6. We must base our authority on God's Word.
7. God showed us how to live by becoming a living example.	7. We must set an appropriate behavioral example.
8. God tells us what His expectations are in clear, positive, specific terms.	8. We also should state our expectations in clear, positive, specific terms.
9. God is consistent.	9. We also have to be consistent.
10. God trusts us.	10. We should trust God, trust our students.
11. God loves us.	11. We must love our students.
12. God reinforces His lessons.	12. We also should reinforce our lessons.

These principles have all been borne out by secular research in teaching little children. God has provided them for us—let's follow them!

Use "life" as your lesson material.

In His teaching, Jesus always met the situation of the moment. When people came to Him, He used everyday examples; when people didn't come specifically to hear Him, He used what they were doing at the time to illustrate spiritual points. When a woman came to draw water at a well where He was resting, He didn't suggest that she leave her task in the middle and have a theological discussion. He spoke to her about what she was doing at the time, and He led her naturally from physical water to living water.

Yet, in spite of this example, with children we often do not respect their interests or tasks, but rudely push in and insist they stop whatever they are doing and listen to us moralize. For example, it is common to impose on children a "Bible story"—a term which is, unfortunately, sometimes applied to any story that sounds religious, whether or not it is based on the Bible.

We need to follow our Lord's example and teach from life,

13

following the lead of the child. What is the child interested in right now? Center on that!

Recently I was teaching a Sunday school class for four and five-year-olds. This particular Sunday, I felt I should give a lesson about following Jesus. As usual, I did not announce my lesson so that I could be more open to God's leading. Did the Lord want me to give the lesson I had tentatively selected, or something else? I looked to the children's interest at the time as part of His leadership.

The children were talking about their toys. I listened, commenting here and there and asking questions.

"Road builders! That's what I have. They're trucks that make the roads," Keith said, illustrating his words with his hands.

"My favorite toy is a racer. It's a super-fast red racer," said Luther, nodding his head enthusiastically.

At that, I turned to the blackboard and began to draw a road.

"What's that?"

"It's a road," I commented, "like Keith's road builders build"—

"Like for my racer to go on!"

I began to draw footprints on the road.

"What's that?"

"Is it a car? No, it doesn't look very much like one. . . ."

"Feet! Is it feet?" guessed Richy.

"You mean 'feet tracks,' " corrected David.

Then I drew two children, Jesus (whose footprints I had already drawn), a cliff in back of the children, and "heaven" in front of Jesus. The children were with me. They wanted to hear about this picture-story.

As for your own selection of meaningful materials, let a little child lead you. Fifteen-month-old Benjamin's first words were "tractor," "bike," "cookie," and "kitty." This vocabulary represented his own firsthand concrete experiences—those that were particularly interesting to him. The young child's interests are lodged in his physical

14

environment. The whole world around you, and all the abundant lessons of life, are your teaching materials. Use them!

2. Teach by concrete examples.

God taught the children of Israel through concrete, physical means. Those lessons of history became their collective concepts. With them, they were being prepared as a people for more abstract spiritual truths. When the children of Israel prepared to break camp and march in the wilderness, they did so in complete battle array. Later, the more abstract principle in the New Testament of putting on the whole armor of God had a meaning to the Jewish Christians that was rooted in actual past events.

So it is today. Whether we are dealing with mathematics or biblical concepts, nature and events give us concrete examples. We need to "plug into" these examples. If we are observant, finding concrete examples in the physical world to illustrate abstract academic concepts is easy. But with biblical concepts there is more required: Unless we know the Word of God and let the Holy Spirit lead us, we will not see the spiritual object lessons around us. The more we know of the Bible, and the more we genuinely want to know God, the more we can recognize His voice in everyday events and the easier it becomes to show the children His ways. Without a real yearning for God, object lessons, even if pointed out to us by someone else, are frequently dead. We, as teachers, need to know the Bible and be open to the Holy Spirit, lest we become "blind leaders."

3. Present concepts in order, carrying the unknown on the shoulders of the known.

Ultimately, it is God who quickens knowledge within us; but enlightenment usually comes after He has prepared us through more elementary concepts and means. Who has not had the experience of hearing a truth, yet not understanding it until other more basic truths had been learned? Then it

15

becomes real.

This appears to be true of all learning. In teaching math concepts to little children, one concept must be built upon another. When a new concept is presented, if the preceding concept is not already a part of the learner, the child will just stare in bewilderment—no matter how concrete the example before him.

4. Follow the natural learning pattern of children.

A child's intellectual as well as physical development follows an orderly progression; there are periods when he is sensitive to receive just a certain type of knowledge. Even a child's art goes through well-defined stages. The teacher needs to know these stages, be able to recognize them in the child, and be prepared to teach accordingly.

Researchers have determined that in language acquisition, for example, the child constructs his own model, constantly comparing it with other models around him. He continues to refine it according to a set pattern of progressive stages. Likewise, in other areas of learning, including the acquisition of reading skills, the child constructs his own knowledge.*

The conclusions of child-development researchers confirm the fact that children learn best by encountering reality and then wrestling with it until they construct their own internal replica, which eventually becomes a part of them. This must be done in step-wise fashion, from simple to complex concepts. I have found that an active approach, in which the child's whole being is engaged in firsthand discovery, best fulfills the requirements of true education. In this approach play and work complement each other, and the teacher acts as a guide, assuming a quiet, humble, nondominating

---

* *Frank Smith, Understanding Reading: Psycholinguistic Analysis of Reading and Learning to Read.* (New York: Holt, Rinehart and Winston, Inc., 1971), p. 50. For further discussion of the research cited here, see Part Two, section v, reference works by DiLeo, Featherstone, Montessori, and Piaget.

16

attitude. The children learn from life.

5. Prepare the physical environment to reflect God's order.

Since young children learn best by firsthand interaction with their environment, the teacher can make their tasks easier by preparing the environment in an orderly way. Orderly presentation of concepts is aided by a classroom environment that reflects a securely ordered arrangement. Furthermore, to be orderly is less fatiguing. It is also more natural. Look at nature; what do you see? Order and precision.

Looking at some classrooms, one occasionally gets the idea that "order" is a dirty word. It is well for the Christian teacher to remember that secular classrooms reflect the world system, and the world system is rapidly heading towards complete chaos. Admittedly, some classrooms reflect this more than others. To want to bring order, reason, and predictability to a classroom environment is a natural, harmonious, and Godly attitude. Don't be intimidated by the world!

6. Base authority on God's Word.

The world would also have us think that "obedience" is a dirty word. But the Bible says, "Children, obey your parents in the Lord, for this is right" (Ephesians 6:1). As teachers, we are acting in place of parents, and children are to obey us. This authority is biblical. It is not an arbitrary authority determined by a self-willed adult. It is God giving us the sacred right to train children. But such authority is a two-sided coin: With it goes responsibility. God will judge us according to how we use His authority—whether according to the flesh or according to the Spirit.

I share these thoughts with the children I teach. I've found that the idea of authority based on God's Word is well accepted, and the children come to expect me to enforce standards when external enforcing is necessary; otherwise,

17

I would be disobeying God! We may all be equal in God's eyes as individuals, but because of different ages and positions, we have different roles. This kind of understanding of who we are in relation to God, and what He expects from us, gives real security. Explaining God's plan for us has brought to my classrooms a relaxed atmosphere, conducive to learning. I have not had to grope for values or ways to interact, because I have applied the values taught in Scripture.

For example, my tape recorder had been accidently broken by a former class. My husband cautioned me not to let the children handle our new one. I explained this to my class and told them God's rules for wives is that they obey their husbands. The children readily appreciated my position and reminded one another not to touch the tape recorder. They didn't think badly of my husband, either. They were beginning to understand that each of us is responsible before God according to the rules that God has laid down for us in our particular roles.

7. Set an appropriate behavioral example.

As a teacher, your major role is to teach by example. You can't expect the children to respond favorably if you tell them to do something and then disregard your own words. The effectiveness of your message depends on how closely your actions parallel your words.

Some teachers misunderstand this role. They feel they must never make a mistake, because they fear they will lose their image in front of the children. Since errors are inevitable, what this amounts to is never admitting to errors. Such teachers are self-deceived. Children are extremely perceptive to nonverbal messages. They are learning all the time, negatively or positively. Whether actions are intentional or incidental, they see it all.

The solution is simple—relax, be honest and straightforward, be transparent. Treat children with the same respect with which you wish to be treated. If you

18

expect children to admit their mistakes and apologize, you must do the same with them. Treat your mistakes and theirs as a matter of course. Admit errors without fanfare, apologize quickly, make amends where amendable, and go on; don't make your mistake or anyone else's a major problem. Errors are part of life, and since they are, it is important that the children learn how to handle them. Your example can go a long way toward making honesty easy.

8. State your expectations in clear, positive, specific terms.

You can make learning easier by positive behavioral suggestions rather than negative commands. This concept was central to Jesus' teaching approach: "You shall love your neighbor as yourself . . . Love one another. . . .Honor your father and your mother. . . .Let your light shine before men in such a way that they may see your good works, and glorify your Father who is in heaven. Enter by the narrow gate. . . ."*

As with the majority of God's commandments, these are concise and positive. When training children, we should follow this pattern.

State the behavior you would like to see in concise, positive terms rather than negative suggestions. For instance, when introducing a book to children, emphasize how pretty and clean the book is, rather than suggesting that the children are not to scribble in it. It's possible the thought of scribbling hasn't entered the minds of some children. Why plant this negative idea and give the children a temptation to fight? Carefully, deliberately, step by step with a minimum of verbal explanation, show them how to use their materials. By your precise demonstration you make it possible for the children to establish effective work habits. If you have done your part, you can expect the

---

* *Matthew 22:39, John 15:12, Exodus 20:12, Matthew 5:16 and 7:13.*

children to do theirs. Ninety-nine percent of the time they will, because they are just as eager to learn as you are to have them learn. And most children are also eager to please.

9. Be consistent.

Consistency is basic to establishing patterns. God is consistent: His nature and values are unchanging and absolute. We can bank on Him. Ages ago, He set in motion His plan for eternal redemption, and that plan is still in effect, unalterably. His consistency calls forth our trust and confidence.

In teaching, much of your own consistency rests on a foundation of preplanning. In order to have consistency you must think out your basic standards in advance, and prepare the environment in such a way as to make your standards possible. You cannot reasonably insist that a child return an article to its place when its place is inaccessible to the child, or different each day. In order to be consistent, careful planning must precede the first purchase, the first day of school, the first move of equipment.

But consistency covers more than establishing physical patterns. It establishes an emotional climate in the classroom. If a teacher consistently displays a stable, positive attitude, the effect is security. Consistency is also basic to establishing personal credibility, and credibility is basic to trust.

10. Trust God, trust your students.

Jesus entrusted His Church with His message. He trusts the members of His Church enough to let them go in His name, to be His ambassadors. He asks us to pray and says He will answer. He calls us His friends. If Jesus, Lord of the universe, so trusts us, surely we should trust our students. After all, if we are where God wants us, and seeking His will, certainly we can expect His help. Because God has stated (2 Peter 3:9) that He is not willing that any should perish, we know He is personally interested in each child in our

20

classroom. And, if we've given out His Word, we have His promise that He is watching over it to perform it (Jeremiah 1:12). Truly then, with the whole situation committed into God's hands, we can relax and trust both Him and our students.

For a short time I worked in a church day-care center where no one seemed to have this trust. The atmosphere was charged with tension. The teachers and director were in constant fear of all sorts of improbable problems which "might happen" at any moment. Consequently, toddlers were confined to their cribs almost all day long. If they walked, it was feared that they might fall and hurt themselves. If they got hurt, the director reasoned, the church or some teacher might get sued.

The teachers did everything for the children, and the children learned practically nothing—except, perhaps, that they were incapable of attempting even the most normal jobs and had to be waited on. Three-year-olds were not allowed to cut with a blunt scissors unless a teacher stood over each child. Usually, the teachers did more than just supervise—they usually ended up doing the cutting for the child. Water play, even outside on a hot summer day, was not allowed because the children would get wet, and if they got wet they might get pneumonia.

If you see yourself in that picture—if you are so worried over your students—you are not trusting either them or the Lord. You'd better quit teaching before you have a nervous breakdown!

There can be little learning of a positive nature unless there is mutual trust between student and teacher. Furthermore, trust undergirds love.

11. Love your students.

Real love starts with God. "In this is love, not that we loved God, but that He loved us and sent His Son to be the propitiation for our sins. We love, because He first loved us" (1 John 4:10, 19). He loves us enough to allow us to use our free will. He lets us develop our muscles, spiritually and physically. He doesn't stifle our urge to explore and to grow. Instead, He provides us with opportunities to learn. He gently woos us to himself.

We should reflect our Father's love and ways to our students. If you sing "Jesus Loves Me," "Oh, How I Love Jesus," or "Jesus Loves the Little Children," you sing about love. Can the children see it on your face, hear it in your voice, see it in your dealings with them and others? If they can, they'll learn that love is more than a word in a song.

12. Reinforce your lessons.

How often and in how many ways does God communicate His love and plan of redemption to man? Over and over He has reinforced His message by revelations, analogies, examples, and symbols. Learning requires reinforcement.

Repetition is one kind of reinforcement. Whether for all of mankind or for individuals, repetition is prominent in God's teaching approach. It is interesting to note that in view of this, He has planted a love for repetition in all of us, especially in the young. Repetition is fun!

Things which are fun to a child are also reinforcing, and learning becomes joyful. If something brings a child happiness, he will continue to pursue the activity without threats or bribes. Teachers have the choice of making any given subject area a chore or a pleasure. Here's where I say, "If it isn't fun, don't teach it." It should be possible to teach anything in a way that's enjoyable to your students.

Children will spend hours breaking secret codes. Isn't that what reading is all about? Why are they willing to spend time breaking a code? So they can read the message. Therefore, reading lessons should always contain a message and not be just a lot of syllable or word drills.

Some teachers dread teaching math. No doubt they never were helped to enjoy it when they were children. But mathematics can be absolutely beautiful! Unfortunately, like so many other teachers, I didn't learn this until I was a graduate student. Little children have a desire for order and patterns. Show them and let them see for themselves the patterns and they will fall in love with math! Then they can appreciate much more the way God made and ordered His universe.

I don't recall any teacher helping me to focus on patterns in math. Besides this, I was not given concrete items with which to work whereby I could discover patterns for myself. Abstract names of operations were given either with no explanation of the terms or with unenlightening verbal abstractions for definitions. Mathematics was not fun for me. It was totally unrelated to anything that was meaningful.

A thing like a number chart can be very dull, or it can be made fun. I added color to such a chart to bring out the patterns. As soon as the children saw the colored chart, they "oooohed" and "aaaahed." By covering certain parts of the chart they became aware of other number patterns. I guided them to the patterns by covering part of the chart and asking them to read down a column—but it had to be their own personal discovery which showed them the pattern I saw. Even if we point something out, it is not the child's until he discovers it for himself.

Pegboards with colored pegs are great for beginning math concepts. Addition, subtraction, multiplication, division, square roots, and numbers can be visualized on a pegboard. A geoboard is a ⅝" board with 1½"-2" nails driven in at regular intervals, on which a child can have fun stretching rubber bands over the nails to show geometric areas.

But can "don't teach it if it isn't fun" be applied to spiritual concepts? Yes, if you apply the term "fun" as broadly as I do. To me, fun is having a zest for life—learning, enjoying, and appreciating all aspects of God's creation. And certainly, spiritual concepts encourage this zest for life, this *joie de vivre*. Jesus said, "I came that they might have life, and might have it abundantly." And Paul tells us to "rejoice . . . always (John 10:10 and Philippians 4:4). I believe that God may want us to change our worldly attitudes about what is fun, but He does not want to deprive us of it. Therefore, as I grow in the Lord, and see things more from His point of view, I expect to have more fun than I ever dreamed possible!

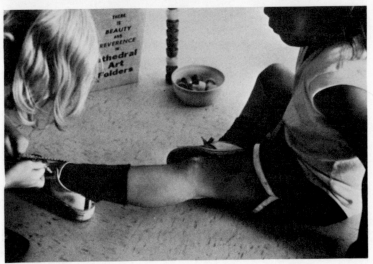

Jesus is all day long.

25

The classroom is a "lab" for practicing Christian living.

4

JESUS ALL DAY LONG

*And whatever you do in word or deed, do all in the name
of the Lord Jesus, giving thanks through Him to God the
Father.*

Colossians 3:17

Translating the twelve "guidelines from God" into a live
program is not difficult. They readily lend themselves to
every situation I've personally been involved with or
observed. But in applying these principles I rely on one
cardinal rule—keep open to the Holy Spirit. This openness is
vital, because you must relate to each individual child, yet
you must also relate to the class as a cohesive unit.

Such openness does not allow for pat answers. Pat
answers seem more comfortable but they are seldom as
effective, because they do not keep pace with life, which is
constantly changing about us. The young child who stands
before you today is not quite the same as he was yesterday.
Only the Spirit of God knows in what way he's changed. Only
He can lead you to deal effectively with your changing
students. And that means a teacher must rely on the Holy
Spirit.

You begin by realizing that, in God's view, there is no
separation between secular learning and religious training.
It's the "how" of your teaching (rather than the subject
matter) that will determine whether or not the children are
pointed towards God.

For a program to be spiritually successful, Christ must be

the cornerstone, the foundation, the walls and canopy through which the program is structured. God can and does use formal Bible studies. But He can also use circumstances throughout the day to drive home His truths and to give us a chance to digest what we have learned. A Bible story may be taught in ten minutes, but the rest of the day will either reinforce the underlying truths or contradict them. Some folks believe that only when they are telling a Bible story are they teaching about God, and that when the children engage in other activities no religious teaching is involved. Because of this fragmented view, we frequently waste much time telling children things they are not ready to hear.

I do not think Christianity should be compartmentalized when instructing a child. I don't think it is good to insist a child listen to the gospel when he does not wish to, and then never mention God again except at grace before meals. I think it is better to bring in godly information as a child moves through life, especially as he enjoys life. If he enjoys the wind as it flies through the leaves and pushes against his face, this is the perfect time to mention that "God made the wind. Isn't it fun? I want to fly with it!" You can build on that: "Can you see the wind? You can't? Well, you can't see it, but can you feel where it is and what it is doing? The Holy Spirit is like that. . . ."

Almost everything in life can be used as a spiritual analogy. Depend on God, depend on life, and what God made. Look to the events He ordered to teach the children (and you!) about himself and His creation. Books are all right, but God can teach directly through circumstances. These are real. These are now. These are lessons from life which demonstrate biblical concepts.

And you, as the children's guide, can help them get in tune with what God is saying. Use every opportunity to teach the children about the things of God. With your students, close your eyes, and listen to the sounds so frequently overlooked. Marvel at the beauty and uniqueness of flowers. Catch bugs and frogs, study them, and then let them go. Observe the

28

ants and follow them to their colonies. Plant radishes and discuss Jesus' words, "unless a grain of wheat falls into the earth and dies, it remains by itself alone; but if it dies, it bears much fruit" (John 12:24).

That's what I did, and it was beautiful. We saw the plants growing towards the light and we talked about us growing towards Jesus who is our light. We drew up a number chart together—slowly, as the children were able to postulate the next number set—and we saw God's systematic order unfold. While we ate, we talked about food and its origin. We were filled with wonder that God knows when a sparrow falls and how many hairs we have (Matthew 10:29, 30)! As we mixed paints, and again, as we added food coloring to water in clear containers, we were delighted to see the sparkling colors in the sunlight. We were continually amazed at the beauty of God's handiwork.

When one child had a small cut, we talked about the built-in healing power with which God has imbued our bodies. And once, when a swing broke at its top momentum, we praised God for His protection of our little boy Corey, who landed on his feet without a scratch! We prayed to the Lord before meals and at other times. We prayed for each other. The children were encouraged by example and comment to voice their own prayers, which they began to do, instead of always relying on memorized prayers.

I brought nonfiction* picture books from the library—books with color photographs. We would look at the pictures and discuss the beauty of God's creation. The children were always extremely curious and interested in the world about them.

Some people feel that children don't understand the biblical truths behind everyday experiences. But God says that His Word will not return empty (Isaiah 55:11). His

---

* I later found that my intuitive choice of more nonfiction than fiction, as preferred by the children, agreed with preferences of children observed by Dr. Montessori. See *The Advanced Montessori Methods*, vol. II, *The Montessori Elementary Materials* (New York: Schocken Books, Inc., 1965), p. 202.

Word, when spoken under the power of the Holy Spirit, produces life (John 6:63).

Children are immersed in a sinful world before they understand it. We must, therefore, under the Spirit's direction, use every opportunity to immerse the children in the Word of Life, so that they may be protected against the onslaught of this present world.

One day, two very young children came up and sat beside me, candidly discussing their ideas about bodily elimination. One child began to berate the other for still wetting and dirtying his pants. Embarrassed, negative attitudes were voiced. The whole conversation was taking a nonproductive turn. Up to then I had been silent, but now I felt things needed to be put in their proper perspective. I explained the function of our bodies in eliminating waste products, using a simple analogy.

"You know when you wash your hands the water that comes off your hands and goes into the sink is dirty," I said. "It isn't good for anything any more and it goes down the drain. Well, when you drink good clean water, your body uses this water to wash itself inside you. But after it is used, the water needs to be let out of your body. If it stayed inside and never got out, we would be very, very dirty inside, and would get very sick. But God made special parts of our bodies to make sure that the used water gets out. . . ."

The children's attitude changed from embarrassment and negativeness to a healthy respect for their bodies. It was no different pointing to the lower abdomen as the site of the bladder than pointing to the chest as the location of the heart, or to the throat as the location of the voice box. The children appreciated this truthful approach and exhibited wonder at how marvelously God had made us. It seems to me that this is a graphic illustration of Titus 1:15: "To the pure, all things are pure. . . ."

I believe that the combination of prayer, Spirit-led spontaneous Bible teaching, and a Christ-centered atmosphere is vital to fruitful spiritual results in the lives of children. If spiritual growth is expected, Bible teaching cannot be relegated to a "time-slot" of religious instruction, after which the things of God are dropped for the rest of the day. God must be seen in all things, and His presence acknowledged throughout every minute of the day.

5

TIMES AND SCHEDULES

. . . The Sabbath was made for man, and not man for the Sabbath.

Mark 2:27

Todd cried violently every morning. He never seemed to adjust. One day Jim Jordan, the director of the center, asked the boy's parents how they awakened their son.

"His sister picks him up by his heels and yells 'time to get up' and then we dress him and bring him here."

Jim asked them to try an experiment. "Wake Todd up very gently, by rubbing his back and talking softly to him. Wake him when you get up—an hour earlier than he is used to getting up—but don't make him get out of bed immediately. Just speak to him off and on so he doesn't go back to sleep." The parents tried this the next morning. When Todd arrived at school he was smiling, and he didn't come in crying after that!

Having a schedule based on the children's needs is basic to a well-run program. If the children's needs are different one day, change for that day. I really enjoyed working at a center where I could say to the cook, "We are running late today" or even, "I know it is lunchtime, but one of the children is making an important discovery, so just leave the food, and we'll pick it up when we are ready." To me, the feeding of the mind is as important as the feeding of the body. Although a child cannot "do his own thing" and make all of us wait for him, there are times when the clock is not all-important. Over scheduling produces boredom; we need a mixture of pattern and novelty.

But there is real value in schedules. Perhaps the major advantage of a basic time schedule is that it lowers the amount of time and energy exerted in continually making decisions. A predictable schedule, with patterns of regularity, enables habits to be established. Habits allow us to do things automatically, with a minimal amount of thought-energy. We are then freed to use our time and talents in creative ways. Thus scheduling, by its predictable patterning, reduces stress and allows us freedom, provided we do not become enslaved to the schedule.

After considering how activities are to be scheduled into time blocks, consider the transition periods between differing activities. Shifting from free time* to community time or to outdoor time can be awkward. What worked for me for the transition from free indoor time to outdoor time was placing a bench near the door. As the children finished their work, they came to the bench and sat down. Here we played finger games, sang, and talked. When all were assembled, we went outside as a group. Of course, if you have an aide in the room, one of you can go outside with the first few children and the other classmates can leave individually as they finish their work.

A similar arrangement can be used when shifting between different activities indoors, such as from indoor free time to indoor community time. The important thing is to have somewhere for the children to sit when they finish their work. Otherwise, while some children are still working, others who are already finished and are awaiting community time will become restless.

One aspect of community time is meal time. About ten

---

* When I say "free time," I mean a block of time expressly set aside for spontaneous individual exploration in a prepared environment. Free-time activities should be enjoyable, goal oriented, and designed to serve developmental purposes through play.

minutes before meals I told the children: "Begin to finish your work now, and don't start any new work. Wash your hands when you finish and come to the table." Handwashing thus actually became the means of transition from free time to meal time. Taking turns, the children were allowed to wash their hands. An aide stood near the washroom and in view of the snack tables. She gave assistance when needed, and in the beginning helped the children remember that they were to sit down at the snack table and wait for the rest to join them.

Some people hate to make children wait, perhaps because it is often difficult to make them do so. But waiting is part of life. It is good for the children to learn this early. (Waiting, of course, should never be unreasonable, such as making children wait while an unprepared teacher searches for her materials.) Two advantages in having the children wait for each other before a snack or meal are: (1) they become more aware of group unity at meal times, so that one child does not take precedence over the needs of all, and (2) they have a space of time to divest themselves of overstimulation from previous activity periods and social interaction. Children enjoy this time of quiet conversation with first one child, then two, then finally the whole group.

Nap time can present its own problem with scheduling. God's schedule, to be sure, calls for rest on the seventh day (Exodus 20:10). But, as Jesus said, the sabbath was made for man, and not man for the sabbath. In our culture naps are expected, and some children do seem to require sleep in the afternoon.* One disadvantage of day-care centers and similar facilities, which must comply with laws and culture, is that nap time is compulsory for all children. All the children must rest at nap time, whether or not they need it. Sending some nonsleepers to another room for play disturbs

---

* *Nap-taking is not universal for young children. When I lived with the Tzeltal people of southern Mexico, the little children got up at 6:30 A.M., two hours after their parents, and were up and about the entire day until they and their parents went to bed at 8:30 or 9:00 P.M.*

34

the schedule of the sleepers and they feel cheated. Another difficulty is that accommodations are often inadequate for individual needs.

In our center, I found books to be a help for nap-time "blahs." We allowed each child to take a book with him at nap time. He could even change books a few times if he couldn't sleep. This made nap time more enjoyable for all the children, the sleepers and the nonsleepers. It also nurtured a love for books. Many times a child would become attached to a particular book and take it day after day.

During nap time I would visit, one by one, the children who remained awake. I would read their book selections to them, rub their backs, sing, and talk. It was a special time of closeness for child and teacher. In the quietness of this time, some of the children prayed to receive Jesus as their own Savior.

Most children awoke from their naps at regular times each day. But occasionally a child would continue to sleep. Unless a parent had requested that we wake the child, I let him sleep. If he were so tired that a room full of active children did not wake him, he obviously needed the extra rest.

This attitude of respect for another's feelings above the dictates of a clock carried over to the children in their dealings with one another all day long. One day as it was getting very late I asked Rosanna, age five, to wake Jeremy, age three. A few minutes later I came to the doorway, but the children were unaware of my presence. Rosanna was kneeling beside Jeremy's cot. As she rubbed his back, she said in a soft voice: "Jerrrremy. Jerrrremy. Wake up now Jerrrremy. It is almost time for you to go home. Come and see the other kids. We are going to listen to the Jesus songs now. Wake up Jerrrremy. . . ."

Rosanna cared for Jeremy. Caring about each other involves responsibility. If you care about people you respect their feelings, you recognize their rights, and you learn from them. And that's what living together is all about.

Nathan creates with paint while Maria examines magnified objects.

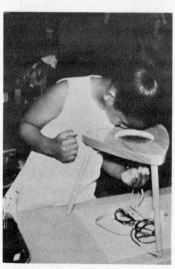

Washing up before our snack makes a good transition from "free time" to "group activity."

6

LIVING TOGETHER

Therefore whatever you want others to do for you, do so for them. . . .

Matthew 7:12

Any time young children are brought together group dynamics come into play, forging in each child's character either positive or negative patterns of behavior towards one another. These forces can be channeled to produce Christian attitudes in interpersonal relationships. But whether they work positively, to foster Christ-like attitudes, or negatively, to create disharmony, depends largely on the framework within which the children work and play, and experiment and learn. In short, the social environment exerts a decisive impact on the lives of all those living together for so many hours each day.

There are several ways a teacher can guide the forces of group dynamics to promote a healthy social environment. The most important of these, to bring Christ into all parts of the program, has already been considered in chapter four. Once this is understood, the following techniques can help you to guide the children's social interaction in your classroom.

1. Establish ground rules and group procedures.
2. Utilize community conversation.
3. Give children opportunities to grow through spontaneous social interaction.

4. Allow for choices in certain areas.
5. Understand how sharing works.
6. Use age and maturity levels to their natural advantage.

1. Ground rules and group procedures

A teacher needs to establish a few basic ground rules which can serve as standards for herself and the children. The more simply they can be worded, the more effective they will be. Jesus himself demonstrated the effectiveness of simplifying rules when He boiled the entire teaching of the law and the prophets down to just two precepts: love God, and love your neighbor (Matthew 22:37-40).

In my experience, I found that only two basic standards were needed to cover our classroom situations:
1. We do not disturb one another.
2. Before we start another activity, we finish the one we have. ("Finishing" includes replacing items in their proper place and original condition.)

The first standard has profound implications on all social behavior. It is, in effect, an application of the golden rule found in Matthew 7:12.

The second standard may initially appear to have little to do with molding Christ-like social relationships. It is a standard which applies directly to the care of the physical environment. Yet this is the very point that makes it so useful. For the environment does, indeed, exert influence on social relationships. Both standards reflect consideration for others, which is vital in any social situation.

When the concept "we do not disturb one another" was applied, I found that there was no need for legalistic lists of "don't hit, don't spit, don't step on crayons, don't throw blocks," and so forth. If a child manifested any contrary behavior, the reminder, "That's disturbing," was usually enough to thwart undesirable actions.

Very soon the child becomes aware of disturbing behavior. He doesn't have to be told that tripping someone is

39

disturbing! He quickly begins to evaluate his action in terms of whether or not it will disturb another. This standard thus avoids a dead legalism. It is fluid enough to penetrate all interpersonal relationships on a moment-by-moment basis.

However, the teacher herself can unwittingly become an offender of this standard. It is tempting, for example, to call to a child from across the room or yard; but that temptation should be avoided. It is better to go to the child and speak softly. If it is not possible to go to him yourself, ask another child near you to go and ask him to come to you.

If you habitually call out to the children, even to compliment them, you break the calmness of the class and disturb individual children's concentration. Besides, you are setting a bad example. What if all the children begin yelling to each other? You can't expect them not to, if you do. The calmer you are, the calmer the class is. Your state of calmness is reflected in both the tone of your voice and its volume.

The children can easily remember the ground rules, applying them to situations both in and out of the classroom. I'll never forget the afternoon the kindergarten children and I were all gathered together singing, when suddenly a rock smashed through the window spraying glass everywhere. The first words to come from the class were spoken by a little girl disgruntled by the unwelcome interruption:

"Dey are disturbing us!"

"Yeah," Jeffrey agreed, "Dat's dangerous! Why, what would have happened if dat rock had busted somebody's head?"

Group procedures, which may seem to a child to be baffling restrictions on his freedom, can actually be a source of class cohesiveness and support, depending on how you, the teacher, communicate to the children the meaning of each procedure. It was difficult for the young children in my class to understand "waiting your turn"—a turn which may not come up for several days. So I posted a schedule just for those jobs which were very popular, such as coloring the

Bible story, saying grace, serving food, and feeding the fish. All of the children relaxed as they saw that they would get their turn when it came around. This schedule also helped them begin to form time concepts.

All group procedures must be chosen with the utmost care, lest they become burdensome and meaningless. For instance, I felt no need of having "line leaders" chosen, as is common practice in most schools. As a matter of fact, we didn't have lines; rather, the children were trained to walk out of the room in a quiet, orderly fashion. True, the first time the children left the classroom without their lines, some literally burst out of the door and ran down the hall. I called them back. I explained: "We must walk quietly so we will not disturb the other classes." They could relate this to our class standard of not disturbing one another. We tried it again; it still wasn't good enough. But by the third time, it was. They responded positively by being treated with dignity and reason. They also wanted to get outside!

2. Community conversation

In my program, time was divided into various community times when the group was brought together, and free time, when the children worked individually on self-chosen projects. We started the day with a community time, which included songs, a Bible story, occasional memory verses, and conversation.

A good way to begin the conversation time is to share enthusiastically some recent event in your own life. "Yesterday when I went home I found that my cat had climbed up a tree and couldn't get down. . . ."

The children can identify with that, and will usually begin telling their own experiences. In most classes, some children are talkers and some aren't. The nontalkers should be drawn into the conversation by asking them, individually, by name, if they have anything to share.

"Leslie, do you have something you'd like to tell us?"

Silence.

41

"Did you go to the park yesterday?"

Shakes head.

"Well, what did you do yesterday?"

"Nothing."

"Did you sleep all day?"

Laughter.

"I watched TV."

"What program did you watch?"

After awhile, perhaps a few weeks in some cases, the child will begin to open up. In the meantime, don't push or intimidate him, just make it easy and possible for him to share. He'll talk when he wants to. If he doesn't want to, respect his wishes. The idea is to make conversation time truly a community time with every member of the class recognized, silent or sharing.

Conversation time is a learning experience for everyone. At first, if I asked a question without stating who was to answer it, everybody, all at the same time, answered! Then I began prefacing my questions with names: "Stephanie, I thought I saw you at the parade downtown yesterday. Were you there?" If others began to chime in, I just reminded them that I had asked Stephanie, and I wanted to hear *her* reply. "Let's all listen to Stephanie." Learning that conversation involves listening as well as speaking is a milestone even some adults have yet to reach!

It takes time for the children to learn that you actually do listen and want to hear what they have to say. At first, children usually respond with self-conscious remarks that they think you want to hear. But their conversation with each other is free and natural. It is as if they have two languages—one for adults and one for each other. To build rapport, you need to crack that language barrier!

Rapport goes both ways—they also need to learn about you as a person. I found out just how remote teachers seem to some children when I had just started teaching kindergarten. One child wanted to know if I ever ate! Another asked if I lived in the school at night! I began eating snacks with them that very day.

Sometimes children's stories are imaginary, and that is fine; any effort to communicate is acceptable. But if a story was clearly fictional, I usually said something like: "That was an interesting story you told us. It's what we call a make-believe story. Make-believe stories are a lot of fun to tell." Sometimes, if I wasn't sure about something being factual, I might ask: "Did that really happen, or are you making a pretend story for us to enjoy?" I stressed the importance of letting us know whether it was fact or fiction so we would know what to believe. Because the children wanted to maintain their credibility, and because there was no stigma attached to made-up stories, within about a week after we began "conversation time," children were readily admitting when their stories were imaginary. Such make-believe stories are delightful and revealing. They are not lies, but you have to keep the record straight.

Conversation time also strengthens verbal skills. You have an opportunity to assess the children's verbal abilities and weaknesses, and they learn verbal skills through natural conversation. By the other children's comments they know if they have been understood, and what thoughts they must clarify or which words they must pronounce better. Thus, the children encourage one another in effective speaking habits.

3. Spontaneous social interaction

Our conversation continued during our morning snack, after which the children began their individual free-time program. Free time, besides giving opportunities for the children to individually gain firsthand knowledge from their environment, also provides spontaneous social interaction. This is another essential to building positive interpersonal relationships, and is an important part of a young child's growth toward God. Social responses become everyday "labs" for the practical working out of Christian values.

While I was teaching in Watts, a five-year-old black girl

with light skin came to me in tears.

"Miz Allis, make 'em stop! Dey callin' me whitey!"

As other children gathered around, some preparing to defend themselves against this accusation, I said, "But that's silly! You aren't a whitey!"

"I know. But dey callin' me one."

"You aren't a whitey, but do you know who is?"

"No! Who?"

"I am."

"No you ain't!"

"Don't say that, Miz Allis!" another child admonished.

"Yes, I am. Look!" I held out my arm next to another child's arm to let the children compare skin tones. The shocked and speechless children drifted back to their individual projects. Meanwhile, as the year wore on, our relations became closer and closer. Race was never mentioned again.

Although prior to this incident we had discussed the fact that God had created all peoples, it hadn't yet penetrated. We sang: "Jesus loves the little children, all the children of the world, red and yellow, black and white . . ." but it was just a song. Not until an incident occurred involving a conflict between what they had been taught and what they felt about me did those words begin to take on meaning. It took a living lesson provided by free interaction to bring the meaning home.

Over a year later, this same student who had been accused of being a whitey gave me a folded paper and rushed back to her first-grade class. The note was a surprise to me, as I expected it to be from another teacher. Instead, the little girl had simply printed:

Dear miss Allison
I love you Because you are
Pretty and you love us.
love Sonja

Children readily apply the Word of God to their social relations. I overheard one child say to another, "I don't like you." But a third child standing nearby commented, "Well, God does!"

Of course, social interaction is not confined to free time; it also plays a part in community time. But it's most often the free-time social encounters that add depth to a child's emerging self-image, and thus make community-time social mistakes more bearable. I've encountered numerous examples of this.

During one meal time, our pineapple server gave himself the first serving, taking a disproportionate amount. Before he finished serving all his class mates lesser amounts, the serving dish was empty and the class was indignant.

"There's not enough for us!"

"Hey, don't we get any?"

"He din't give me enough!"

"Look how much he put in *his* dish!"

"Yeah. Look how much Steven got! That's not fair!"

Immediately, the embarrassed Steven removed the excess from his dish and shared with his classmates. Steven was learning the effect of his selfish actions. Yet, he was not overwhelmed by this embarrassment. Free time, conversation time, and the general atmosphere of the class had given him a broad base of experience with his friends, who were also in the process of learning to make wise choices.

4. Children's choices

In courtesy to one another, at mealtimes, we had a saying: "The one you touch is the one you take." It was very effective. One mother laughed and said that it was too effective, for when she went shopping and felt some fruit to make her selection, her child cautioned her, "The one you touch is the one you take!"

Learning to make right choices is a part of Christian growth. By making provisions for individual choices, the physical, temporal, and social organization of a home or classroom can aid the child in his early decisions. Choices can be made with regard to eating, activities, and playmates. Yet, by controlling the environment the range of choices can be limited so that they are not overwhelming.

Choices by an individual child, that affect him only, are good practice for the preschooler; he has the opportunity to learn from the consequences of his decisions. But at this early age, choices thrown open for group decision making are an invitation to chaos. Because the children are so new at group socializing, they need a firm guide for group activities. Therefore, the clearer the rules for this mode of social behavior, the easier the adjustment. I have learned that the fastest way to total bedlam is to offer the group alternatives!

"We have five minutes left before you go to your next classroom. What would you like to do? Would you like to stay here and listen to a story, or go out in the hall and get a drink from the cooler?"

To this, the children reacted as individuals and not as a group. They each interpreted the alternative to mean, "the teacher doesn't know what we should do now and is asking me what I want to do." Seemingly, in less than a second, the once-calm students scattered as if they were playing hide-and-seek. After that, the group as a whole was not given choices to make.

5. Sharing

On the other hand, individual choices that affected only the individual making the choice were respected. If a child wanted to work with an item that another child was already using, he would have to find a different activity. Besides a child's right to work with unique equipment, his choice of working alone or with someone else also was respected. In other words, a child was not forced to share. I believe that the security children have in knowing that they will not be forced to share materials helps them respond more quickly in learning to share. They don't have anything to resist.

Sharing was subtly incorporated into certain parts of our program. For example, some art materials were purposely limited so that sharing was necessary and there was no need for direct intervention. The environment dictated the solution. If two people wished to paint with tempera they shared the same paint box, which contained the individual color paint cartons and brushes. In tissue lamination it got a bit cozier. Two children, each with his own brush, shared the same starch container. And in collage, it was even "stickier." Two children learned patience as they waited to share the same glue bottle.

Sharing involves a natural developmental pattern. It can be tacitly encouraged, but not forced. Nonvoluntary sharing isn't sharing at all. It's a powerful adult usurping the child's right to decide and giving "his" material to some unwelcome classmate.

6. Age and maturity levels

Having children of mixed ages in one class also encourages sharing. Older children frequently are willing to share with younger children. They like to act like "the teacher." And the younger children learn more quickly by the older children's example.

In every class of mixed ages I have observed, the older children develop a "brotherly affection" for the younger ones. The mocking phenomenon—teasing, name-calling, etc.—which characterizes classes separated by chronological age has not occurred.

I enjoy classes of mixed ages; they seem so much more sensible to me. Life is made up of people of mixed ages. I think our school rooms should reflect that reality. In my opinion, a contributing factor to suspicions between different age groups is this artificial grouping of people by chronological age. Why build unnatural barriers? Weren't even Jesus' disciples of varying ages? God first spoke to Samuel when he was three years old. God first spoke to Moses when he was eighty.

In my class at the Norman day-care center, children ranged in age from just under three to six years old. They all displayed a high degree of follow-through without adult supervision. In other, younger classes, there were children up to three and a half, older than some in my class. Yet, because they were not ready to assume the degree of independence and freedom the children in my class could handle, they remained in a younger class.

Although the skill level of ages three through six varies widely, I have never encountered any problems with this because of the wide range of graded materials that we used in our program. Our children were free to choose from the items they already knew how to use. Their free choice was based on knowledge, not idle curiosity. If a child wished to choose an unfamiliar object, I would show him how to use it, provided it was not too advanced for him. If it were clearly too advanced, I would explain that it was for older children, but when he mastered his present material, I would show him how to use it. This approach minimized the risk of failure and provided enticement for advanced learning.

I have found that children with similar levels of social maturation work well together. In fact, social maturation rather than chronological age could be a valid criterion for forming classes or groups within your class. Even making two classes of the same wide age range, or adding more teachers to a large class, might be better than arbitrarily splitting the class into younger and older categories. Generally an overlapping system, as diagramed below, fits the needs of children more adequately than strict age groupings.

Thus, if you have a wide age span in your class, use it to its natural advantage in fostering healthy social relationships. If you are obliged to teach one age level, be sensitive to the different levels of maturation, and possibly group them for a more harmonious social atmosphere. If you can select your class composition, divide classes along "readiness" lines rather than age.

Bases for Grouping

Figure 1. Traditional approach: chronological age

3 mo.   1 year 2 years 3 years 4 years 5 years 6 years 7 years

Figure 2. More workable approach: social maturations with graded
material for varying skill levels

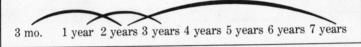

3 mo.   1 year 2 years 3 years 4 years 5 years 6 years 7 years

When a teacher is able to distinguish between situations which call forth positive social responses and those which do not, she can then begin to use the forces of group dynamics to channel the children's responses. She will no longer need to watch helplessly as social situations arise which provoke and reinforce negative responses. Rather, by subtle structuring of the social environment, applied with God-given wisdom, the teacher can guide her students into harmonious relationships with each other. Thus the teacher can, and should, be God's instrument for leading the children to experience Hebrews 10:24: "And let us consider one another to provoke unto love and to good works" (KJV).

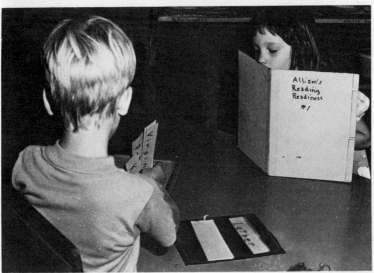

Older or more advanced children like to act as "Teacher." Children learn from one another.

51

7

THIS ENVIRONMENT
UNDER CHILD MANAGEMENT

*See that you do not despise one of these little ones, for I
say to you, that their angels in heaven continually
behold the face of My Father who is in heaven.*

Matthew 18:10

It was my first day at Jim Jordan's day-care center. I saw
a child with a plastic capital letter.

"Where do you keep those letters?"

"What?"

"That letter you have in your hand. Are there any more
like it?"

"Uh-huh. I mean, there was some. Maybe they're in that
box."

"Well, let's find them."

"Why?"

"Because those letters are very useful. If you can find all
of them, I can make you an exercise which will help you
learn to read."

"We gotta find those letters! Come on!"

Rosanna scampered off to the box. Others joined her in
the search. Some letters were in the box, but not all. Since
the children were now aware of the letters, they kept on
finding them during their normal activities.

Three days later a child announced to me, "Here's another
one."

"That's it," I exclaimed. "The last letter! Now that they
have all been found, I'll make the exercise I told you about."

Excited looks were exchanged. Spontaneous clapping burst forth. "We found them! We found all of them!"

In the meantime, I had found the small metal board that went with the set, and Jim, the director, had purchased a set of lower case, magnetized plastic letters. Someone had donated an unpretentious 18" by 24" tin sheet with safe, rounded edges. With a felt tip pen, I drew lines across the tin and wrote all the letters, capital and lower case, in alphabetical order (Aaa, Bbb, Ccc, Ddd etc.). When the children saw the letters so displayed, there was considerable interest.

"Wow! We have so many letters. I didn't know there were that many."

"A, B, C . . . where's S? My name starts with S."

"Here's S."

"S! S! My name starts with S!"

"Hey! They stick! They stick to the metal!"

"Now you have a place to put them back," I said. "So, after you use them, if you always put them where each letter has its place, you'll always have them and be able to use the exercise."

"We won't have to look for them."

"We won't lose them any more."

"When you want to make a word, you use this little metal board and put the letters of the word on it. You can spell your names. Just get your name cards from this tray. This tray of name cards and the small metal board go with this exercise. They are to be used together."

Rosanna reached for a name card.

"Okay, here's my name. Let's see, where is the R? Oh, here it is. . . ."

The children watched in rapt attention as Rosanna proceeded to give her own informal demonstration.

"There. I did it! I spelled my name! See, R-o-s-a-n-n-a. Now I'll spell your name, Corey."

"Now," I interrupted, "you must first put the letters from your name back. Then you can get the letters for Corey's name."

"Gotta put them back so we won't lose them."

"Yeah, they cost Jim a lot of money," Tammi put in.

"This is hard! Where's the R go?"

I pointed to the R.

"Okay. Let *me* put them back."

Rosanna was still used to a teacher-active approach, where the teacher does everything but grow for the child, rather than a child-active approach.

"Don't worry, I'll let you find their places. As a matter of fact, to use this exercise you'll have to be able to put the letters back yourself." Rosanna looked puzzled. I continued, "Anyone who cannot replace all these letters can't work with this exercise, unless he finds someone to work with him who knows how to find the right place for each letter."

"You know where the letters go. Will you help us?" Rachael asked me.

"If I'm not busy I will. But it will be better if you can find another child to help you. Anyway, since this exercise is new, I'll be the one to help you today. After that, I'll let you know if you can work with it alone, or if you'll need to work with someone else. But probably, after I work with you today on it, you won't find it too hard."

As it turned out, with only one exception every one of the four-, five- and six-year-olds in the class could replace the letters after the first or second trial. When younger children wanted to use the alphabet board, they asked an older child to assist them. They were not allowed to use it alone because they could not replace the letters without an excessive amount of energy (or frustration), which made the exercise too much for them.

Through this exercise the children learned to spell and to write their own names, the names of classmates, and other words of their own choosing. The exercise retained its popularity and value. None of the letters was lost. If, for a time, a letter was missing, a glance at the board revealed its absence.

"The H is missing."

"The H is missing," the children echoed. They spontaneously began to look around for the H. After a few minutes it turned up.

Missing letters weren't missing long because it was so easy to spot a missing piece immediately. The same is true for puzzles. If you insist that puzzles must be completed before returning them to their place on the shelf, pieces just don't get lost.

Everything having its exact place, from materials to the individual parts of any item, promotes efficiency, order, security, harmony, consideration of others, and care of the materials. Disorder brings a low level of learning; produces frustration, insecurity, and boredom; and wastes energy, time and equipment.

With everything in a set place, children can be trained to manage their own environment. This helps them to develop a sense of responsibility as well as a sense of their own worth and capacities. Order is present; it's natural. A child can quickly learn to keep it that way.

Parents have frequently asked me how old a child must be to understand what it means to put things away. My experience suggests that it can be learned early.

When I was filling in for another worker in a nursery, I was given charge of infants under one year. An eleven-month-old baby, just learning to walk, found some detached crib wheels with potentially dangerous projections. As I was seated feeding a three-month-old baby, I could not immediately intervene. And, being used to older children, I simply said, "Amy, please put those back." She looked at me, then at the wheels and then began to replace them where she had found them! I'm not sure if she really understood the verbal command, but somehow she got the message!

In classes with two-year-olds, I found that these youngsters were quick to notice if anything was out of place or missing from our organized shelves. From the age of two-and-a-half, children could generally be counted on to replace objects after use. I suspect that children could learn this habit even younger than two-and-a-half if they were consistently encouraged to put things away, and if their physical environment permitted child management.

Putting away material immediately after work was not a "tack on." As I've stated earlier, the replacement of items was part of the work. A child was not finished using something until it was returned to its place exactly as found. This procedure trained the children to complete their cycle of activity. Also, squabbles over materials were avoided. If a child was using some material and had to stop temporarily, he could leave his work out. When he returned, his work was still there waiting for him. Another child would not take it, since the children were not allowed to take materials except from the shelves where they were stored when not in use.

Child management of the environment also trains the mind. Here are the steps a child has to organize mentally in order to water-paint.

First, he must see if the water paints are available (they might be in use by another child). After securing the paints he must take them, and a piece of watercolor paper, to a table. Then he must get a cup, fill it with water, and take it to the table. Finally, he has to get a paint shirt and put it on.

When he finishes his painting, he has to take it to the drying area, then throw out his water, rinse the cup, and return it to its cupboard. Next he must rinse his brush, clean his paint tin, and replace both. Then he must take a cloth to the table, clean the table, rinse out the cloth, and hang it up to dry. He must also wash his hands and wipe off the sink area, then find someone who will assist him in removing his paint shirt so that he can either put it in the laundry or put it where he found it. Later, when his picture is dry, he needs to put it in his own box. I've seen children under three years old capable of this routine.

Through the care of the environment and materials, good stewardship is also learned. It was not permissible to waste or abuse material. If a book or other item were chewed on, thrown, or otherwise misused, the item was taken from the child. If a child could mend what he had damaged, he was required to do so. As one might expect, problems of this nature were very few.

I've found that after training the children, I could trust them to conserve materials. Our children would use only one paper towel, or only a few drops of liquid glue. They would not fold or mutilate the IBM cards in the back envelopes of library books.

I remember Donny. When he first came to the center, he used to pull out the IBM cards from the library books he chose for nap time and throw them away. After a few days, he grew fond of the books and one book in particular. Up to this time I had said nothing to him about the cards; he had had enough new adjustments to make without one more. By now he was eager for me to read his book to him before he went to sleep. One day, as I was about to read to him, I turned to the back of the book. The card must have annoyed him, for he immediately took it out and threw it on the floor. When I picked it up he said, "No."

"Don't you like this card, Donny!"

"No."

"Well, Donny, even though you don't like this card, if it doesn't stay in the book we can't have the book any more."

He looked at me in surprise.

"You see," I continued, "the book doesn't belong to me or to Jim or to anyone here at the center. It belongs to the library. Do you know what a library is?" He shook his head. "The library is a building with lots and lots of books inside. This book, the one you like, came from the library. The people who work in the library let me take some of their books and bring them here to the center so you and the other boys and girls can see them. But when they let me take them, I have to promise to bring them back after a little while. The card in the back reminds me of my promise and tells me when I have to bring them back. Then, when I take

57

them back, the people open the books and look for the cards. If they are not there, they will be upset with me and make me pay them money. They might not let me take more books out. So if you want to see this book again, you'd better leave the card in it because the library people need to see that it's still there when they get the book back."

Donny let me know he didn't want the book going back to the library! He wanted it at the center. He agreed to leave the card in so the library people would let me recheck the book, and he even wanted to see the library.

Good stewardship also extends to ecology. When we are careful in the use of God's creation, we are honoring Him. Once the class and I discussed that paper comes from trees, and that God made the trees for us to use. But it takes a long time to grow a tree. The question of how long came up. For the answer, we turned to class experiments with plants.

"Golly, plants grow slow!" Tammi observed after some days.

"So think how long it takes for God to make a tree!" Rosanna exclaimed.

"Wow! A long, long, long, super-long time!" James agreed.

"Forever?" Cindy inquired.

"Not quite that long, but trees do grow slowly. Like children. . . ."

"Golly, if they cut down all the trees to make houses and slides and paper, then what will happen to all the trees?" Rosanna was becoming ecology conscious.

"There won't be any more!" Steven was getting the picture.

"Then how will we get our paper for drawing?" Rachel asked.

"We won't have any," Corey summed up.

After that, the children generally were more cautious in their use of paper and they even kept an eye on each other to check possible extravagance.

Before age six, patterns are being formed which will

remain for life. The example set at school can and does carry over to the home. A mother told me that her son, age three-and-a-half, after being in our program just three weeks, began to take an interest in keeping his room at home neat and orderly. One day he cleaned and tried to organize his belongings by taking them out of his closet and placing them on his partially bare book shelves. His perceptive mother decided to have shelving put up to help him. She saw that the toy box encouraged disorder, carelessness, and broken toys, so she wisely discarded it.

A working mother told the director that the reason she had placed her almost-four-year-old son in the day-care center was that he made such a mess of the house. Donald had never been trained to put anything away. When I tried to show him how to put some things away after he had used them he was rebellious, not understanding why he just couldn't leave the mess as he had always done before. But I firmly insisted that he stay while I showed him how to replace the items. Halfway through the demonstration I asked him to try also, but he said, "Can't," which I interpreted to mean, "Don't want to." He continued to watch, and after more encouragement, finally attempted to reconstruct a puzzle-like apparatus he had used and abandoned. His success surprised him. As he put the last piece in place he looked at me in astonishment, and then back at his orderly accomplishment with satisfaction. He had made the discovery that he could contribute to order instead of to chaos!

As a matter of fact, children prefer order to chaos. When I visited one mother of three preschool children, two of whom had just started in my program, she related, "You won't believe this! We cleaned the children's playroom, and now they don't want to mess it up! So they're taking their toys to the living room to play!"

Parents have an alternative to a messy playroom. They can set up the playroom so that their children can manage it, and after showing the children how, they can expect them to follow through. The playroom need never be in a mess, even when its equipment is in use.

But teachers really don't have any choice. In school there are many children from different backgrounds and there's usually more equipment to keep in order. If there isn't some system whereby the children are involved in keeping their environment orderly, they become unhappy and constantly squabble; the materials are frequently lost and broken; the noise level usually rises until it jangles the nerves; and the teacher becomes exhausted, since she spends more time being referee, maid, and "missing items detective" than teacher. What teaching she is able to do will probably have to be done en masse rather than individually. And she will have little or no time to observe her students, to assess their needs, or to evaluate her program's adequacy.

Child management of the environment also promotes a sense of unity. When we initiated cleaning, some children asked, "Why do we have to?"

I answered, "Because you live here most of the day. It is your room and my room. We are the ones who live in it. We work in it, we dirty it, and we need to keep it clean."

One girl who was at first most reluctant to participate later explained to a newcomer: "We keep our room clean, and on Fridays we take everything off the shelves and clean all that too, because we live here, see, and now you'll live here too, so you have to help us keep our room clean!"

Individually, the children were expected to aid in maintaining the environment, from washing their hands before handling any material, to cleaning up their own spills.

Corporately, the children participated in the Friday afternoon "scrub in" and vigorously attacked dust, dirt, and grime in the form of fingerprints on the walls or glue on the tables. Paint brushes were washed and set out to dry for the weekend; materials were removed from their shelves, dusted, and put back on shelves which had themselves just been cleaned. The room was ready for the weekend, and so were the children and their teacher!

Our room had five basic areas: sensorial and academic, manipulative, roleplaying, unit blocks, and art. Within each physical area, every piece of equipment had its own place. Some of these were marked with tape or contact paper on low, open-sided, moveable shelves.* Individual paper "mail boxes" were taped to the wall to provide a temporary storage place for the children's work. Thus, the children always knew where things were to be found and to be replaced.

In order to promote the most effective use of materials, objects from one area were not allowed to be used in other areas. Blocks were for construction, math cubes were not. Math cubes stayed in the academic area and were used for building math concepts, not buildings.

In free time, I've found that the "academic" part of a program is the "protein"; art blocks and manipulative activities (such as miniature models and various construction materials) the "fat"; and dramatic roleplaying, sand and water play, and other outdoor activities the "carbohydrate." All are necessary for a well-balanced learning program, but when the carbohydrates and fats are present with the protein, they tend to replace it. (Especially the carbohydrates!) Therefore, separating the location and time of these activities is helpful for the child's assimilation. Also, the more structured materials require individual concentration, which is hard to achieve when other children are too near and are engaged in socially oriented activities such as dramatic roleplay.

---

* *After we marked places for materials, I discovered the following statement by John Holt in* Freedom and Beyond *(P. Dutton and Company, Inc., New York, 1972), pp. 29-30:*

"Children . . . like to put things into places especially made and fitted for them. Woodworking shops where tools are stored on a pegboard with a silhouette for each tool, or according to some other plan in which the child can *see* where each tool goes, and that no other tool can go there, tend to be neater than those where storage is more haphazard. . . . Putting something away becomes . . . a puzzle itself."

One does not need a large collection of expensive playthings. In fact, too many choices overwhelm children. How the materials are presented and physically organized also has a great influence on how effectively they will be used and how many will be necessary. I have found it beneficial to introduce only one new item at a time, and that not too often. (Of course, when beginning a new program, it is necessary to introduce perhaps three or four new exercises almost every day over a period of about a week and a half.)

When materials are presented to the children, they should be clean, attractive, and whole. It is unreasonable to ask children to keep materials clean and neat if they are dirty or broken to begin with. Attractive equipment is appealing to the children and encourages proper use.

In order for children to manage their environment well, the proper use of all materials and the operation of any exercises must be clearly presented. On the mornings when I presented a new exercise, I would keep it in a box or cover it with a cloth so that it wouldn't distract the children during the first part of their community time, and so the exercise would be introduced as dramatically as possible. Presentations were usually made in silence. I would remove the article from its cover and slowly and precisely go through the steps in using it. I tried to be alert to the child who showed the most interest and who I felt could do the exercise with relative ease. After the presentation, I would place the object on its shelf and select the child who showed the most interest to work with it first.

It is very important for the teacher herself to understand the purpose and function of new materials. She must carefully run through the presentation beforehand so as to establish exactly how she wants the children to work. If she fumbles around in front of the children she will confuse them. This is true for both group and individual presentations. Certain items, like sandpaper letters, must be presented individually because the teacher needs to assess the child's readiness to use the letters as she gives the lesson. If the child is not ready, the teacher must put away the materials and try again in a few weeks or a month. Only when the child is able to complete the exercise should she say: "Now you may use these letters whenever you wish." For every two or three new letters, another presentation is required. The child may only work with those specific letters which he has successfully mastered during the presentation.

With the exception of books, puzzles, some cleaning materials, individual chalk boards, and a few art materials, each item should be unique and complete within itself. If an exercise requires a stencil, two colored pencils and paper, these should be placed neatly in a tray or box. That way, when a child wishes to use the exercise he does not have to see if someone else is using part of the equipment. Everything he needs to complete his work is there.

I found that there are several advantages to having "one-of-a-kind" materials. First, a child will select the item because of his own inner impulse to do so, not because another child is doing that activity. Jealous competition between children is avoided. Second, when a child selects an item because he alone wants to use the item, he usually works very well with it and learns to concentrate rapidly. Not only does concentration train the mind, it also promotes a quiet class. The quietness comes from the children—not from an adult trying to enforce it. Third, a variety of training materials can be purchased for the same amount of money required for several sets of the same article. Variety, of course, must not take precedence over the effectiveness of the materials. It's not how many different materials you have, but how effective they are that counts. Finally, with all the children working away on projects of their own choosing, the teacher is freed to observe and to fill the role of "consultant" when the children need her.

Teachers have asked me, "But how is it possible to make sure the children are learning what they are supposed to, when each child is working on a different exercise at the same time? How can I possibly teach twenty different

63

lessons at once?" You can't. But the materials can, if they have a built-in "control of error." Proper materials will train the child by letting him know when he is successful in completing an exercise. For instance, if a blindfolded child is working with a sandpaper letter, tracing its shape with his finger, and his finger slips off the sandpaper, he immediately feels his finger on the smooth surface and knows he was inaccurate. He does not need a teacher to remind him of what his finger has told him. Therefore, he can remove the blindfold, practice again, and when he feels confident, replace the blindfold and continue.

Even simple, everyday actions can be turned into exercises with a control of error. For example, the control of error in replacing a chair under a table comes from the noise or lack of noise the chair makes as it is moved. If a child is clumsy, and scrapes the chair along the floor, the noise tells him that he needs to practice this exercise until he has learned to judge his movements correctly.

In summary, here are seven tips for setting up an effective, child-managed enviroment:

1. Have a specific place for each item in the environment.
2. Show the children how to use the materials before making them accessible.
3. Present clean, attractive, and whole materials to the children.
4. Give the children access to the cleaning equipment and instruct them in their use, so that the children can be responsible for the care and management of their own environment.
5. Teach the child that his work is not completed until the material he is using has been replaced as found.
6. Select unique items, without duplicates, which serve specific developmental needs.
7. Let the child work on his own to discover what the materials are designed to teach him.

Everything having its exact place promotes harmony, security, consideration of others, and care for our environment.

To use these letters, you have to know how to put them back in order by yourself.

65

Steven serves the pineapple, judiciously.

We dirty it, and we need to keep it clean.

8

MATERIALS AND BOOKS

One generation shall praise Thy works to another,
And shall declare Thy mighty acts.
They shall speak of the glory of Thy kingdom,
And talk of Thy power. . . .

Psalm 145:4, 11

Many different types of learning experiences are possible, both indoors and out, which do not require physical materials. Pantomime, singing, storytelling, exploring nature, field trips, walks, creative movement, rhythmic clapping, conversation, treasure hunts, listening to sounds for identification, and simple games*—these are all good learning experiences that need no equipment.

Some teaching approaches—highly successful ones at that—shun the use of too many materials. Sylvia Ashton-Warner, teaching Maori children in New Zealand, preferred only chalk and chalkboard, paper and pencils, clay and paint, guitar and piano, books and charts, and the great outdoors. In Mexico, I taught—successfully and happily—with even less than that. (As a matter of fact, our classroom was held in a part-time chicken coop. The students and I used it in the daytime, the chickens at night!) Even if you do prefer to work in a well-stocked environment,

---

* *Structured games and sports must be used sparingly with young children, who need much time to interact individually with their environment and with each other. Socialization of children follows a slow but natural process which should not be "pressure rushed."*

don't limit yourself to it.

Art, music, and creative movement provide needed opportunities for expression and are especially helpful to a child who, in the past, has been desensitized by television, too many toys at once, etc. Remember that in early childhood the process of creativity is far more important than the product. It is only after children have had much freedom to experiment with art materials and learn a medium's limitations that they can begin to create. After a time, children will impose their own standards on their work as they develop towards accurate self-expression. Imposing adult standards of realism on a child's artwork stifles growth in art and in observation. If the child is helped to develop his own powers of observation, his art will reflect the deepening of his mind and soul.

In the Resource Handbook included in this volume you will find a chart of activities that foster creative expression in a child, as well as learning exercises. For each activity I have listed the purpose, or skills developed by that activity, as well as the materials required and where you can find them.

In designing your program and selecting preschool equipment, you can hardly escape the influence of Jean Piaget and Maria Montessori. Dr. Piaget of Switzerland is famous for his observations of young children during the past fifty years. He believes that each child passes through specific stages in his mental development. His studies indicate that the rate at which a child may pass through the stages varies with the individual and may be altered by environment. Piaget states that materials which are most helpful for intellectual stimulation are "active" materials which force the child to stay on the "leading edge" of his newly emerging developmental state. Maria Montessori's materials accomplish this.

Dr. Maria Montessori was Italy's first woman medical doctor. After her graduation she worked with mentally retarded children. Through keen observation and continued study she discovered ways to help these children learn. The institutionalized children passed Italy's primary education examinations—a feat thought impossible. Dr. Montessori reasoned that if these retarded children could pass the examinations, something must be wrong with the education of normal children. She therefore began working to advance the learning capability of children with normal intelligence.

Dr. Montessori developed special didactic materials and child-sized furniture which were so revolutionary that they are still influencing manufacturers today. However, to use her materials for the greatest benefit to the child it is necessary to understand her observations and methods (see bibliography of reference works in the Resource Handbook). She uses the term "freedom" for the child, but her meaning is not the same as that which educators currently attach to the word. Her system fosters responsibility, self-discipline, and a love for learning in children.

Piaget and Montessori both emphasize sensitive learning periods or developmental stages, psychological and physical environments which encourage the child to learn, and the necessity for the young child to participate physically in his own learning.

The key to effective classroom equipment is in selecting those things with which the children must *act*. I have seen excited parents give an expensive battery-driven train set to their preschooler. After two minutes, the child turned away in favor of tearing up the wrapping paper! And why not? All he could do with the train was turn it on, place it on its track, and watch it go. There was nothing to do to it, or for it. Preschoolers want and need sturdy materials that demand the use of their muscles, minds, and creativity.

Christian teachers have to observe one important caution in choosing preschool materials: even playthings are transmitters of culture and values. What is their nonverbal message? Evel Knievel carries one message, a woodworking set carries another. Barbie and her boyfriend Ken stimulate one kind of play, baby dolls another.

What about miniature cars, trucks, and other toy vehicles? Children love them. But in the classroom environment, model vehicles speeding across the floor from various directions can be a pain in the ankle, to say the least. The teacher who supervised my internship, Carol Stickler, had a solution. After the children learned to work well with unit blocks, the vehicles and other objects were introduced as "accessories" to be used in their construction projects. The children would build something with the unit blocks, and then go to Carol and tell her what they had built. She would write what the children called it on a strip of paper (house, fire station, freeway, hospital, farm, etc.). She put tape on the back of the paper and the children affixed it to one of the blocks in their project. The posting of this sign allowed the children use of appropriate accessories. For houses, these included wooden people and dolls; for farms, wooden or plastic animals; for freeways, cars, trucks, and buses. If the construction did not merit accessories, she would suggest that the children needed to continue working on their project.

By insisting that such accessories be used as part of a creative project, their use also became creative and imaginative. I liked that! The construction materials demanded physical and mental activity, and the teacher challenged the children to find new and creative uses for the toys or accessories. That's an illustration of how class equipment can benefit the children.

At the other extreme is television, which can work incredibly more harm than good in a child. Whereas children grow through mental and physical activity, television stunts their growth by promoting mindless inactivity. And what is even worse than stifling their creative thought, television brainwashes the children with non-Christian values. Consider, for example, the cute kiddie cartoon shows that look so innocuous to many adults. If the cat runs the mouse over a cliff, naturally the mouse is expected to "get even" by running the cat over the cliff—and if he can make a huge boulder fall on top of him besides, so much the better, because that's the system of justice which is insidiously programed into the current generation of television watchers. It is difficult, if not impossible, to teach children about the things of God if their minds are filled with concepts that are, at their core, ungodly. In general, non-Christian television programing teaches the false values of a world hostile to faith in God.

When I first arrived at the day-care center, the children had been used to watching television during the day. They told each other macabre stories, apparently provoked by the influence of TV. We had the set removed. The first day without it, one child suddenly realized it was gone.

"Hey, where's the TV?"

"We removed it. We won't have it again."

"Why? Did it break?"

"No, it didn't break. We took it away because you won't have time to watch it any more. You are going to be doing all sorts of new things."

"What sorts of new things?"

"Artwork you'll do all by yourself, like painting and. . . ."

"Painting!"

"We get to do painting!"

"When?"

After that, no one ever mentioned television again.

In another experience, the children taught us how unnecessary television was to them. In Watts, after our kindergarten program had been going about two months, we brought a television set into the room so the children could watch a specific program ("Sesame Street"). This program was aired during the children's free time, and as such was just another activity from which the children could choose. But by now children were really "plugged into" learning from life, so they ignored the television. When it first arrived, about six children sat down to watch it. Within about five minutes the work in the classroom proved more inviting and, one by one, they forsook the set.

71

In these days of increasing social erosion, even books designed for preschoolers need to be carefully screened. Gone are the days when a conscientious parent can drop into the friendly neighborhood library, randomly select a few children's books and then hurry home, secure that the selections are appropriate. There are today an increasing number of enticingly beautiful books for very young children which hold values that are not only anti-Christian, but are actually anti-God. I watched one mother hurriedly pick up a book, flip through its brightly colored pages, and tell her four-year-old, "I'll get this one for you—its pictures are so pretty." This mother never realized that the themes of that beautiful book were rebellion, robbery, and suicide!

As I was reviewing picture books for the bibliography in this text a young woman, eyeing my stack of children's books, jokingly remarked: "You must be a teacher or you must like children's stories a lot." To this I replied, "Well, I am a teacher, and I do like children's literature too." Thinking I was being facetious, she added, "Oh—right! They have such good plots!" She, like so many people, failed to appreciate the vast amount of good literature that is available in children's picture books.

But such books, some of which have a great influence on children, must be carefully chosen. Books which are "written down" to children in "primerese" (Look Jane, look!) do a disservice to our children, whereas books written as good literature can enrich children's lives.

In the first seven years of life, language is being formed. Children are hungry for words and desire the liberating tools of self-expression. Therefore, they need adequate models of a full, rich language, not an impoverished vocabulary. Rather than insipid stories written by uninspired writers, they need (and enjoy) both good fiction, which captures their imagination and expands their perspectives, and nonfiction, which adds to their knowledge. They need to see that art has many dimensions and conveys the feeling of the story as well as the artist's interpretation. In short, they need to see and to hear good literature which can serve as a base for later creativity.

It is true that a young child may not understand all the words nor grasp the subtle innuendos, but in well-chosen children's literature, it is of small consequence. The natural flow of well-written material will accustom the child to language used effectively, and will help him to learn it. Unknown words become understood as they are continually confronted in a variety of contexts. Language awareness is acquired through much experience in dealing with it—by listening, by speaking, by piecing together clues and experimenting with them, and later by writing. Our job, as teachers and as parents, is to provide the clues the child needs to construct his own internal language system, and one way this can be done is by choosing literature wisely.

Picture books, like other books, are written on different levels; some are more sophisticated than others and require the listener to have greater experience in life. Generally, when reading to a group of children, the selection should be geared to hold the attention of the least mature. But when reading to children individually, one may choose books which fit the development of each particular child. In fact, one may include some selections which are slightly above the current level of the child's understanding and in that way aid his language and concept development. The bibliography in the Resource Handbook lists the most appropriate ages for each book; however, these ages are given only as a guide, and when reading to just one child they may be almost disregarded.

In considering books for the bibliography, I used the following criteria:

1. Christ is glorified, or could be glorified through the story or subject treated.
2. Subject matter is presented with good taste, balanced views, and values consistent with the Christian faith.
3. Writing style provides rich imagery and

73

language-learning opportunities.
4. Art work is aesthetically pleasing.
5. Format is clear, uncluttered and interesting.
6. Illustrations are multiracial where appropriate.
7. Subject matter is understandable and interesting to children.
8. Subject matter is presented with uniqueness and creativity.
9. Text is concise.
10. Illustrations are in full color.

Most of the books meet all of the above guidelines. A few miss perhaps one or two, but are included because their overall value was not diminished if they lacked, for instance, full color. I know that 425 books seems like an overwhelming number to choose from, but why choose? If you read one new story to your children every day, this list will take you just beyond a year!

Besides teaching language, books also contribute to a child's general knowledge and provide ideas, insights and directions on which he may base future actions. Many busy teachers and parents have quickly scanned books at the library—even recommended books—only to find when reading them to their children that the books presented objectionable values. One of my major purposes in compiling the bibliography of children's books has been to list books which are not in conflict with Christian values or good taste, and to present books which fill the child's mind with good, true, and praiseworthy ideas.

Not only is it difficult to find worthy books without hours of research; it is also hard to find companies which provide specialized, high-quality educational products. It is not that there aren't many such companies—there are—but locating them is a different matter. I once spent two hours poring over the Chicago telephone directories to obtain the address of a company whose name I had forgotten, but which I felt sure I would recognize if I saw it again. As it turned out, the company which made the educational products was listed under its main product—chemicals!

The Resource Handbook, which is Part Two of this volume, represents hours of "digging." As I began to accumulate data, I became aware that other people—fellow teachers, parents, administrators, educators, librarians—could also profit from some of my "finds." The Handbook, therefore, is offered in the hope that it will spare you, whether you are a new or an experienced teacher, much time-consuming (and sometimes fruitless) searching. Fundamentally it is a labor of love, and its information should be of value to anyone concerned with the teaching and training of young children. The materials and books we provide can be powerful aids in transmitting to our children a love for life and a sense of wonder at the glory of God's kingdom.

Choose those materials which cause the child to act.

A puzzle can be done correctly only one way.

"Control-of-error" means the exercise itself will let the child know if he has done it incorrectly.

77

Math concepts are quantities that can be seen and handled.

78

9

TRAINING A CHILD IN
SELF-DISCIPLINE

Train up a child in the way he should go,
Even when he is old he will not depart from it.

Proverbs 22:6

Child management of the environment fosters self-discipline and, indeed, requires it. But the environment, per se, cannot do all of the training. It is the teacher who must train the children to work harmoniously in her classroom. If she does her job well, situations which call for external discipline will be very, very few. But if discipline is a problem in your classroom, don't give up! The solution may be simpler than you think.

Most ordinary discipline problems seem hard to solve because the teacher's focus is wrong. She's looking at the result—the unruly behavior of her students. She needs to focus on the cause. The cause may be her program.

The program can make it easy for the children to learn self-discipline—or almost impossible. Check your expectations against the provisions for the children to meet those expectations. If your program captures the children's imagination, and channels their creative energies, you'll find that most discipline problems just vanish. If, on the other hand, your program doesn't meet the children's needs to explore, to become independent, and to engage in activities which are meaningful to them, the children's behavior will let you know.

79

In an adequate program, normal children—that is, healthy children with reasonably secure and happy home lives—seldom have discipline problems. These children are good barometers of the overall program. When their work becomes sloppy, that is your first clue that the program may not be meeting their needs. When interpersonal relationships become unpleasant, that's your second clue. After that, restlessness, disorder, and destructive behavior towards the environment, as well as disruption of class unity, will occur. This downhill spiral happens when your program is no longer meeting the changing needs of the children. Before you judge your students too harshly, look for precipitating causes in your program. Once corrections are made, balance will be restored.

One area where external discipline is seldom the answer is that of children's conflicts with each other. Intervention by an adult "referee" is rarely needed—even when requested. Generally, adult interference deprives the children of working through their own problems and retards their social and spiritual growth. Also, adults often project their own fears into the situation, magnifying the problem until it is too big for the children to solve for themselves.

Children's arguments are usually short-lived, energetic, and uncomplicated. The minute an adult steps in, either as referee or on the side of one child, the situation becomes unnecessarily complex. Since simple personal problems are easier to solve, let the children solve them. Once you are in, you must solve a much more complicated situation.

Of course, the teacher can give guidance. But the lessons you give in how to deal with social problems should be presented before or after the problem occurs, rather than during the problem itself. This timing allows the lessons to be absorbed in a calm, unemotional state.

One way of presenting lessons in social relations is with puppets. During a community time, let hand puppets do the misunderstanding, bickering, and problem-solving. Your scripts can be made from situations you've observed in your own classroom. That way, they are certain to be relevant, yet they avoid adding new negative ideas of which the children may not yet be aware. To make the puppets more realistic, alter your voice dramatically for each different puppet. By this means you can dramatize the children's own problems and fears while teaching them ways to handle such situations.

Make it clear, as with the children managing their own environment, that you expect them to manage their own social affairs. By your nonintervention, good example, biblical teaching, class conferences, and practical Christianity in action, the children will have enough input to begin working through their own interpersonal relationships. Let them do so.

In one small nursery school three-year-old Lisa came to me with a complaint: "Mindy scratched me."

"Oh," I said nonchalantly, as I continued working with another child. Lisa stood near me, waiting for me to take action against Mindy. I looked at her: "Lisa, you'll have to work it out with Mindy." Surprised, Lisa stomped off to Mindy.

"Mrs. Allison says you have to say you're sorry and you won't do it again," Lisa chided.

Shy little Mindy, convinced she had been convicted without a trial or even a glimpse of the judge, resigned herself to the verdict and buried her head in her arms on the table.

I confronted Lisa. "What did I say, Lisa?" She jumped in surprise, wide-eyed to find me standing behind her so quickly. "I said, 'Go work it out with Mindy.' "

Mindy, head still on her arms, slowly turned her face to look at me. She stared at me in wonder, while Lisa looked bewildered.

Children are so accustomed to adults demanding apologies, believing one child over another, and making quick judgments, that they seldom expect a "fair hearing." Adults stress things like, "Say 'I'm sorry,' " but rarely demand a token of forgiveness on the part of the "victim." Thus the "victim" gets the adult on his side, tipping the scales in his favor, and gloats over the other child's punishment. He has used the teacher to get back at "the kid who hit him." Is this the attitude we want to promote in children? The Bible clearly shows us Jesus' attitude towards the sinner. He loves him. And, even when the sinner brings punishment on himself, Jesus doesn't gloat, he sorrows.

John accidentally knocked Peter over while he was sitting on a tricycle. John's first reaction was to help Peter, but before he carried through, he saw me, his new teacher, and momentarily froze. Then, instead of continuing to help Peter, he started up the grass towards me, mentally readying his defense. Before he could speak, I said, "Too bad you boys had an accident. Go ahead, John, as you were going to. Help Peter." Then I left the scene. Out of the corner of my eye, I saw John race back down the slope and put his arm around Peter, then pick up his trike. Peter, only slightly shaken, jumped right back on and pedaled off.

It is sad that children don't generally expect to be understood by adults. They expect to be condemned. If we take ourselves off the pedestal as "children's judge and arbiter" we can relax and keep things simple.

Another technique to reduce discipline problems is the class conference. During community time, discuss relevant problems and project possible outcomes.

"Lately I've noticed the toilet has not been flushing very well. . . ."

"You need Jim to fix it," Tammi suggested.

"Well, Jim and I have looked at it, and Jim says it's not the toilet's fault. It isn't broken."

"Well, it still doesn't work right," Rosanna put in.

"I know. Since it's not the toilet's fault, it must be our fault. Perhaps we are using too much toilet paper."

"I saw Jeremy put a paper towel in it," Tony said.

"And we are not always remembering to put paper towels where they go. Where do they go?"

"In the trash!" the children chorused.

"What do you suppose will happen if we keep using the toilet as a trash basket?"

"It will break."

"The water will come out."

"Yes. And we don't want that to happen, do we?"

The class wrinkled up their noses at that statement. "If the water overflows, it will be very messy, won't it . . . and it might even stink." The class grimaced at the thought. "And the children using the toilet will have to help mop it up. . . ."

"Yuk! Ech! Icky, icky!" the children protested. "Make Jeremy do it!"

"But it's not just Jeremy. It's all of us. We all have to put less toilet paper in the toilet, too."

"And not throw paper towels down it!" Cindy responded.

"And flush it. . . ." another child remembered.

After this discussion we had no further problems with the toilet.

A class conference can also be effective when the problem is not a general one, but centers around a disruptive child. With such a problem, you need the help and understanding of the whole class. Without mentioning names, discuss the problem with all the children.

"One of us has very disturbing behavior. He can't seem to remember what work is his and he takes others' work."

"I know! It's—"

"Let's not mention names."

"But I know who it is!"

"Perhaps you do, but let's not embarrass the person. You wouldn't like it if someone embarrassed you. Besides, maybe others don't know who it is. Anyway, what do you think we can do to help this person—or any other child—to remember not to take other children's work?"

"Whip him!"

"Send him to the principal!"

"Tell his mom!"

"Well, we could do that . . . but would you like to be whipped? Or sent to the principal, or have your mom told how you've been acting?"

"No!"

"Well then, let's try to help this person first. What can we do to help him?"

"Tell him it's our work, not his."

"Tell him to do something else."

"He should do his own work."

While this discussion is going on, you can be sure the little offender is listening with both ears. He sees that the whole class is against his behavior. No one thinks he is funny; no one is amused. Hopefully, he will also see that the class is for him. They wish to help him so that their drastic suggestions given at the beginning of the conference won't be necessary. This may take some conversational steering on your part. Sometimes children are delighted to think of a classmate, especially an unpopular one, getting punished. So the learning situation is directed at the class as much as the offender.

In most of my classes, I have had one or two very emotionally disturbed children. I used this discussion technique, but added another class discussion when the child was absent. The opportunity to talk to the class in the absence of the disturbed child evolved naturally. The first time this occurred was when the child, in a hysterical rage, had to be removed from the class. While he was calming down in the nurse's office, the other children in my class were very excited about the situation and were talking about it among themselves. They were glad that the child had "gotten in trouble" and had to be removed from the class. Therefore, I felt a class conference was needed right then.

The class readily agreed that the student had a problem, and because of that problem he was unhappy and hadn't yet learned how to get along with many people. Therefore we shouldn't add to his burden, but rather we should help him by being friendlier and kinder, and by not complaining about him to me and others. The children agreed not to come to me every time they had a run-in with the child but to try to ignore most of the problems he caused. I told them that since I already saw how the child did disturb others I did not need to be informed of this.

This approach helped in several ways. First, it made the students see that the misbehaving child was not the teacher's problem, but a class problem. Second, it gave the students something positive to contribute to the child and to the whole class situation. Third, it took away the negative reinforcement some children may have been getting from me by their bid for attention when they reported the latest happening to me, always at the expense of the disturbed child. Fourth, it helped the children see the problem more sympathetically. Finally, it taught a Christian response to people who trouble us. The result was a marked drop in tension, and the problem-child's behavior improved.

In class conferences I frequently refer to the Bible, for the children know that the Bible is the standard authority in our classroom; its words are final. Its words are also backed up by the Holy Spirit's convicting power which convinces children more than any worldly wisdom could possibly do. The children are often amazed to learn that the Bible pinpoints their very own needs and problems, and then also gives solutions. What a wonderful discovery to make as a little child! As four-year-old Keith said, "God's words are full."

Sometimes a discipline problem is bigger than it should be because no one is communicating. When the teacher talks with her children, the burden can be carried by the whole class, not just the teacher or the misbehaving child. Talking together can "clear the air" and help to create understanding among individual members of the group.

Often, confrontations demanding discipline can be avoided altogether by simply telling the child what he should do. Reminders stated in positive, specific terms are more helpful to children than negative or general remarks. For instance, "Be good" does not communicate much to the child because it is so broad that the child does not know how to translate this request into his everyday actions. "Put the material in its place" or "Please sit down" are concrete, specific statements which the child can readily put into action.

Instead of constantly nagging the children to "Be quiet" or "Don't talk," they should be told calmly to: "Sit down," "Fold your hands," or "Put on your listening ears." Phrases such as "I like the way Corey is sitting," tell another nonconforming child the specific behavior you want to see and of which you approve. Motivation is provided also, for the child desires to win approval, especially in front of the group. Calling attention to a child who is sitting attentively during a directed activity not only rewards that child for his positive behavior, but also encourages other children to emulate their complimented classmate. Thus, not only are they shown by example and words how to act, but positive behavior is being rewarded.

This is not to say that we can avoid the use of "don't" altogether, but by applying other alternatives when given the opportunity, children have a chance to correct their behavior themselves before most "don'ts" become necessary. The fewer the negative injunctions the fewer the possible power struggles, and the fewer the discipline problems.

In working with children, many potential areas of friction can be reduced just by a knowledge of child development and by seeking God's help in applying this knowledge to individual children. By knowing individual weaknesses and by providing alternative ways for the child to act, head-on confrontations are appreciably diminished. As a result, it is easier for the child to eliminate unacceptable behavior.

I remember a bright little five-year-old who was suffering from a lack of parental affection and from sibling rivalry. She was sulky and aggressive and refused to admit mistakes.

This caused her a great deal of trouble in interpersonal relations and scarred the classroom atmosphere of congeniality. To channel her abilities positively, I gave her opportunities to teach the other children art processes that I had already shown her. As her leadership abilities were recognized by the class, her aggressiveness became channeled into responsible leadership, and she began to respond to other phases of the program. Day after day she asked questions about God and tested me for fairness. Eventually she asked Jesus to come into her heart. Slowly she began to change. One evidence of her changed personality was her ability to admit her mistakes. After having a squabble with another girl, she stomped off—which was usual behavior for her. But within five minutes she was back, admitting her wrong and apologizing. Her sincere, spontaneous apology was joyfully and immediately accepted, and the two little girls hugged each other.

10

WHEN ALL ELSE FAILS!

For whom the Lord loves He reproves,
Even as a father, the son in whom he delights.

Proverbs 3:12

So you've evaluated your program and corrected its weaknesses. You've had class conferences and puppet plays. You've established boundaries and given reminders. You've admitted your mistakes, and made honesty easy. You've set a calm example, and used a soft voice. You've introduced Bible stories and initiated memory verses.

Yet, sometimes Johnny still refuses to cooperate! He "does his own thing" at the group's expense. Obviously, some other measure must be taken to help him develop his own internal sense of social regulation. External discipline may be the needed measure.

External discipline need not be grievous. Instead, it should aid in orienting Johnny to the complexities of life, like other people's rights and feelings. But to discipline him requires rapport.

Rapport is based on love. Discipline without love is cold, harsh and usually ineffective, for it fails to establish positive behavior patterns. Instead, it can embitter children. Conversely, discipline with love corrects imbalances that the child is temporarily unable to correct. This kind of discipline does not break rapport; indeed, it is born naturally out of the established rapport. The child accepts this, and he learns. In the end, the child-teacher relationship becomes stronger.

In practice, these measures and outcomes are not easily realized. Like most adults, at one time or another I found discipline a difficult problem. What does one do about a misbehaving child? Looking for answers I read many books, each of which offered different advice. For a time, I become thoroughly confused.

The commandments in the Bible were clear enough: Do not provoke your children to anger; but bring them up in the discipline and instruction of the Lord (Ephesians 6:4); "He who spares his rod hates his son, but he who loves him disciplines him diligently." (Proverbs 13:24). The public school system allowed no choice in the latter: I had to spare the rod. And I was not sure how to apply the former!

Because of my uncertainty about handling discipline situations, I was slow to react, always wondering, "Are my expectations reasonable?" This indecision made matters worse, and I fell into an uncomfortable predicament.

If a parent or teacher becomes annoyed at a child's behavior, but lets the behavior continue before he puts a stop to it, the behavior continues to deteriorate and tension builds. It builds in the adult, for he is irritated; it builds in the child, because guidelines come too late and too indecisively. In his book *Freedom and Beyond*, John Holt calls this phenomenon the "behavior gap"—that is, the time it takes the adult to enforce limits after he has become annoyed at the behavior. The longer the gap, the greater the tension; the shorter the time, the calmer the class.

Clearly, I was on the long side of the behavior gap. I began to feel depressed and earnestly sought the Lord for guidance. Shortly thereafter a minister loaned me a booklet, *Dare to Discipline*, by James Dobson. It describes how, in a futile effort to avoid uncomfortable situations, some teachers frequently fail to respond to situations which demand confrontation. As a consequence, they lose control of their classes. The limits either are not decisively set or, if

Behavior Gap*

Figure 1. A small time gap promotes security in the child.

Ideal Behavior . . A B . . . . . . Problem behavior.

Figure 2. Too Long a time gap promotes tension in both the child and the adult.

Ideal behavior . . A . . . . . B . Problem behavior.

A=point at which behavior annoys adult
B=point at which adult imposes restrictions on undesirable behavior
A-B=time interval between points A & B (behavior gap)

they are, they aren't enforced when challenged, so the class wavers at the teacher's hesitation.

For a tension-free atmosphere, children need to understand clearly their reasonable limits. To accomplish this the teacher must be decisive. The teacher or parent must clearly communicate his expectations to the children without timidity.

The approaches I finally adopted are advocated by many authorities, including medical doctors, pyschologists, and educators—Christian as well as non-Christian.

---

* See *Freedom and Beyond*, by John Holt (New York: E. P. Dutton and Company, Inc. 1972) p. 13.

1. Talk with the child and explain the inevitable consequences of his unwise behavior.
2. Reinforce desirable behavior.
3. Find the hidden "rewarding motivation" in undesirable behavior and extinguish the motive by removing the reward.
4. Allow the natural consequences of the behavior to occur.
5. Enforce predetermined, precommunicated, logical consequences of behavior when there are no natural consequences (or when the natural consequences would be too harmful).
6. Physically spank when all else has failed. (This final step, of course, must be omitted where it is legally prohibited within the public school systems.)

By using these methods under the guidance of the Holy Spirit, the teacher gives the child a chance to learn directly from his own choices. The child learns to discern cause and effect, and power struggles—so costly to the adult-child relationship—are avoided. Besides being sensitive as to when and how to apply these methods, the best way for an adult to teach correct modes of behavior is to be a good model for the child to follow. Certainly, the setting of such an example is the responsibility of every Christian parent and teacher.

But because each child is different, there is no one way to handle all situations. One must truly rely on God's guidance and seek discernment from the Holy Spirit. With one child, only a glance will cause him to alter his behavior; with another, nothing short of a spanking will work. One maladjusted child may be a chronic offender. Another child with no previous history of behavioral problems may suddenly become rebellious. Methods of discipline must not only fit the child, but the situation.

If a child with few behavior problems suddenly seems rebellious, one needs to seek the cause. Sometimes a behavior problem can emanate from something that occurred at the breakfast table at home. Before you get all set to try your latest discipline theory, talk to the child and try to find out the reason for his sudden change in behavior. If he feels you are on his side, that you understand, the need for him to act out his frustrations in a destructive way may vanish.

Perhaps because so many teachers and parents have misused corporal punishment, applying it too freely and without just cause and thereby brutalizing some children, most states have now outlawed its use in the schools. Some type of substitute for this measure is needed.

We found a "time-out chair" to be the answer at the day-care center. With this method, the child was taken out of circulation and deprived of participation in activities for a short period. The time-out chair is an example of a "logical consequence."

Any chair can be used as a potential time-out chair. I used whatever chair was handy at the moment. I didn't want to traipse across the room to the child and back again to a specific chair located in a fixed place.

The misbehaving child would have to sit on the time-out chair during his own free time for as many minutes as he had misused the community time (or disregarded the standards). In this way, he learned to make a distinction between a time for group activity and a time for individual activity, between constructive use of the environment and destructive use, between harmonious social relationships and unpleasant relationships.

The child in the time-out chair was always in view of the other children. He was not socially cut off, could converse if he wasn't disturbing anyone, and could watch the other children. Outside, I would designate a time-out area—a tire, a tree, or whatever was handy.

Sometimes the time-out chair leads the child to redirect his activities. For example, two boys suddenly jumped up from their block work and, with a whoop and a holler, began running in my direction. As they raced towards me, I stepped in front of them.

"Steven! Tony! Remember we walk inside, and your voices need to be quieter."

This reminder seemed to work. But a minute later, there they were again, tearing around the classroom. Grabbing two chairs and two little hands I said, "Okay, Steven and Tony. Take time out. You boys need to find some work to do. When you think of some work you'd like to do, you can get up and go do it."

"We need to find some work to do," agreed Steven as he sat down.

The boys, not the least perturbed by being seated in the time-out chairs, set their minds on possible activities. Within a few seconds Tony, with a burst of new excitement, announced, "Puzzles! I'll do puzzles! Ya wanna do puzzles, Steve?" (Steven shakes his head.) "Hey Karen, I'm gonna do puzzles, okay?"

"Fine."

Steven continued to weigh the possibilities. For five minutes he did not move from the chair. Then his face lighted up with an idea. "I'm going to paint now," he said half aloud, as he headed to the art area.

In situations that call for external discipline, I try to give the child a chance to cool off and rethink his position. This is also one function of the time-out chair. But I never suggest that "God will surely punish you," nor pressure a child into asking for forgiveness at the height of his. emotion. An apology should be spontaneous and sincerely felt. Otherwise it cheapens repentance and encourages hypocrisy. The phrase "I'm sorry" should not become for the child a convenient way out of a wrong which he has committed. We must not force a child to ask for forgiveness before he is ready to be forgiven.

Probably the two most difficult times for a teacher to administer discipline are during meals and during Bible lessons (or other devotionals). These times are touchy because of the negative overtones disciplining may produce, both in the offending child and in the total group. We do not wish to inject unhappy feelings in situations designed to be positive. Yet it is possible to discipline during these times without spoiling the activity or without feeling guilty.

During mealtimes we accomplished discipline by social isolation. I explained beforehand to the children: "Mealtimes are happy times when we are all together, and for them to keep on being happy times, each of us needs to have good manners—courtesy toward one another."* After that, if a child was rude and disregarded the established rules of courtesy, his dishes were removed and placed on another table, where he finished his meal standing up, about twenty feet away but in full view of the main table. He was not verbally chided or ignored and he still enjoyed the benefits of being served by the servers. This method of discipline worked well for us at the center.

No child was ever disciplined for not eating, or for poor selection of food, because we respected individual choices. The children were encouraged to eat without cajoling, threatening, or bribing, through natural conversation about the food.

"My, these carrots are good!"

"How do we get carrots?"

"God first made the carrot. It grows in the ground, and the green leafy part, which was cut off and not cooked, is all you can see. The orange part we are eating was buried in the ground. It is the root part of the carrot plant."

"Buried in the ground!"

"Right."

"I'm glad God made carrots! I like them!"

"I'm glad too, because my eyes are happy every time I eat

---

* Good manners at mealtimes with preschoolers means simple courtesy and not specific use of eating utensils. Correct techniques in handling utensils are encouraged by example and occasional explanation. But correct handling of knife and fork cannot be expected, for some of the children's small-motor hand muscles are not yet capable of such feats. Specific table manners quietly develop as the children themselves desire to become more adept.

carrots."

"Your eyes are happy?"

"Yes, because God put something special inside the orange carrot root, called vitamin A, and vitamin A helps my eyes to see, even when it is very dark at night."

"I want some more— so I can see better!"

"Let's thank Nancy for cooking carrots for us today."

One time a little boy was being very fussy about food. As each server offered him a particular item, he turned it down. To make certain he understood what the ultimate consequences of his behavior would lead to, he was reminded that if he refused every item on the lunch menu, he'd end up with an empty plate and a hungry stomach. Nothing more was said, and he continued to turn food down until all the servers had finished. He sat at the table looking more and more mournful as we continued to eat and make our usual comments about how good the food was. The child was learning the power of his own words and decisions. It was a lesson that never had to be repeated by any of the children. In a short time, without pressure, external discipline, or bribes, the children all adopted healthy appetites for nourishing food!

Group harmony and cooperation are required for Bible lessons and other directed activities during community time. All the children must be involved so that none will be distracted and the feeling of unity lost. It is unrealistic and unfair to children to always let them have their own way, for life is simply not like that. But directed activities * need not be an unpleasant restriction to the child. Rather, they offer him a broader base of experience from which to form concepts and learn community life.

I would have been dismayed if the Bible story time had been burdensome to the children. As it happened, the Bible

_____

* Directed activities are those which are pre-planned by the teacher, such as Bible lesson time, to meet specific needs not adequately met by free (nondirected) time alone.

95

never became distasteful, and on the few days I did not present a story, the children reminded me to have one the next day for sure! This happy attitude would not have been possible in a chaotic class, without the discipline needed to promote group participation and cooperation.

Situations that call for discipline often lead to opportunities for greater understanding of spiritual truths. A bright five-year-old girl was coloring the creation story, which I had drawn on a large poster during the Bible story. Prompted by the student's questions, I had also touched on the fall of man. I told the child that she could color everything in the picture except the stylized dove because, as I had explained earlier, the dove in this picture was there only to remind the children that the Holy Spirit was present during creation. He was really invisible in this story. But before the girls had finished coloring all the various items of creation, she began to color the dove. I reminded her again. However, she insisted on coloring it and during the process turned and looked at me in defiance. I told the child:

"What you did is a little like what Eve did. I told you that you could color everything except one thing in the picture. God told Eve that she could eat anything in the garden except one thing."

The little girl looked at the picture and then at me: "She didn't have to eat the fruit. She could have done what God said!"

"That's right. And you didn't have to color the dove."

That little girl gave a look of sudden comprehension, but said nothing.

I continued, "People haven't changed much since then, have they?" She reluctantly agreed. "God had to punish Eve. Because she didn't obey, she couldn't be trusted to stay in the garden. So she had to leave. Neither can I let you finish coloring the story. It will just have to stay unfinished. Now, go to the time-out chair and sit there for five minutes."

I showed her my watch and where the hand would be in five minutes. After the time had passed, I gave her the choice of participating in class activities, but she was not permitted to return to coloring the story for that day. The child took all of this very seriously. I had a chance to observe her over several weeks. She became a happier child, less defensive, and freer to enjoy life. She became increasingly interested in what God had to say, and eventually asked Christ into her heart.

Spanking, time-out chairs, and related methods are not the answers to discipline problems. They are temporary measures to be used in special circumstances, usually involving clear acts of rebellion. The answer to discipline problems lies in the child's ability to learn self-discipline. One's whole approach should be geared around training a child to be a self-disciplined person.

As the children in our day-care program began to understand what was expected of them, less external discipline was needed. They began to believe that God loved them, even though they were imperfect. They began to respect themselves as worthy, because God had created them. Their self-respect was a result of scriptural truth, not deceptive flattery, which so often is man's way of trying to promote a good self-image.

Only in Christianity is it possible to develop a positive self-concept which is related to reality and based on truth. God doesn't allow an individual to overlook his shortcomings, yet He gives each person a positive self-image because of the value He places on people. The personal sacrifice of Jesus Christ to pay for man's sins and to bring him to salvation is God's final statement of man's value. Our personal worth, then, is not measured by what we do, but by who we are. A child shouldn't have to look to his I.Q. score to be self-accepting. He can look to God and know he was created with innate, infinite worth. If God has given such worth, the child should learn to discipline himself to live in accordance with it.

The disciples were scared. They thought
they were about to drown. They woke Jesus up.
Jesus came to the side of the boat and He
stopped the thunder and the rain and the
water went down.

Mark 4:37-39

A whole bunch of people came to see Jesus.
The mothers brought their children to Jesus. He
was busy the people said. Jesus said, "I
love little children. Please bring them to Me."

Mark 10:13-16, Luke 18:15-17

Zaccheus was so little he couldn't see Jesus. He climbed up a tree and Jesus saw him in the tree. Zaccheus went home and cooked supper. The crowd didn't like Zaccheus and they didn't want Jesus to go home with him. Zaccheus cheated people. But, after Jesus ate with Zaccheus, he was good. He gave back all the stuff he cheated. Jesus loved him even when he was creepy.

Luke 19:1-10

The man sat by the gate and he couldn't walk. John and Peter came along, and he could walk. Because Jesus answered their prayer.

Acts 3:1-10

11

AFTER ALL, WE *ARE* A CHRISTIAN DAY-CARE CENTER

In all your ways acknowledge Him, And He will make your paths straight.

Proverbs 3:6

"And, of course, there are to be Bible lessons, because, after all, we *are* a Christian day-care center. I consider this program part of the church's outreach."

"Any particular way you want me to teach these lessons?"

"Well, we are so new . . . we haven't got any materials yet . . . just tell us what you want and we'll try to get it for you."

What did I want? What would I need? How does one teach the Bible to such young children in a meaningful way? Isn't that too advanced for them?

"Lord Jesus, what would you do if you were conducting this class? How would you teach these little children? I start tomorrow, and I don't know these children—but you do. And you are the One who's put me here. Please let your love reach through me to the children. Show me the way, and thank you for letting me be the one to share your love with them."

The morning dawned dewy-bright and promising. As I drove to the school I continued my conversation with the Lord; I was filled with a calm expectancy.

In the church classroom the children, from just under three through six years of age, gathered about me. As I saw

100

them, I felt love for them. I was jubilant! I had to share with them the Lord's answer to my prayer about them!

"I talked to God about you."

"About us?"

"Uh-huh. You see, I don't know you all yet. I'm your new teacher. But God knows you, each one of you. And each one of you is special to Him. There is nobody like you in the whole world.

"God sent me here to you to be your teacher for a little while. He sent me to tell you that He loves you and wants you to know more about Him and His world.

"Right now, God has given me love for you. Even though I don't know you, He does, and He has put some of His love into me for you. That's a miracle! To love someone you don't know! And I love you!"

There were smiles on every face. I don't know if all of the children understood all my words, but one thing was certain: They knew I was really glad to meet them, and that God was the reason that I was so glad.

"It's a beautiful day! Let's sing! I'll teach you 'This is the day that the Lord has made.' "

"He did?" Trevor asked.

"Yes!"

"Oh!" Trevor's eyes shone with the secret of it.

The next day I continued: "Remember I told you yesterday that God sent me here to help you get to know Him better?"

"Yeah. When ya gonna teach us about God?"

"Right now." I picked up a Bible. "Do you see this book? It is called the Bible. The things written down in this book are things God wants to say to people. He doesn't want people to forget these things, because they tell us how to live. Some of the things in the Bible are rules. There are rules for mothers and fathers, and all grownups, and for children too! If we know and follow these rules we will be happy, and God will be happy with us also."

"What's a rule for children?"

I opened the Bible to Ephesians 6:1. Pointing to the verse, I read, "Children, obey your parents in the Lord, for this is right." We talked about what that meant and how to apply it in life. It became our first memory verse. I wrote it down in front of the children, and they tried to read it. I noticed how positively they responded to seeing the verse written as they watched.

"There are many more things in the Bible, stories that really happened to real people and children. I'll write these things down for you, like I did the verse, so we can have our own record, our own copy of the Bible!" It will be a book just for you—the children's Bible!"

It may have been news to the children that "this is the day which the Lord has made," but it was news to me that we were going to have a children's Bible! The idea had come to mind just as I spoke to the children, and I had vocalized it so quickly that I was surprised myself. Little did I know how greatly the Lord was planning to use this in the lives of the children.

The next day I affixed a large sheet of white paper to the wall with masking tape. When the children came in, they were immediately curious. I began to draw a scene, illustrating the story of Peter and John healing the lame man at the gate Beautiful (Acts 3:1-10). I told the names of the characters as I formed them. Then I told the story, up to the point I had illustrated. I added one final figure—the lame man healed, now leaping joyfully—and I told the climax of the story. Finally I asked, "Can you tell me the story you have just listened to?"

"The man sat by the gate and he couldn't walk," one child said.

"Right!" Then I pointed to the other figures, asking, "What about these men?"

"John and Peter came along."

I began to write down their remarks, repeating them as I wrote. Soon we had our own paraphrase of the story. We read it back together and then sang a song to recap the story:

"Silver and Gold Have I None."

The drawing I had made was composed of simple, cartoon-style figures. During the children's nap time, I colored this rather plain-looking illustration. When the children awoke they noticed how much better the picture looked, and some of them said, "You did a nice job of coloring. Can we color one?" They stood around the story talking about it among themselves. Some sang the song we had learned and then asked me to "read the words we said." Thus, in the spontaneity of the classroom, utilizing some old ideas and some new ones, a simple but highly effective idea was born for teaching children the Bible.

After a few days, Jim felt guilty about my having to draw all my own visuals. "I'll order materials just as soon as our budget allows," he said.

"No . . . I don't think I'll need them now. Unless you'd rather I use preprogramed lessons."

"Oh, no! I like what you're doing. But I thought prepared stories and materials would make it easier for you. I mean, how long can you keep drawing each lesson?"

"Just as long as the Holy Spirit leads me to continue this way. It's really fun!" I was just beginning to get a taste of Spirit-led teaching, and it was exciting. Each lesson was a step of faith for me.

A year later I was in the Philippines. While passing through Manila, I happened to have a conversation with a missionary, trained in Christian education, who was serving with another mission board.

"We've been here weeks already, and who knows when we will be able to start our work. It's so frustrating, especially after seeing the great need, just to have to sit and wait."

"But why can't you start now?" I asked.

"Because my visuals are somewhere on the ocean. I've shipped a whole crateful, hundreds of dollars' worth, actually. But they are still on the ship, and we don't know when they will arrive. Not only that: when they finally get here they'll have to clear customs, and that means more waiting, so you can see why I'm so frustrated just having to sit and wait. I don't know how anyone can teach without visuals!" I was tempted to remind her of the lack of visuals in the first-century church, but she was convinced. There was nothing I could add.

My thoughts drifted back to a hot and dusty little Indian village in southern Mexico. There I had labored, armed with only a few Tzeltal phrases, struggling to teach literacy. The first time I saw my "classroom" I was aghast: It was a thatch-roofed, dirt-floored, mud-walled, one-room affair. My teaching materials consisted of a tiny blackboard precariously hanging on one nail from a pole wall support, some chalk, a few 18" x 24" sheets of paper, ten small sheets of construction paper, a dirty map of Mexico, several broken crayons, and some simple Tzeltal primers. The hut also came fully equipped with chickens, rats, fleas, and an occasional stray dog, but at least the pigs did not venture into this abode of higher learning. My twenty students ranged in age from five to twenty-three years old. Because of the range of both age and previous lessons, as well as the fact that there was only one table (smaller than a picnic table, with two wobbly benches), I held three different classes daily.

The previous teachers had told me that I could expect the attendance to drop off quickly. "After the first week, the novelty of having a new teacher wears kind of thin," they sighed. This was discouraging news to me.

I had never before taught under such primitive and limiting conditions. Prior to this I, too, had been used to visuals and a plethora of equipment. Moreover, I was used to talking my way through lessons, and now I could speak only eight or ten sentences in the Tzeltal language. Shortly I was to learn that even words were unnecessary.

After the first day I formed a rough assessment of the students' strengths and weaknesses. One thing was certain: they were tired of the primers. I set a behavioral goal which I hoped the students would achieve before I left. Now the problem was to implement that goal. I prayed about that; I prayed hard.

It was out of this situation that I really began to understand that "life" was my teaching material, visuals and all! For geography, the students and I made our own maps. We started with a floor plan of the room. Next came a map of the village, which we drew up as we paced off each house and section. Later, we postulated an area map and from there we used the map of Mexico. For math, I used money, corn kernels, a number chart, and a homemade calendar to bridge the gap between the abstract and the concrete.

For reading, I drew sketches of actual village happenings.* Then the students supplied their own sentences about the pictures, after which they would read them to each other. Gradually they began to have the confidence that they, not just *Americanos*, could compose stories. And that was my behavioral goal for them: creative writing!

There were many other things we did and each step, I felt, was guided by the Lord. But most importantly, I made a "material breakthrough" by learning that I did not have to rely solely upon educational aids "made in U.S.A." As for the students, they were exhilarated at the discovery of being able to write out their own thoughts. (And attendance never did drop off!)

The lessons I had learned in Mexico—allowing the students to create their own relevant materials—stuck with me; and, with the Lord's guidance, the child-dictated Bible stories came into being at the Norman day-care center.

The Bible stories continued for several weeks, and they maintained their popularity throughout with the children. But time was running out. Soon I would be leaving for my

---

* *The Tzeltal children did not draw spontaneously. After watching me, some of them would shyly attempt to draw. If drawing had been indigenous to their culture, or if they had wished to do original work, my approach would no doubt have been different. But drawing was new to them. It proved fascinating to the children. Occasionally I used geometric shapes and built my figures from those. This pleased the students, for they could readily copy my figures and adapt this technique to their own early attempts at sketching.*

Philippine assignment with the Wycliffe Bible Translators.

"But who will do the Bible lessons after you go?" Rosanna asked.

Jim, the director, wondered too. "The Bible stories just flowed, did they?" he asked.

"Yes, most of the time they really did."

"Effortless Bible teaching!" he mused.

"Spirit-led Bible teaching."

Looking around at the story-lined walls he continued, "The kids really go for them, and so do I. And some of the parents have commented about them also. Why don't you write down some of your main points for the next teacher so we can continue them?"

Jesus started shining Jesus friends were scared. And a cloud came and God was in the cloud. God said, "This is My beloved Son, listen to Him!" And Moses and Elijah were with Jesus.

Mark 9:1-7

You have to follow Jesus. Jesus asks you to follow Him. We have to decide.

John 12:26

Jesus knocks on the door:
"Can I come in?" The children asked
Him into their hearts. Their hearts are
happy.
Revelation 3:20 & John 10:10

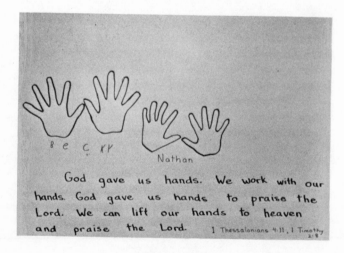

BECKY

Nathan

God gave us hands. We work with our
hands. God gave us hands to praise the
Lord. We can lift our hands to heaven
and praise the Lord. 1 Thessalonians 4:11, 1 Timothy 2:8

12

SPIRIT-LED BIBLE TEACHING: NINE SUGGESTIONS

But the Helper, the Holy Spirit, whom the Father will send in My name, He will teach you all things, and bring to your remembrance all that I said to you.
John 14:26

1. Select the story.
2. Pick an appropriate time of day.
3. Illustrate the story.
4. Tell the story.
5. Write down the children's words as they retell the story.
6. Read their story aloud.
7. Color the illustration.
8. Review the finished stories.
9. Plan related activities.

1. Select the story.

The most important aspect of story selection is to let the Holy Spirit guide you. Relying on the Spirit, though, doesn't mean you come into class empty headed. In order to be prepared to respond to the leading of the Holy Spirit, you must have a deep reservoir of Bible lessons within you. Therefore, the best lesson planning you can do is your own personal study of God's Word. Then the lessons will come spontaneously.

To select my lessons, I listened to the children. Maybe during outdoor playtime a situation would occur that brought to mind an example in the Bible. It was a knowledge of the Bible, quickened to me by the Holy Spirit, that matched up the children's needs and the biblical message. Perhaps the next day I would tell the biblical example that had illuminated yesterday's playtime situation. Although I always had a lesson in mind, or perhaps two or three tentative lessons, I never committed myself to teach it until I actually was ready to begin. If this lesson was the one the Holy Spirit wanted me to teach, often the little children's conversation naturally led into it. I would wait for their interests to become clear to me. Then I would begin to draw the story or items suggested by their interests. The children focused their attention on the drawing as it began to take shape and guessed what the story might be about. The story I drew might be the one I had already planned, or it might be something that the Holy Spirit had just given me.

For example, at one Sunday school class for four- and five-year-olds we had a lesson on deciding to follow Jesus. The children understood that they must *choose* to follow Jesus, but what then? I wanted the children to know what following Jesus meant on a practical, moment-by-moment basis. I felt that this continuing aspect of following Jesus needed to be made clear. But just how I was going to be able to clarify it, I wasn't sure.

Saturday I awoke in the middle of the night with an impression. "Following Jesus is like a game of following the leader: you go where the leader goes and do what the leader does." The next day as the children and I went from the church sanctuary to our classroom, we played "follow-the-leader." I thought all the children would be willing to talk about the unusual way we got to class, and I unhesitatingly remarked: "I bet you wonder why we played follow-the-leader this morning." But apparently no one did, for they ignored my remark and began talking about fishing and the beach!

I pushed my intended lesson over to one corner of my mind and shifted mental gears. I began to draw a beach scene and

110

some fishermen. Just where this unplanned story would lead, only the Lord knew! As I formed the picture, the children began to discuss it and to guess what it might be about. At this point, the story of Jesus calling Peter and Andrew to follow Him and become fishers of men came to mind. It fit the children's needs in several ways. First, it tied the story to the previous lesson. The Holy Spirit can be trusted. He has a way of fitting what might at first glance seem to be disjointed lessons into a logical pattern that parallels the children's interests. Second, the story related to the children's immediate interests. Third, it provided a beautiful introduction to following Jesus in daily life.

After the children had finished dictating the story back to me and I had written down their words, I underlined *"Follow me."* I said to them, "You said Jesus told the disciples to follow Him. What did He mean by that? What does it mean to follow someone?"

"See what they do and do it," answered Jay.

"Like the game follow-the-leader?" I pursued.

"Yes. You have to watch what the leader does," Jay replied.

"Well, we can't see Jesus," said Richy.

"But Peter and Andrew saw Jesus," reminded Stephanie.

"Yes, Peter and Andrew did see Jesus when He was on earth. They saw what He did and tried to be like Him. They went with Him and watched Him. But Jesus wants us to follow Him too, so how do we know what to do, since He has gone back to heaven for a while?"

The children shrugged their shoulders.

"I want to follow Jesus but I don't know how," admitted Stephanie.

"Well, here's how to follow Jesus. When Peter and Andrew and other friends followed Jesus, some of them wrote down what they saw Jesus doing. What they wrote down is in the Bible. So when we read the Bible, we can find out what Jesus did and what we should do also. Jesus doesn't ask us to do anything that He would not or did not do. And besides that, if we want to follow Him and be like Him, He

111

sends us His Holy Spirit to live in us and help us to do the things He did. Would you like to know something He did so you can follow Him?"

"Yes."

"One thing He did: He always obeyed His Father who is God. What does 'obey' mean?"

"To do what God told Him to do."

"Right. Was it easy for Him to obey His Father? Did He always feel like doing what His Father asked Him to do?"

The children didn't know.

"Do you always feel like obeying your daddy or mommy?"

"No."

"How about the time God told Jesus to let men nail Him to a cross?"

"And He died on the cross," Keith broke in.

"Yes. He even died on the cross. Do you think He felt like doing that?"

"Uh-uh."

"But He did it anyway. He wanted to obey His Father even when He didn't feel like it.

"So if we want to follow Jesus—to do what He did—what is one thing we can do?"

"We can obey God," Luther summed up.

"Yes." I picked up Richy's Bible. "And it tells us in the Bible what God wants us to do. He doesn't want us to die on a cross; that was only what He asked Jesus to do, no one else. But look what it says here—something God wants children to do: "Children, obey your parents in the Lord, for this is right." I showed them the passage and they were quite impressed that the Bible remembered children, too. Ephesians 6:1 became our memory verse, which we tried several times on the tape recorder and then played back. Some parents later told me that their children came home happily saying their memory verse.

Teaching that's open to the leading of God's Spirit welcomes the children's comments and uses "interruptions," as Jesus often did, to good advantage.

112

One Sunday, between songs, Luther produced a toy soldier from his pocket.

"I have a soldier!" he proudly announced.

"I see that you do. May I please hold it for a while?" He handed me the soldier. Holding it up for the class to see, I asked, "Do you think there will be soldiers in heaven?"

"No," one of the children said.

"Yes!—I mean, the good soldiers," another protested.

"What about the bad soldiers?" I pursued.

"No!" they chorused.

"All soldiers are bad. They kill people," Jay said.

"No, that's not right, Jay," corrected Luther. "Some soldiers are good. Like the ones who protected us." Luther had lived in Vietnam.

As the lively conversation continued, we consulted the Bible to answer the questions and disagreements. The children concluded that: (1) Jesus loves both good and bad soldiers; (2) Jesus wants to see bad soldiers become good; (3) to be a soldier who gets into heaven, the soldier needs to have Jesus in his heart and follow Him; and (4) when the soldiers who want to follow Jesus go to heaven they will have to have another job, because people don't kill each other in heaven and they don't have war in heaven.

The Holy Spirit is not likely to guide you in a way that is contrary to the natural mental capacities and developmental stages of children, for then He would be working against the way He himself has obviously created them. Thus, stories that can be taken literally are understandable to little children (although they understand them in terms of their own experience), while stories with oblique meanings, rich in symbolism, demand reasoning of which preschool children are largely incapable. Indeed, for any of us to comprehend something new, we need to relate it to something within our experience. (The unknown must always be carried on the shoulders of the known.) Therefore, it often happens that when children hear something new, confusion results because of their limited reservoir of knowledge.

"Why do we sing about Rosanna in that song?" Mike asked.

"What do you mean?"

"You know—'Rosanna, Rosanna, shout unto God with the voice of triumph!' "

The correct version of this song is, "Hosanna! Hosanna! Shout unto God with a voice of triumph!"

Another child, when told that "Jesus came to earth" converted the message into "Jesus visited the school!"

And in a class of all black children, I was asked: "God didn't make us out of dirt, did He?"

Every eye in the group was suddenly fixed on me. I replied, "The Bible says that when God made the very first person, He used the clay of the ground."

"He must have made *you* out of white clay!"

If a story is related to the children's own current thoughts and happenings, fears and joys, it will be remembered and pondered. The stories will sink down into their souls, where change is born. This is why I seldom plan lessons more than a day in advance—and sometimes, even at that, I will drop a planned lesson and do another, or none at all. The lessons have to be fresh. Let the Holy Spirit be the curriculum planner, because He is the One who knows the daily needs of us all.

2. Pick an appropriate time of day.

The timing of formal Bible instruction for young children is important. I chose the first part of the morning, about nine o'clock. At this hour the children were fresh and better able to concentrate than later on. By having the Bible story early, a God-centered attitude was set for the day. At the end of the day, we had another short community time reviewing Scripture memory verses, reading stories about God's creation, and singing songs about Jesus. Thus, the day ended on a note similar to that on which it began.

3. Illustrate the story.

There are several ways to illustrate the stories you teach. Flannel boards (and similar equipment) have been used successfully by many teachers. Simple, on-the-spot sketching is another method that is highly effective, and one that I have personally found the most adaptive to Spirit-led teaching. You don't have to be an artist to outline simple forms which convey meaning. I use cartoon-like figures (stick figures are fine, too) and largely ignore perspective. I don't want to lose the children in irrelevant detail.

As an example, in picturing Jesus' post-resurrection appearance (as given in Luke 24:36-43 and John 20:19), I included only the disciples, Jesus, a barred door and window, and some fish. I added no outline of the room, or any furniture. What was included was enough to help the children remember the significant parts of the story.

Since I use only figure outlines for my illustrations, all of my subjects look basically alike. So I decided to place lines radiating from Jesus' head to distinguish Him from others. To convey the brilliance of His transfiguration, I used radiating lines for His whole body. After His resurrection, Jesus was noted by marks on His hands and feet. The Holy Spirit was pictured as a dove. God the Father was symbolized by a semi-circle of radiating lines from an invisible source.

Once I use a particular symbol, I use it consistently. These simple symbols are all explained to the children as the story is being told.

If a flannel board is used, one needs a rather complete selection of figures and scenic items, so that a wide variety of illustrations can be produced. Figures of Jesus and of the individual disciples in various poses, houses, fences, wells, grass, water, lakes, seashore, clouds, and other items can be used to create a spontaneous scene, illustrating the story at hand. A bit of practice with this technique should provide the ability to illustrate almost any scene.

Meaningful illustrations can also be created by using concrete, physical analogies of spiritual concepts. When viewing a story that employed the picture symbols I use for God the Father, God the Son, and God the Holy Spirit,

115

Rachel asked the inevitable question: "Are there three Gods?" I held up the marking pen in my hand.

"How many pens do I have in my hand?"

"One!"

"Right! One pen. But it has parts. See the part which I am holding? I don't get ink on my fingers because I am holding this part. It protects me. Look at this other part—it's the top. What would happen if I didn't put it back on when I finished using the pen?"

"It would dry up!"

"Then do we need the top?"

"Yes!"

"What is this part?"

"The part that writes."

"That's right, the part with the colored ink. Now let's count the parts: the holder, one; the top, two; the ink-felt, three. How many parts altogether?"

"Three!"

"Right, three parts. How many pens?"

"One!"

With this start, we talked about the analogy between the pen, which was part of their experience, and God in three persons.

These suggestions for illustrating stories are representative of the many possibilities awaiting a creative teacher open to the Holy Spirit's leadership. You will find many more as you step out in faith.

4. Tell the story.

Be lively, understandable to the children, and believable. When telling a Bible story, a teacher should use her most expressive gestures and tone of voice. How can we be less than enthusiastic while relating the living Word? God's Word is exciting and alive. You must feel this fact. If you do, the children will feel it also.

Explain vocabulary and cultural trappings in terms of the children's own experience. Take the raising of Lazarus from the grave as an example. Have any of the children been to a mortuary or a funeral? Talk about it. A discussion of burial customs, old and new, may be needed. Dying is part of this present world. The children accept this and are much more matter-of-fact about it than most adults.

Credibility involves making a clear distinction between fact and fiction. It is imperative for children to understand that Bible stories are not make-believe, that they are true events which God wants us to know. When teaching Bible stories I constantly stress their reality. When, in a school program, I occasionally read a fictional work, I tell the children that such stories are made-up, "pretend" stories, unlike the real stories in the Bible. It cannot be overemphasized that it is essential to stress this point with children.

Little children want to know what they can count on; they do not want to be fooled. Since they have limited experience, what they are told is very important to them. By the time a child is five years old he usually has already had the painful experience of trusting himself to things he was told which have proven to be false. At this tender age he is old enough to be skeptical, and sometimes even cynical. Therefore it is not surprising that it sometimes takes a while before a child is willing to believe the Word of God.

I learned this from the children when I taught kindergarten. After having told them day after day for weeks that the Bible tales were true, I was surprised to hear a boy say, in response to a story, "Did that really happen?" The truth that God cares about individuals and does step into peoples' lives to save, heal, and guide began to break through to him. If God cared about a blind man, and sent His Son to heal him, God also could care about this little boy. It was a revelation to the child!

To maintain credibility, you must be consistent with the children in all areas of life. You cannot expect children to trust the Word of God as truth, if their teacher tells them that other things are also true which are not. This will inevitably be discovered, and the child will distrust all he has been taught.

Many children are taught by parents and teachers that Santa is real. Some parents unthinkingly point to the fat man in the red suit and say, "Look, there is Santa!" when they should be saying, "Look, there is a man dressed up as Santa Claus." Perpetuating the Santa Claus myth in this way can have unfortunate results. A little girl with big brown eyes was asked, "Who is Santa, honey?" Full of trust and conviction she responded, "He's God."

Most of the lessons I give are directly from the Bible. But don't overlook the lessons of what Jesus is doing today. He still answers prayer, heals the sick, protects people, provides financially, and performs other miracles. I was thrilled as I read the account of God's protection of a group of Otomi Indians, in Mexico, who were new believers.* As they prayed for protection from neighboring villagers who were intent on massacring them, God literally surrounded them with angelic hosts. Their enemies, coming toward the village in the dead of the night, saw it surrounded by torches and thought that soldiers had been called out to protect the villagers. But the believers saw no one except their fleeing enemies. "The angel of the Lord encamps around those who fear Him, and rescues them (Psalm 34:7)."

Encourage your children to look for God's working in their own daily lives. If you, yourself, have had a definite answer to prayer which illustrates a promise of God, it can be a valuable lesson. Firsthand accounts of God's majesty, power, and compassion are the most compelling lessons of all. Jesus Christ is the same yesterday and today, and forever. Let your students see that this is literally true!

5. Write down the children's words as they retell the story.

Four-, five-, and six-year-old children are quite able to

---

* *Ethel Wallis, Otomi Shepherdess* (Huntington Beach, CA: Wycliffe Bible Translators, n.d.).

dictate sentences in retelling a story. Generally, three-year-olds are not quite ready to verbalize on this level; but if the story is short and direct enough, they follow with rapt attention and learn much from their older classmates. Therefore, the children should be asked to tell the story in their own words while the teacher writes it down where they can see it.

This is an important step, for it allows feedback from the children so that the teacher immediately knows if they have grasped the lesson. It also helps the children to internalize the story, aiding them in building their own inner value structures.

Sometimes the sentences come so fast that it is necessary to ask the children to wait. The words of the children should be repeated as they are written down. This way the children see the written form of each word take shape. Some of the five-year-olds are beginning to be aware of spelling, and it's not at all unusual for them to ask questions like: "How do you just *know* how to spell all that?"

The Bible lesson is not a grammar class. It's more important for the children to learn to verbalize concepts that reinforce the Word of Life, than to confuse them with unfamiliar grammatical forms. Therefore, acceptance of the children's words is part of my method. However, if a misinterpretation of the story occurs I help the child to correct it immediately, for it is equally important not to let erroneous ideas take root. Sometimes the sketched illustration helps to clarify a mistake. If such is the case, I direct the child's attention to the picture, where he usually spots his mistake and quickly corrects it himself.

Nothing breaks communication faster than embarrassing the child who has made a mistake. "No, Johnny, that's not what I said" may be true, but it is also a big "put-down." Let the Holy Spirit lead you to clear up any misunderstanding.

During a lesson about deciding to follow Jesus, one child dictated: "The children in the picture are following Him, but they do not want to follow Him until they see how He gets into heaven." I was surprised. This thought had never occurred to me, but I wrote his words down anyway. The comment gave me insight I may never have gleaned in any other way about this child's thinking. After reading the story together, I explained that we do know how Jesus got into heaven and then I related the account of His ascension. The following week we did the story of His ascension to reinforce this vital lesson.

Like a master weaver training an apprentice, you can work with mistakes as part of the overall design. That is the only way to keep the class genuinely open and able to voice their thoughts. And in order to teach your students, you need feedback concerning what they are actually thinking.*

Eliciting story retelling from the children is not always an easy process, especially from children whose verbal skills are weak. The shorter and simpler the story the better they

---

* Another way to deepen feedback from children is to ask specific, probing questions. For instance you might ask, "If that had happened to you, what would you have done?" Or, "When such-and-such happened, how did you feel?" If the children's reaction is different from that of the person in the story, you might want to ask why the biblical person reacted the way he did.

But do not press the children for answers. Not every question must be answered right then. Sometimes it is well to leave the question to ferment in the children's minds. This will give them the chance to try to construct the reasonings for themselves. In thinking through the possible reasons, the story becomes much more real to them and relevant to their own lives. To be sure, this step is not to let the children pick and choose what their values will be, but rather, to give them a chance to wrestle with God's absolute truths, and consciously and freely make them their own.

You may wonder, "Do little children ponder questions until they are resolved to their satisfaction?" Consider the following example: Four-year-old David asked his mother why we had a new president. His Christian mother, not knowing how to answer him in a way that seemed appropriate for one so young, just said that the previous president had been bad. But David persisted, "Why was he bad? What did he do bad?" Again the mother answered, "He was bad so he did bad things." Unsatisfied, he fell silent, but continued to wrestle with the problem. Hours later he told his mother, "I know why he was bad—he had a bad heart." This answer shows the integration into an actual situation of what he had been taught about the human condition.

Value Clarification by Simon, Howe, and Kirschenbaum (New York: Hart Publishing Company, 1972), gives a thorough (though humanistic) discussion of this subject.

will understand it, and the easier it will be for them to supply the text. Teacher assistance is sometimes necessary.

Each story should be completed, but occasionally it may take more than one lesson before the children are able to provide the text. When the children have been unresponsive (and it does happen), I suspect that I was not sensitive enough to the Holy Spirit when I selected the story. Even then, it has been my experience that children do not like a story to be unfinished. During the day they'll look at the picture and remind me that we wrote no words and no one colored it. When it was necessary to spend another lesson on one story, I simply said that we needed to listen really well so we could think of things to write. The children became acutely aware of their responsibility, and they would try to supply the missing text. It became my practice, therefore, not to give a new story until the current one was completed.

6. Read their story aloud.

I had the entire group "read" the story aloud by repeating my words. This step gives the children a strong sense of accomplishment in being able to reconstruct the story. Incidentally, it is beneficial to the development of language and prereading skills.

7. Color the illustration.

If the illustration is a line sketch, one of the children should be allowed to color it. If a flannel board is used, an alternative to the large wall sketch is a mimeographed line drawing of the story for each child to color the next day. Or the coloring step could be replaced by letting the children use the flannel board individually during their free time to reconstruct the story.

I am aware that, according to some current theories, coloring in an outlined form is said to block a child's creativity. If coloring the Bible stories were the only art experience available to the children, this possibly would hold true. But in our program the children were constantly free to experiment with various media every day. Usually, everyone spent a portion of each day working at some creative art project of their individual choosing.

For coloring stories I provided broad, felt-tip colored pens, because I found that these were less fatiguing than crayons. The pens were reserved for the Bible stories and for occasional special art projects. This led the children to feel that it was a special treat to color their own Bible story pictures. Sometimes there is a thin line between the familiar and the common—I wanted the children to look at these stories as something extraordinary.

The children were not required to finish the coloring of a picture, though practically without exception they did. Generally a child would spend from thirty minutes to two hours on each picture! Sometimes the children would get tired and put away the pens, saying, "I'll finish after nap time." That's fine. If they don't finish, that's fine too. But I gave them only one day to work on their story. Finished or unfinished, the next day was for someone else and a new story.

One of the major reasons for coloring is that it fixes the story in the minds of the children. It also has the advantage of increasing child participation. I allow the child who colors the picture to put his name on it, or I write it on for him if he can't write. The stories each child colors become especially important to him.

It is true that a young child's coloring may spoil the picture. But although it is not unreasonable to expect effort on the part of the children, it is unreasonable to insist on their meeting an arbitrary standard. While I suggest that the children try to retain the forms of the figures, as long as the children are genuinely trying to do a good job I do not bother them or try to assist them once they start.

Some of the younger children may start within the lines and then get so interested in the mechanics of drawing that they go over and over the same figure, gradually going beyond the outline and obliterating it. Nevertheless, as long

122

as they are intent on their work I don't disturb or reprimand them.

Corey had a habit of starting within the lines, then going outside of them to draw his own squiggles. But as he drew his various doodles, he told himself the story over and over, using his squiggles as symbols. Once he was working on the picture of Revelation 3:20. Two hours after he had all but obliterated the picture of Jesus knocking at the door, he asked Jesus to come into his heart!

8. Review the finished stories.

Our finished illustrations were placed on the walls in the room and hallway where everyone could readily see them. This way, the pictures served as continual reinforcement.

One day there was a terrific storm. At first the children were merely excited. But when the lights failed, and playground equipment outside began toppling over, the children became really frightened. I reminded them of the story of Jesus calming the storm when the disciples were frightened. At once the children dashed across the room to the wall where that particular Bible lesson was hanging. They said, "Please read us the story again." Afterwards they discussed it, and we began to sing choruses and repeat Scripture verses. Soon the children became calm and regained their confidence, all because of the Word of God. This experience showed me the value of leaving the stories where they are accessible to the children at all times.

9. Plan related activities.

I frequently use songs and Scripture memorization as related activities to reinforce the Bible lessons. If I know a song that relates to the day's story, I'll introduce it after the story. (Again, it pays to be open to the Holy Spirit's leadership. If the story evolves into a discussion, it is sometimes better to wait and share the song later, perhaps at the closing community time.)

I recorded many Christian choruses, especially those with

Scripture verses set to music, on a cassette tape recorder.*
We played these just before the end of the day. The children
always responded very positively to the songs. All of them in
our program, without direction or any coaxing whatsoever,
memorized all the taped songs as well as the other classroom
songs. And Steven consistently refused to go home until he
heard the Jesus songs on the tape recorder!

With some of the songs I used creative movement to
reflect the words and music. This kinesthetic expression
helps to further fix concepts in the minds of the children. The
movements I used are very simple and largely repetitive. I
think the experience provides a beautiful means of
worshipful expression towards God, and a silent heightened
sense of unity.

Of course, no pressure to participate is ever applied. As
the music is played, those who care to join in creative
movement do so; those who do not, continue to listen or sing.
But even those who are only watching usually enjoy the
activity.

For Scripture memorizing, a cassette tape recorder is also
great fun. The children can keep track of their own progress,
both as a group and as individuals.

As they become familiar with the verses and songs,
children tend to punctuate the atmosphere with them at
various times throughout the day. They do this at home, too,
and on several occasions this witness of the children has led
parents to seek salvation for themselves.

Other methods of lesson reinforcement include acting out
the Bible stories, student use of flannel boards to
reconstruct stories, and models of biblical people for solo

---

* It is interesting to note the children preferred the music of two nonprofessionals
to that of professionally recorded artists. The songs they preferred were the
so-called "Jesus Songs" sung by two of my friends, one of whom played the guitar
as they sang. Perhaps the children preferred this music because it was simple,
repetitive, and free from gimmicks like the affected voices that are so prominent in
music for children. The children were also impressed with the fact that these
singers were friends who had recorded the songs especially for them.

play. These all heighten the children's concentration on the stories they've heard. And so, free-time or "play" activities can reinforce the life-changing concepts that are being learned while the children (and you) are having fun.

The Holy Spirit gave me these nine techniques for bringing Bible truths into the reality of a child's present world. If you ask Him, He will show you what approach you should take to meet each need at hand. Spirit-led teaching can never be confined to a nine-point formula.

Being sensitive to the children's immediate interest is one way the Spirit directed me to present the lessons, but this was not the only way I have been led. At other times, I would search the Scriptures to find out what God had to say concerning a particular need the children had. And, as I searched, I found such thrilling answers that I found it hard to wait to share my "finds" with the children!

So, armed with the Bible, notes, and verse references, I didn't wait to see what turn the children's conversation would take, but rather announced that God had showed me some things from His Word that were especially for them, things that they needed to know, things that would help them.

These lessons frequently involved deep teachings that were not easily illustrated. Nevertheless, I wrote key words down as I went, partly so I could give a coherent summary at the conclusion of the lesson, and partly to emphasize the points as I gave the teaching. Among the topical lessons I have given are "The Word of God," "Avoiding Foolishness," "God's Attitude towards Grumbling," "Praise and Worship," "The Fear of the Lord," and "What God Wants from Us."

Impossible, you say! Not suited to preschoolers! If I expected the little ones to understand every word, then, true, these subjects are not suitable. Yet these topics represented and met the personal and current needs in the lives of the children. From listening to the Word of God as I read, explained, and reread it, these children were able to understand the major point of each lesson. They appreciated this approach and were attentive. (I encouraged this attentive, reverent attitude by not allowing any disrespect, i.e. disturbance, silliness, extraneous comments and so forth during the reading or discussing of the Word of God.) But, beyond that, these lessons seemed to produce changes in the children's attitudes and behavior, and so impressed them that they frequently related the main points to their families and playmates. So don't be afraid to teach even preschoolers directly from the Word of God. It's powerful!

Select the story and draw the picture.

Tell the story. Be lively, understandable, and believable to the children.

127

Let the children re-form the story in their own words. Write down the children's words.

Read the finished story together.

13

THE ADVENTURE IS
JUST BEGINNING

*For I am confident of this very thing, that He who began
a good work in you will perfect it until the day of Christ
Jesus.*

Philippians 1:6

So there you have it, the adventure I've had as a teacher of
little children, learning to point them to Christ. Whether the
subject matter was mathematics, natural science,
geography, reading, or the Bible—always, in every field,
I've endeavored to reveal God to them through His
handiwork.

"Dear Fellow Teacher," began the letter I addressed to
my successor. "It is with both sorrow and joy that I release
this work to you. Sorrow, because I surely will miss these
children, whom I love. Joy, because I know the blessing you
will receive from God as you work with them. And I am
assured for the children, that He who has begun a good work
in them will perfect it until the day of Jesus Christ.

"The Lord has taught me many things as I have worked
with these children. One is to rely on the Holy Spirit. . . ."

That is as far as a teacher can go. She can present the truth
about God in all its variegated beauty; she can describe the
love of Christ for little children; she can explain the way of
salvation. But only God can give a child spiritual birth. When
a teacher has faithfully taught all she can, she must leave it
in God's hands to bring forth spiritual life in the child's heart.
And He does.

One little girl asked recently, "Why do we always have to have stories about Jesus?" This is a question none of us likes to hear. Nevertheless, an honest question deserves an honest, unembarrassed, undefensive answer. In this case I explained: "You'll have to decide whether you want to follow Jesus, who loves you, and be with Him forever in heaven, or whether you want to live forever without God, in some other place besides heaven. If you don't know about Jesus, and what He has already done for you, how will you be able to follow Him?"

At that the girl shrugged her shoulders. The idea promised interest.

"We also need to hear about Jesus because He made us, and He knows us, and He wants us to know all about Him. When we get to know Him, then we will know why we were made and what we are supposed to do with our lives."

This child became eager to hear Bible stories and was overheard saying to others, "We gotta listen to these stories. They're important so we'll know how to follow Jesus and go to heaven!"

In this same class, after a relatively short time of teaching God's Word to the children on a daily basis and promoting a Christ-centered atmosphere throughout the day, statements of commitment to Jesus were made spontaneously. Various children made such statements as:

"I want to follow Jesus; how can I do that?"

"I want to go to church."

"I want to ask Jesus to live in my heart."

"I want to go to heaven and live with Jesus and all the people He's making houses for: Peter, James, John, Jim, Saunny. . . ."

When children voiced such statements I would personally talk with them, asking questions to determine the level of their understanding and whether or not they were truly ready to enter into a genuine commitment to Christ. If a child gave evidence of understanding, and conviction that he must commit himself to God through Jesus, it was a simple matter to ask him if he would like to invite Jesus to come into his heart. If the child gave a positive response to this invitation, we prayed right then.

There are a few precautions to be observed when leading such young children to Christ. We need to recognize that it is sometimes hard for little children to express themselves verbally on an abstract level. We should be sensitive to what the child is actually trying to say within his limited vocabulary. Conversely, some little children have memorized religious-sounding answers and desire to please the adult, but the words are not meaningful to them yet. We need discernment regarding these matters. If a child exhibits an awareness of his sins, expresses a desire to be forgiven, and realizes that only through receiving Jesus, who paid for his sins, will he go to be with the Father in heaven, certainly this child is ready to pray—and who would deny him that?

After children pray to receive Christ, their consciousness of a new relationship to God is usually reflected in their lives and words. I have overheard these babes in Christ say:

"Who will live in heaven with us?"

"Jesus is in my heart now."

"I wish He'd come back right now!"

Spiritual growth will be evidenced little by little, until one day it will seem as if you have a kaleidoscope of change occurring right in your own classroom. It's an amazing and beautiful thing to see this occurring in the lives of even the smallest children.

During one lunch time the five-year-old table setter, Rosanna, had a mixture of shiny and not-so-shiny flatware. She put the shiny pieces at her place, but she gave the less attractive pieces to others. Four-year-old Tammi complained:

"I want a shiny spoon and fork. Give me the shiny ones!"

"I don't have any more," Rosanna answered.

"You gave yourself some shiny ones," Tammi said tearfully.

Then came the forceful defense, "Yes, but there aren't any left—and anyway, I am the table setter today. I can set the table the way I want to. I decide who gets to have the shiny ones and who doesn't, and I would have given you shiny ones, but there aren't enough. See?"

Rosanna continued, loudly and uncomfortably, "I *would* have given you some, but I ran out before I got to you. . . . When it's *your* turn to be the table setter, then you can do it *your* way. *And stop that crying.* You're not a baby!"

At the word *baby*, Tammi began to cry even louder.

The table setter explained to me, "There aren't enough shiny ones. I don't know why she's crying. It's not *my* fault."

Obviously troubled but not admitting it, she finished setting the table in a silence broken only by the sobs of her unhappy friend. Then, unobtrusively, she went into the kitchen and asked the cook if there were any more shiny utensils. Returning with the extra pieces, she thrust them at Tammi: "All right, Tammi—here! Now don't cry any more!"

Learning to cope with one's fallen nature in a Christ-like manner isn't easy for any of us, and the struggle can be seen in children as young as this. Selfishness and pride die hard. But the evidence of God's Spirit at work will be clear.

I'll never forget the lesson of love red-headed Steven taught us all. We were singing "God is so good, He's so good to me" when Steven, with arms wide apart, interrupted.

"Us!" he cried. "He's so good to *us! All* of us!"

Steven was getting the message of corporate love, love for the whole Body of Christ.

As the time neared for me to leave the day-care center, the children began to evidence anxiety about who their next teacher would be. I reminded them that God had sent me, and that He would provide a new teacher for them. I told them that the director was praying for God to send a teacher who would be the one He wanted. As the children talked about this, they came to the conclusion that God really had provided before and that He would continue to provide. Their attitude gradually changed from one of worry to one of expectancy.

As the children grew in Christ they reached out to others in a natural, straightforward way, as only children can do. One day a mother who was very troubled with personal problems entered the room. She wanted to pray, and her needs were so critical that we prayed right then. As we finished praying, a little girl looking straight at us began to sing "Rejoice in the Lord always and again I say rejoice!" The sensitivity of little children to the needs of others is remarkable!

Children are also completely candid and direct in witnessing to others. Tammi frankly advised her three-year-old classmate, Cindy, to ask Jesus into her heart, so she would someday live in heaven with her and a host of others whom she began to name—both biblical characters and saved classmates. Perhaps such openness and directness is one of the characteristics Jesus referred to in Matthew 18:3: ". . . unless you are converted and become like children, you shall not enter the kingdom of heaven."

When it finally came time for me to leave the day-care center, the children asked again why I had to go. I reminded them of why God had sent me to them, and told them that now I had finished my part of the task. God was sending me to other children who lived in a far corner of the world and did not know that He loved them, but needed to know. The children discussed my leaving and began convincing one another that people living in a jungle far away also needed to know about God. Shane, who was not quite three, was cautious: "I don't think I'd go to the jungle; I might get all tangled up in it." But Tammi was reflecting. . . "Maybe someday when I'm grown up I'll go to the jungle so they can hear about Jesus, too."

And so we grew—the children, the staff, the director, and myself. Children were saved; parents, too, were moved toward God. And I, who in my pre-Christian days had looked on schoolteachers with disdain, cried when I left.

PART TWO:

RESOURCE HANDBOOK FOR RUNNING YOUR OWN PRESCHOOL PROGRAM

135

Learning comes through physical participation.

I. ACTIVITIES-SKILLS-MATERIALS CHARTS

The purpose of these charts is to offer guidance as to preschool activities and exercises which are most helpful to a child's early development and cognitive growth. More than enough suggestions are given here to provide a rich and varied program which will develop a wide range of skills, stimulating the child's learning pattern both mentally and physically. (An "activity" may be performed by one or more children and is usually unstructured, while an "exercise" is performed by only one child and is often structured with a predetermined goal.)

Activities are designated as free (F), structured (S), or teacher-directed (T) on the charts. A "free" activity is unstructured. It involves imagination and/or experimentation, and does not have a predetermined, patterned goal. For example, the finished product of an art project will vary from one child to another. A "structured" exercise, on the other hand, is to be done only in a prescribed way to achieve a predetermined goal. A puzzle, for example, can be correctly done in only one way. Materials for these exercises usually have a built-in "control-of-error" feature; if not, the teacher should check the child's work.

Some activities may be either free or structured. A geoboard with rubber bands is a free activity, but when the student follows patterned cards to make his designs it becomes a structured exercise. A "teacher-directed" activity may be either a group activity directed by the teacher or a project which requires teacher supervision, such as cooking on a stove.

The ages given in the charts indicate the best age ranges for introducing a particular activity, or the usual period of highest interest in a given activity.

The "location" column show whether an activity is most suitable for indoors (I), outdoors (O), or either (I/O). Thus, if you are looking for an art activity to do outdoors, you can see from just a glance at the chart which ones to consider.

The skills, or purpose, are what is taught by the activity, or why it is included in a preschool program. An activity is said to be "therapeutic" when a calming effect, or a release of emotions, is seen in the child. All the activities are therapeutic to some extent, but those that are especially so are noted.

Materials and equipment listed are all that you will need for each activity. The use of place mats and floor mats helps focus attention, reduce sound, and keep the child's activities confined to a certain space. Each mat should be of a solid color rather than patterned, so small objects can be easily seen. Most of the materials called for are common household items, and many can be made by hand. The source of manufactured items is indicated by three letters of the company's name, and company addresses are listed in section II, "Sources of Materials and Information," immediately following the charts.

BOW = Bowmar Publishing Company
BRM = C. Baroni & G. Marangon
CRP = Creative Playthings
CPU = Creative Publications
DLM = Developmental Learning Materials
EPT = Educational Playthings

ETA = Educational Teaching Aids
LCM = Lakeshore Curriculum Materials
NIE = Niehuis
SDE = Skill Development Equipment Company

ACTIVE PLAY

Activity/Exercise	Type	Skill/Purpose	Age	Materials/Equipment	Area
water play	F	experimentation, therapy	1½-3½	large basin, nearby water source, containers, toy boats	I
sand play	F	construction, experimentation, dramatic play, measuring, therapy	2-5	sandbox, sand & covering, a few toy trucks, funnel, sieve, containers of various sizes, cookie cutters, sand combs (EPT)	O
making suds	F	observing a gear, turning a handle, therapy	2-4	egg beater, basin, sudsy detergent	O
pantomime	F	dramatic representation, confidence	3½-6		I/O
puppet play	F/T	dramatic representation, social relations lessons, verbal skills, therapy	4-6	hand puppets (DLM), box made into a stage or TV (optional)	I/O
dramatic play	F	role playing, socialization, verbal skills, therapy	3-5	cardboard boxes, hollow blocks or snap walls (EPT, LCM), 1 or 2 dolls, teddy bear, various types of hats, a few garments that lend themselves to imaginative play, small closet or hooks for clothes	O
obstacle course	S/T	responding to verbal commands, vocabulary formation	4-7	objects for the obstacle course, such as a chair, sawhorse, hollow blocks, small table, etc.	I/O
musical games	S/T	learning body parts, responding to verbal commands, rhythm	3½-7	live or recorded music of "Hokey Pokey" or "Did You Ever See a Lassie," etc.	I/O
mirror	F	body concept	all	full-length mirror (EPT) or 3-way full-length mirrors (LCM)	I

Activity	Type	Purpose/Skills	Age	Equipment/Materials	I/O
riding	F	pushing, pulling rocking, bouncing, large muscle control	1-3½	rocking horse or Spring Mates (EPT)	O
jumping & leaping over obstacles	F/S	timing perception of space	3½-6	hollow blocks (EPT, LCM), tire tubes, etc.	O
walking on tiptoe	F/S	balance, grace, strength in legs & feet	2½-4	line or balance beam (EPT, LCM)	I/O
overhand swinging	F/S	coordination, strength in arms & hands	2-6	horizontal ladder (EPT)	I/O
climbing	F	coordination, large muscle control, therapy	2-5	climbing cube, sculptured shapes, barrel tunnel, slide, trees, etc.	O
swinging	F	pumping, therapy	4-6	swings (EPT, LCM)	O
riding tricycles	F	coordination, strength in leg muscles	2-4	Big Wheel (or similar) tricycle	O
pulling carts	F	pulling, socialization	2-4	cart or wagon (LCM)	O
target practice	F/S	throwing, hand-eye coordination	4-7	target board, bean bags & box to store bean bags	I/O
playing ball	F/S/T	throwing, catching, hand-eye coordination, socialization	4-7	ball at least 6" in diameter	O
hula hooping	F	muscle control	4-6	hula hoops	O
jumping rope	S	timing, jumping	4-7	long, heavy jump rope or clothesline	O
construction	F	hand-eye coordination, balancing, lifting, socialization	3-6	hollow blocks (EPT, LCM)	O
clay	F	experimentation, creativity, therapy	2½-5	clay or play dough, small board or heavy cardboard covered with vinyl or oilcloth, cookie cutter (optional)	I/O

ART

The skills and purpose of all art activities include hand-eye coordination, strengthening and control of muscles, experimentation, creativity, organization of materials, responsibility, logic, observation, color sense, and therapy.

Work on large tables and protect them and the floor with drop cloths (plastic sheeting, oil-cloth, or newspapers). Protect children's clothing with smocks (old adult shirts with cut-off sleeves) and provide hooks for hanging them up or a basket for storing them.

Hang wet artwork with clothespins on clothesline or wire fence, or spread on flat surface to dry.

When using old magazines, remove offensive pictures beforehand.

In the following chart, "paints" are tempera paints which may be purchased dry and mixed, as needed, with water and a bit of detergent or liquid starch for desired consistency. "Brushes" are short-handled paint brushes with ½" bristles. "Paper" is construction paper. "Cups" are small milk cartons or tin cans used individually by the children.

Activity/Exercise	Type	Age	Materials/Equipment	Area
gadget printing	F	3-6	paint and tray, paper, objects to print with—spools, carved potatoes, lemons, etc.	I/O
leaf printing	F	4-6	paint, brushes, cups, paper, natural articles—leaves, shells, twigs, rocks, etc.	I/O
hand & foot prints	F	2½-5	tray, paint, newsprint or old wallpaper catalogs	I/O
painting own body silhouette	F	4-7	wall or door, brushes, cups, paint, newsprint or butcher paper, crayons or felt-tip pens, masking tape	I/O
straw painting	F	3½-6	paint, cups, paper, straws	I/O
splatter painting	F	2½-5	floor or ground, paint, brushes, cups, paper	O
squeeze painting	F	2½-5	3 plastic squeeze bottles, paint, paper	O
tempera painting	F	2½-6	easels (optional), paint, brushes, cups, newsprint	O
watercolor painting	F	3½-7	watercolor paints, watercolor brushes, cups, watercolor paper	I
finger painting or monoprint	F F	2-5 3½-6	prepared finger paints or liquid starch mixed with dry tempera paint, slick paper, wiping cloth or paper towels	I/O

Activity	Type	Age	Materials	Setting
cut & paste	F	2½-5	blunt scissors, paste, old wallpaper catalogs or magazines, paper	I
cutting strips or shapes (for paper mosaic, weaving, etc.)	S	4½-6	blunt scissors, old wallpaper catalogs, magazines, colored tissue paper, newspaper, etc.	I
paper mosaic	F/S	4½-7	glue or paste, old wallpaper catalogs or magazines	I
paper weaving	S	4½-7	paper strips, paste, paper backing	I
paper chains	S	3½-6	paper or wallpaper strips, stapler or glue	I
collage	F	2½-5	blunt scissors, liquid glue or paste, paper, yarn, fabric scraps, or natural articles —leaves, shells, twigs, rocks, etc.	I/O
torn paper collage	F	2½-5	paste, paper	I
yarn pictures	F	4½-7	blunt scissors, liquid glue, paper or cardboard, yarn or fabric scraps	I
stitchery	F	4½-7	large blunt needles, yarn, fabric scraps, burlap	I
3-D tissue	F/S	3½-7	liquid glue, paper, colored tissue paper, scrap of heavy paper for glue (blunt scissors and crayons optional)	I
3-D paper sculpture	F	3-6	blunt scissors, glue or paste, paper or old wallpaper catalogs or magazines	I
tissue lamination	F	3-6	liquid starch, brushes, cups, paper, colored tissue paper	I
papier-mache ornaments	F	5-7	old bucket or basin, liquid glue, balloons, newspaper strips	I
dip-dye	F	3½-6	paper towels or fabric scraps, food coloring, containers for dyeing	I/O
screen rubbings	F	3-5	screen-covered cardboard, newsprint or fabric scraps, crayons	I
coloring	F	2-6	newsprint, crayons	I
chalk drawing	F	2-5	floor, ground, paper, or chalkboard with eraser, chalk	I/O

BIBLE

Activity/Exercise	Type	Skill/Purpose	Age	Materials/Equipment	Area
Bible story with child dictation	T	recall of story, sequence of events, verbal & listening skills, left-to-right eye movement	3–6	chalk & chalkboard or a large sheet of paper & felt-tip pens	I/O
memorizing Scripture	T	memorization, pronunciation	3–7	Bible, tape recorder (optional)	I/O
singing	F/T	memorization of Bible verses, tone perception, pitch control, therapy	2½–7	piano or other accompaniment (optional)	I/O I/O
creative movement or drama	F/T	Clarifying, reinforcing, & appropriating concepts; therapy	3½–6	music, songs	I/O
reconstructing stories	F	recalling Bible lessons, reinforcing concepts	3½–7	flannel board & cut outs or models, miniatures of Biblical scenes & characters	I
walks, excursions, etc.	F/T	recalling Bible lessons, appreciation of God's creation	3–7		O

144

MANIPULATIVE EXPERIENCES

Activity/Exercise	Type	Skill/Purpose	Age	Materials/Equipment	Area
pouring water	S	hand-eye coordination, muscle control, precision	3–4	drying cloth or sponge, two small clear pitchers, a few drops of food coloring added to the water (optional), tray	I
lids & jars	S	visual perception of size, control of hand muscles	2–4	6 different-sized jars with screw-on lids, storage container, place mat	I
construction	F	balancing, large motor control, geometric concepts, creativity, therapy	3–5	unit blocks (EPT, LCM), storage container	I
puzzles	S	logic, small motor control, preparation for grasping a pencil, visual perception	2½–4	wooden puzzles with knobs of varying degrees of difficulty (inset puzzle strips LCM, perception puzzles ETA), place mat	I
standing puzzles	S	balancing, logic, hand-eye coordination	3–5	equilibrium puzzles (ETA)	I
block construction (2 or more building together)	F	balancing, large motor control, socialization	3–6	hollow blocks (LCM, EPT)	O
woodworking	F	use of tools, large motor control, creativity, precision, experimentation, safety	4½–7	sawhorse (LCM), clamp, safety block, saw, hammer, nails, sandpaper, scrap lumber, box or cart container	O
body puzzle	S	body concept	3½–7	large body puzzle (DLM), large floor mat	I

MATHEMATICS

Activity/Exercise	Type	Skill/Purpose	Age	Materials/Equipment	Area
30 pegs	S	size perception large muscle control, 30 concept, 5 x 6=30 concept	3-5	peg grading board (EPT)	I
peg board	F/S	exploration, patterns, counting, serration, small muscle control, number concepts & operations	4-7	small peg boards & pegs & box (EPT), pattern sheets, pencil & paper (optional), place mat	I
counting cube rods	F/S/T	number concepts and operations, vocabulary (equal, unequal, less than, greater than, etc.), symbols, serrations, counting, place value, exploration	3½-7	counting cubes glued together (and varnished) to represent 1 to 10 units per block, or Unifix cubes in one color (LCM), pencil & paper (optional), place mat	I
cubes & grid	S	constancy of number, number concepts	3-7	Unifix operational grid, number group and analysis cards, light blue & red cubes place mat (LCM)	I

golden beads	F/S/T	number concepts & operations, counting, place value, small motor control, exploration	3½-7	golden beads, box & rack (BRM, NIE), place mat or floor mat	I
number rods	F/S	exploration, serration, carrying of long objects, counting, numeral recognition	3-5	number rods (BRM, ETA, NIE), numeral cards & box, floor mat	I
number line	F/S/T	counting, number concepts, exploration, vocabulary (forwards, backwards, more, less, adding, subtracting	3-6	number line painted by squares on floor or cement	I/O
logic	S	logic, number concepts, counting, large motor control	2½-5	Bead & Rod (EPT) or Add-A-Rack (LCM), basket, place mat	I
number sorting	S	logic, number concepts, counting, serration, dexterity	2½-4½	Number Sorter (CRP)	I
number-numeral	S	number concepts, counting, numeral recognition	3-6	Number-Numeral Triple Tiles (by Playskool), place mat	I

147

MATHEMATICS (cont.)

Activity/Exercise	Type	Skill/Purpose	Age	Materials/Equipment	Area
number chart	F/S	counting recognition of patterns & numerals, games	4½-6	large sheet of paper affixed to a wall (1-100 numerals), different-colored felt-tip pens	I
prediction tunnel, (See *Thinking Is Child's Play*, by Evelyn Sharp, in reference bibliography.)	F/T	prediction, logic, order	3-6	3 different colored spools & bowl, a long shoelace, cardboard tube, place mat	I
fractions	S	part-whole relationships	4-7	fractional geometric insets, equivalent figures (BRM, ETA, NIE), place mat	I
standing fractions	S	part-whole relationships	3½-7	Fraction Skittles (NIE), place mat	I
geometric insets	S	kinesthetic sense, vocabulary of geometric shapes	3-5	set of wooden geometric insets (ETA, BRM, NIE)	I
geoboard	F/S	observation of areas & shapes, vocabulary of geometric shapes, exploration	3-6	geoboard & rubber bands (CPU, LCM), box for rubber bands, pattern cards (optional)	I
scale & weights	F/S/T	prediction, exploration, addition, subtraction, vocabulary (more, less, lighter, heavier), reading scale	4-7	metric or English scale with metal weights (ETA), place mat	I

weight scale	F/T	prediction, size-bulk-weight relationship, weight measuring, reading scale	2½-5	bathroom scale (metric scale, CPU)	I
measuring	F/S	exploration, reading a ruler, logic, size relationship concepts	4-6	ruler, yardstick (metric rulers & metersticks from CPU, primary yardstick from ETA), paper & pencil (optional)	I/O
height chart	F/T	height measurement, growth over a period of time, reading a number line	2½-5	height measuring chart or a measuring line drawn on wall or door	I/O
dry measure	F/S	exploration, volume measuring, reading volume measures, large muscle control, addition	3-5	set of dry measuring cups, tray, sand or rice & container	I/O
liquid measure	F/S	volume measuring, addition, subtraction, exploration, hand-eye coordination	4-6	set of metric or English measure containers (ETA, CPU), tray	I/O
equal volume measuring	S	constancy of volume	5-7	set of liter-volume clear containers (CPU), tray	I/O
clock puzzle	S	clock sequence	3-6	Fit-A-Clock (EPT), place mat (optional)	I

MUSIC

Activity/Exercise	Type	Skill/Purpose	Age	Materials/Equipment	Area
listening	F	auditory perception, therapy	all	music, live or recorded	I/O
creative movement	F/S	coordination of large muscles, awareness of moods & tempo in music, therapy	3½-6	music, live or recorded	I/O
rhythmic clapping	T	auditory perception of rhythm, timing	4-7	music, live or recorded	I/O
music box	F	observation	3-7	see-through music box (CRP)	I/O
rhythm band	F	dramatic play, therapy, socialization	2½-5	rhythm band set: tambourine, shakers, triangle, wrist bells (CRP, EPT, LCM), container	O
bells	S	auditory perception, reading music, vocabulary (musical notes)	3½-7	2 sets of tone bells & mallets (BRM, ETA, NIE), music pattern cards (optional) box	I
playing piano	F	exploration, vocabulary (musical notes, high, low), auditory perception, therapy	2-5	piano	I
drawing to music	F/T	auditory perception, therapy	4½-7	music, live or recorded paper, crayons & container	I

PRACTICAL LIFE

Activity/Exercise	Type	Skill/Purpose	Age	Materials/Equipment	Area
hand washing	S	self-reliance, establishing a routine, sequence of action	2½–4	basin or sink, soap & container, towel, trash basket if paper towels are used	I
correct use of toilet	S	self-reliance, courtesy	2½–4	rest room & toilet paper	I
scrubbing nails	S	self-reliance	2½–5	small bowl, soap or detergent, child-sized nail brush or old toothbrush	I
hair brushing	S	self-reliance, hand-eye coordination	2½–5	brush, comb & mirror	I
manicure	S	small motor control, self-reliance, sequence of actions	4½–7	small bowl, soap or detergent, child-sized nail brush or old toothbrush, orange stick, nail file	I
shoe polishing	S	self-reliance, care of shoes, wiping, brushing, buffing, sequence of actions, therapy	3½–6	newspapers for floor or table, polish & applicator, brush, container	I
buttoning	S	small motor control, coordination, self-reliance	2½–4	large & small buttoned dressing frames (BRM, ETA, NIE)	I
zipping	S	small motor control, coordination, self-reliance	3–5	jacket zipper dressing frame (ETA, NIE)	I

PRACTICAL LIFE (cont.)

buckling	S	small motor control, coordination, self-reliance	3-5	buckling dressing frame (BRM, ETA, NIE)	I
pinning	S	small motor control, coordination, self-reliance	3½-6	safety pin dressing frame (BRM, NIE)	I
bow tying	S	small motor control, coordination, self-reliance, sequence of actions	4-6	bow tying dressing frame (BRM, ETA, NIE)	I
lacing	S	small motor control, coordination, self-reliance, sequence of actions	4-6	lacing dressing frame (BRM, ETA, NIE)	I
drawer closing	S	coordination, large motor control	2½-4	dresser or cabinet with drawers	I
chair & table moving	S	grace & ease, large motor control, accuracy in judging distance	2½-5	child-sized chairs & tables	I/O
carrying objects	S	grace & ease, confidence, large motor control, precision & care	2-4	vases, dishes, trays, etc. (BRM, NIE)	I/O

Activity	S/T	Skills	Age	Materials	I/O
setting table	S	remembering a set order, classifying, responsibility, precision	3½-6	all needed utensils, plates & napkins, place mats or table cloth, flowers & vase, or other decoration	I/O
serving finger food	S	courtesy	2½-4	plate & finger food	I/O
pouring beverages	S	hand-eye coordination, precision	3-5	small pitcher and glasses	I/O
serving hot food	S/T	carrying, courtesy, care & precision	4-6	serving plates & utensils, tray (optional)	I/O
clearing table	S/T	carrying, courtesy responsibility	3½-5	all plates & utensils	I/O
scraping dishes	S	responsibility, classification, stacking dishes properly	3½-5	all used plates & utensils	I
washing dishes	S/T	teamwork, care & precision in handling soapy dishes, self-reliance, responsibility	3½-6	sink or basin	I
rinsing dishes	S/T	teamwork, care & precision, responsibility	3-5	sink or basin	I

PRACTICAL LIFE (cont.)

Activity/Exercise	Type	Skill/Purpose	Age	Materials/Equipment	Area
drying dishes	S/T	care & precision, team-work, responsibility	3½–5	dish drainer, counter, drying cloth	I
putting away dishes	S	classification, order, teamwork, responsibility, lifting & carrying	3½–5	cupboard	I
cooking	T	confidence, self-reliance, measuring, teamwork	4–7	stove, utensils, ingredients, cleaning materials, recipe book or cards	I
correct use of clothespins	S	squeezing, small muscle control & strength	4–7	clothespins, clothesline or wire fence	I/O
cleaning chalk-board, easels	S	responsibility, control of sponge & water	3–5	container for water, sponge	I/O
cleaning eraser	S	responsibility, therapy	2–4	chalkboard eraser	O
cleaning paint-brushes	S	responsibility, care of environment, sequence of actions, therapy	3½–5	container for paintbrushes, cloth or sponge, sink or basin	I/O

154

Activity/Exercise	Type	Skill/Purpose	Age	Materials/Equipment	Area
folding	S	responsibility, therapy, precision	2½-5	small towels, wash cloths, napkins	I
rolling up mat	S	responsibility, precision	3-5	place mats used for some exercises and/or floor mats	I/O
cleaning	S	self-reliance, care of environment, sequence of actions, therapy	2½-5	container for water, small scrub brush & sponge (NIE), drying cloth, plastic apron, detergent, small bucket or basin for all the above	I/O
dusting	S	observe that dust accumulates daily, care of the environment, large motor control	2½-5	dust cloth, spray or liquid polish (optional)	I
sweeping	S	care of environment, large motor control, responsibility, therapy	2½-5	child-sized broom & dust pan (BRM, EPT, NIE)	I/O
mopping	S	care of environment, responsibility	3½-6	child-size mop & bucket, detergent	I
cleaning the mirror	S	care of environment, large motor control, therapy	3-5	container for water, apron, cloth or sponge, window-cleaning agent drying/polishing cloth	I/O

155

PRE-READING AND READING

Activity/Exercise	Type	Skill/Purpose	Age	Materials/Equipment	Area
parquet patterns	F/S	exploration, visual matching to a pattern, therapy	3-5	Large Parquetry (DLM) pattern sheets (optional), floor mat or place mat	I
faces	S	visual perception of same pattern & matching	3½-5	Matching Faces (CRP), floor mat or place mat	I
alphabet board	S	letter matching, spelling of names	4-5	metal board with letters drawn on with permanent ink, magnetic letters in one color (LCM), small magnetic board, name cards & box	I
ring the peg	S	left-to-right movement, sequencing, spatial orientation, hand-eye coordination, small control	2-4	Spatial Orientation & Sequencing Board (DLM), box for rings	I
sequence stories	S	sequencing	4-6	Sequence Cards (LCM), floor mat or place mat	I
alphabet puzzle	S	sequencing, small motor control	3-5	alphabet puzzle (LCM), place mat (optional)	I
sandpaper letters	S	phonics, kinesthetic memory of letter shapes	3-5	sandpaper letters & container (BRM, ETA, EPT, LCM, NIE) place mat or floor mat (optional)	I

movable alphabet	S	word attack through phonics, spelling	4-7	movable alphabet & compartmentalized box (BRM, NIE), floor mat	I
Talking Typewriter	F/S	learning alphabet	4-6	Moore's Talking Typewriter, word cards (optional) & container	I
picture file	F	independent research, classification, therapy	3½-7	box with pictures mounted on cardboard & covered with clear contact paper, & filed under various classifications, floor mat	I
read & do	S	reading for meaning	4-7	box with little rolls of paper, each containing a command the child reads & carries out	I
looking at books	F	proper handling of books, appreciation of books, reading	2-7	20 picture books, plus 10 rotating library books	I
individual dictionary	F	sight reading of words with emotional impact to a particular child	4½-7	student notebooks for the recording of words which are especially meaningful	I
reading student stories	F	socialization, reading for enjoyment & meaning	4½-7	student notebooks to be filled with their own stories (the children read each other's notebooks)	I

PRE-WRITING AND WRITING

Activity/Exercise	Type	Skill/Purpose	Age	Materials/Equipment	Area
chalkboard	F	large & small muscle control, therapy, hand-eye coordination	2½-5	chalk, pavement or chalkboard (individual or large) & container for the chalk (LCM) eraser or cloth for chalkboard	I/O
coloring	F	therapy, large & small muscle control, hand-eye coordination	2-3½	crayons & container, paper	I
pegs & peg board	F	small muscle control, therapy	3½-5	small peg board, pegs & box (EPT, LCM)	I
puzzles	S	grasping of knob in preparation for grasping a pencil	2½-5	wooden puzzles with knobs: inset puzzle strips (LCM), perception puzzles (ETA), map & flower puzzles, geometric and leaf insets, (BRM, NIE)	I
cutting on a line	S	hand-eye coordination, small motor control, strengthen hand muscles	3-4	1 pair blunt scissors, paper bisected by a straight line, tray	I
outlining & filling in geometric forms	F/S *	small motor control, abstracting form concept, exploration with multi-shapes & possible designs	3-5	metal geometric insets (BRM, ETA, NIE) or clear stencils (DLM), 2 colored pencils, tray	I
sandpaper letters/numerals	S	kinesthetic memory of writing as motion	3-5	sandpaper letters/numerals & container (BRM, ETA, LCM, EPT, NIE), place mat (optional)	I

trace a line	S	small motor control, hand-eye coordination	4½-6	mimeographed sheets with continuous, spiraling, dotted lines representing basic geometric shapes, pencil, tray or box	I
name tracing and printing	S	small motor control, hand-eye coordination, practice in writing names (own & classmates') sense of achievement	4½-6	piece of heavy cardboard or wood, with a heavy clear plastic strip affixed on three sides to the upper half of the board, and a pile of paper strips stapled at one end on the bottom half of the board, name cards (which are inserted in the plastic window & traced over), grease pencil (taped to a string), soft cloth for cleaning plastic, tray or box	I
dictation	T	observe words take shape	3-5	paper, & crayon/pencil/pen (child dictates sentences to teacher, who writes them down)	I/O
composition	F	creative writing	5-7	individual students' notebooks, pencils, child's dictionary	I

* Unlike most F/S exercises, this one proceeds from "structured" to "free." As the children are able to manage outlining and filling in the shapes, they are allowed to use more than one at a time, thereby creating their own geometric art forms.

SCIENCE

Activity/Exercise	Type	Skill/Purpose	Age	Materials/Equipment	Area
finding places on globe	F/T	beginning research, exploration, geographic concepts	3½-6	tactile globe & continent globe (ETA, BRM, NIE), set of continent maps, floor mat (optional)	I
map making	T	reducing reality to two dimensions, observation, objectivity	5-7	paper & felt-tip pen, compass (optional for floor plans & simple maps	I/O
map puzzle	S	logic, geographic concepts, preparation for grasping a pencil	4-6	puzzles of the world, continents, countries, states/provinces, & puzzle stand (ETA, BRM, NIE)	I
peg village	S	map reading, small muscle control	3½-5	Landscape peg set (Playskool)	I
magnet	F/S	experimentation, classification	3½-6	Super Magnet (LCM) or other magnet, things to classify & boxes (optional)	I/O
magnifying glass	F	exploration	2½-5	large magnifying glass set on wooden tripod (CRP, LCM, EPT)	I/O
light	F	exploration	3-6	mirror, flashlight, tray	I/O
prism	F	exploration	4½-7	prism (CRP), white card	I/O
color mixing	F	experimentation	3-6	3 clear jars for primary colors, other jars for mixing colors, food coloring in red, yellow & blue	O

activity	type	skills/concepts	age	materials	I/O
nature studies	F	observation	2-6	clear jar with holes in lid, stray bugs caught	I/O
caring for pets	S	responsibility, observation, therapy, sequence of actions	3-6	birds, hamsters, fish, rabbit, duck, turtles, chickens, etc.; cages hutches, pet supplies & food, newspaper cage liners	I/O
caring for plants	S	responsibility, observation, appreciation of beauty, experimentation	2½-5	plants, either indoors or outdoors or both	I/O
sprouting seeds	S	observation, time concepts	3-6	seeds, container & water	I
growing vegetables, flowers	S	responsibility, observation, time concepts, therapy	3-6	garden, seeds, small gardening tools, water source	O
listening to my body	F	observation,	4-7	stethoscope (CRP)	I
wall chart		location & size concepts	4-7	outline of child's body with transparent overlays of specific internal organs	I
flower puzzle	S	vocabulary (parts of a flower)	3½-5	flower puzzle (BRM, NIE)	I
group parachute	F/T	air experimentation, strengthen arm muscles	2½-6	parachute (without cords)	O
blowing bubbles	F	air experimentation, therapy	all	bubble solution & wire loop	O
kite flying	F	air experimentation	3½-7	kite, paper to send up string (optional)	O

SENSORIMOTOR

Activity/Exercise	Type	Skill/Purpose	Age	Materials/Equipment	Area
mystery bag	S	stereognostic sense	3–5	bag with various common objects, blindfold	I
geometric solids	S	stereognostic sense, vocabulary (geometric shapes, analysis of form in relation to the base form cards)	2–4	set of geometric solids & basket (ETA, BRM, NIE), base form cards & container (NIE), place mat, blindfold	I
fabric swatches	S	tactile sense, matching, vocabulary (fabric names & qualities	3–5	2 sets of 6 or more different textured fabrics & container EPT, ETA, NIE), blindfold	I
rough & smooth board	S	tactile sense, vocabulary (rough, smooth, comparative & superlative forms), serration	2½–4	board with 5 different grades of sandpaper (BRM, ETA, NIE), blindfold	I
sound	S	auditory sense, matching, vocabulary, serration	3–5	2 sets of sound cylinders & container (NIE) or matching opaque jars filled with different substances	I
bells	S	auditory sense, serration, vocabulary (musical notes, high, low)	3½–7	2 sets of tone bells and mallet (BRM, ETA, NIE)	I
weight tablets	S	baric sense, vocabulary (weight comparison words)	3–5	10 sets of 3 different weight tablets & divider box (NIE), blindfold, place mat	I

Activity	Category	Skills	Age	Materials	Type
thermal bottles	S	thermic sense, vocabulary (temperature comparison words), matching, serration	2–5	2 sets of metal bottles containing various temperatures of water, & container (BRM, NIE)	I
thermic bar	S	thermic sense, matching, vocabulary (temperature comparison words), serration	2½–4	2 sets of bars of various materials such as wood, glass, stone, metal, & container (NIE)	I
smelling	S	olfactory sense, matching, vocabulary (names of substances)	2½–5	2 sets of opaque bottles with holes in lids & various aromatic substances inside, container, place mat	I
smelling flowers	F/T	olfactory sense, vocabulary (flower names)	2½–5	various kinds of fresh flowers, blindfold	O
tasting	S	taste sense, vocabulary (sweet, sour, salty, bitter)	2½–5	bowls of sugar, salt, lemon juice, & coffee (ground, powdered or liquid), disposable tasting tabs or spoons, tray, blindfold	I
pink tower	S	visual sense, serration, carrying, balance, large motor control	2½–4	pink tower (BRM, ETA, NIE), floor mat, blindfold	I
cylinder	S	visual sense, serration, preparation for grasping a pencil	2½–5	set of 4 different cylinders (present 1 then add the others, 1 at a time) (BRM, ETA, NIE) place mat or floor mat, blindfold	I

SENSORIMOTOR (cont.)

Activity/Exercise	Type	Skill/Purpose	Age	Materials/Equipment	Area
knobless cylinder	S	visual sense, serration, small motor control	3-5	set of 4 different knobless cylinders & boxes (BRM, ETA, DLM, NIE) place mat or floor mat, blindfold	I
broad stair	S	visual sense, large motor control, serration, carrying objects	2½-4	broad stair (BRM, ETA, NIE), floor mat	I
long stair	S	visual sense, serration, practice in carrying long objects, large motor control	2½-4	long stair (BRM, ETA, BIE), floor mat	I
wooden geometric inset	S	visual sense, vocabulary (geometric shapes, abstracting reality to 2-dimension pattern cards), preparation for grasping a pencil	3-5	wooden geometric insets & case, pattern cards (BRM, ETA, NIE), floor mat, blindfold	I
square/circle puzzle	S	visual sense, serration, size & order concepts	3-5	Fit-A-Square, Fit-A-Circle (EPT), blindfold	I

Activity		Concepts/Skills	Age	Materials	
colors	S	visual sense, color sense, vocabulary (color names), serration, matching	3-6	2 sets of 64 color tablets & container (BRM, ETA, NIE), floor mat	I
color sorting	S	visual sense, left-to-right progression of layout, color classification, small motor control	3-4	8 basic colors of chips, paper, buttons, crayons, etc. & container, place mat (optional)	I
size sorting	S	visual sense, size classification, small motor control	2½-4	various sized buttons of the same color & container, as many bowls as there are sizes (optional), place mat	I
shape sorting	S	visual sense, shape classification, small motor control, top to bottom & left-to-right progression of layout	2½-4	various geometric shapes, place mat or floor mat	I
mixed classification game (1 to 4 players, non-competitive)	S	visual sense, time concepts, listening skill, socialization, teammanship	3½-5	stop watch, various sizes & shapes of colors, box	I
triangles	F	visual sense, geometric concepts, exploration	2½-5	constructive triangles in 4 boxes (BRM, ETA, NIE), place mat or floor mat	I

A floor mat or place mat helps to focus the child's attention on one activity.

II. SOURCES OF MATERIALS AND INFORMATION

Many firms send their expensive catalogs only to schools, churches, or other similar organizations. If you are a parent, and are denied a catalog, ask if your local school, college, or library has one. If not, they might be glad to order one for themselves which you may borrow.

Manufacturers, Distributors, and Publishers

Academic Therapy Publications
1539 Fourth Street
San Rafael, CA 94901
Publishes *Academic Therapy,* an interdisciplinary journal focusing on the inefficient learner. Also offers reading programs, materials, pamphlets, books and screening tests, most of which are geared to helping children with language, motor and perceptual problems. Descriptive list of publications on request.

Addison-Wesley Publishing Company, Inc.
Reading, MA 01867
Publishes a variety of educational books, textbooks, and children's literature, preschool through elementary. Black-and-white posters from *What's Inside the Egg?* and *The Birth of Sunset's Kittens* (see listings under "Picture Books Little Children Like") are available. This company has republished many famous children's books in its "author collections." Also of interest is a study series for preschool through seven years consisting of seventy-two small, laminated covered, paperback books covering different subjects. These little books were developed in England and tested there. They can be purchased as a set or in separate package of six different titles. Discounts on all books to schools and libraries. Catalog on request.

American Guidance Service, Inc.
Publishers' Building
Circle Pines, MN 55014
Offers a variety of tests, materials, and instructional programs, including the Peabody Language Development Kits (ages 3–9½) used in many public schools.

Army Surplus Outlets
(Check your telephone book for local listings.)
 Sometimes parachutes (without cords) are available. These are good for air experiments with groups of children.

Baroni & Marangon
Montessori Materials
Gonzaga, Mantova, Italy
 Produces fine (but expensive) authentic Montessori material. First commissioned by Dr. Montessori. Free, full-color catalog and price list on request.

BFA Educational Media, a division of CBS
2211 Michigan Avenue
Santa Monica, CA 90404
 Produces and distributes educational films (8 mm and 16 mm), film strips, study prints, audio-visual hardware, and multi-media kits for elementary through secondary grades. Their expensive films can be purchased or rented, and prints of the films are available for study before purchasing. Their AV hardware is only sold in quantity. Many children's books, including Dr. Seuss's *The Cat in the Hat*, are available on film. Many of the films and other materials are available through various state university film libraries (listed under "E., Miscellaneous").

Bowmar Publishing Company
722 Rodier Drive
Glendale, CA 91201
 Offers large, laminated picture-posters of young children and their activities, as well as books, records and cassettes (which go with several of their books).

Child Evangelism Fellowship Press
Box 1156
Grand Rapids, MI 49511
Offers full-color picture books, flannel boards and backgrounds, flannel stories, pictures, music, visual aids and a bi-monthly magazine, *Evangelizing Today's Child*, all of which deal with Biblical themes and events. Child Evangelism also trains people to conduct "Good News Clubs" for reaching children with the gospel, and helping new Christians to grow. Their materials are available in most Christian bookstores and at their Good News Club training sessions. Write to them regarding their work and materials in your locale.

Childcraft Education Corporation
20 Kilmer Road
Edison, NJ 08817
Markets "toys that teach" which are made by many different manufacturers. Their selection is not limited to young children but also includes babies through adults. Catalog lists prices.

Children's Book and Music Center
5373 W. Pico Boulevard
Los Angeles, CA 90019
This unusual retail outlet carries quality phonograph records, books, multi-media and enrichment material for children of all ages, parents and teachers. Their materials may be previewed at their showroom. Large descriptive catalog lists prices.

Children's House
Box 111
Caldwell, NJ 07006
Publishes a bi-monthly magazine, *Children's House*, which focuses on Montessori schools. Also stocks various books of interest to parents and teachers, sells

new and used Montessori equipment, and provides various services for Montessori educators.

Constructive Playthings
1040 E. 85th Street
  Kansas City, MO 06431
  and
11100 Harry Hines Boulevard
Dallas, TX 75229

Makers of educational wooden playthings and a few Montessori items, and distributors for other firms' school products. Of interest are their "tactile letter blocks" in which half-inch thick wooden numerals and letters fit into molds cut into a wood base which provides a 3-D kinesthetic experience. Also, they carry a wide selection of children's and teachers' books including books on special education and Montessori. Instructo science displays and specimens are also available through Constructive Playthings. (Catalogs for individuals are not usually available.)

The Continental Press, Inc.
Elizabethtown, PA 17022
(Offices also in Elgin, IL; Atlanta, GA; Dallas, TX; Portland, OR; and % Voroman's, Pasadena, CA.)
A good source for liquid duplicator masters, workbooks and transparencies for grades preschool through high school, and special education. Teacher guides accompany material. Also offers AIMS, prereading and phonics programs, and a few filmstrips and kits. Catalog on request. Lists prices.

Creative Playthings, A Div. of
Columbia Broadcasting System, Inc.
Princeton, NJ 08540
  Showroom:

Toy Center
200 Fifth Avenue
New York, NY 10013

   Manufactures quality products, many in wood, for babies through children of twelve years, but concentrated on eight years and younger. Each toy is marked with the suggested age for use. Full-color catalogs or brochures are sometimes available at low cost at toy shops. Catalog includes price list.

Creative Publications
Box 10328
Palo Alto, CA 94303

   Makers of quality wood, plastic, metal and rubber materials for learning math. Full-color catalog lists prices.

Cuisenaire Company of America
12 Church Street
New Rochelle, NY 10805

   Makers of the famous "Cuisenaire rods" used in teaching math. Elementary catalog and news letter on request.

Dennison Manufacturing Company
Dept. J 24
300 Howard Street
Framingham, MA 01701

   Offers low-cost craft books: *Collage with Crepe Paper*, *Paper Arts and Crafts* and *Cut Your Own Flowers*.

Developmental Learning Materials
7440 Natches Avenue
Niles, IL 60648

   Carries material for elementary-school children. Of particular interest are their clear plastic individual geometric stencils; graduated, sized, wooden perception puzzles; life-size body puzzles; bilingual materials; and programed activities for body- and self-awareness and visual perception. Full-color catalog lists prices. Includes a cross-reference skill chart.

Developmental Vision Associates, Inc.
2950 Hearne Avenue
Shreveport, LA 71103
Source for the Russell Perceptual Sorting Program, which provides training in visual discrimination. Descriptive brochure on request.

The Drawing Board
256 Regal Row
Box 505
Dallas, TX 75221
Primarily an office supply manufacturer. Also offers a beautiful Christian calendar done in watercolor, as well as several exceptional religious Christmas cards suitable for decoupage projects.

The Economy Company
Box 25308
1901 N. Walnut
Oklahoma City, OK 73125
Offers a kindergarten program, materials, and elementary-level reading programs. Used in many public schools.

Ed-Nu, Inc.
5115 Route 38
Pennsauken, NY 08109
Offers hula hoops (Groovy Loops).

Educational Aids Ltd.
72, Kew Road
Colombo 2, Sri Lanka (formerly Ceylon)

and
Cabdev Inc.
31 Progress Avenue, Unit #9,
Scarborough, Ontario, Canada

Manufactures Montessori material. Although their materials are far from inexpensive, they are, nevertheless, generally lower priced than some other companies. They offer a ten percent discount on first orders. Small catalog on request. Price list included.

Educational Digest
416 Longshore Drive
Ann Arbor, MI 48107
and
Educational Playthings
418 E. Main Street
Richmond, VA 23219

Makers of wooden playthings, school furniture and outdoor equipment. They also carry carefully selected educational items from Giant Blocks, Instructor Curriculum Materials, Mead Educational Services, Hohner Instruments, Milton Bradley, Trend, Lauri, Playskool, Learning, and Play Learn Products. Of interest are their spring-mounted outdoor riding toys. Catalog lists prices.

Educators Publishing Service
75 Moulton Street
Cambridge, MA 02138

Offers information, screening tests, prereading, and reading programs primarily for dyslexic children. Among the approaches offered are the Slingerland Multi-Sensory Approach to Language Arts, Orton-Gillingham materials, and the Color Phonics System. Information about where the "Specific Language Disability Summer School Workshops" are held is also given by this group.

ETA (Educational Teaching Aids)
Daigger Chemical Company
159 W. Kinzie
Chicago, IL 60610
 Offers some Montessori materials (which are
 expensive), Frobel cubes, special education, scientific
 instruments, and other preschool through eighth grade
 learning materials. Catalog lists prices.

Ginn & Company
Western Regional Office
2550 Hanover Street
Palo Alto, CA 94304
 Produces prereading and reading programs and
 materials. Many public schools have adopted their
 materials for official public instruction.

The Horn Book, Inc.
Dept. 9
585 Boylston Street
Boston, MA 02116
 Publishes *The Horn Book Magazine*, a magazine about
 children's books.

Houghton Mifflin Company
2 Park Street
Boston, MA 02108
 and
551 Fifth Avenue
New York, NY 10017
 Source of "Interaction," a student-centered language
 arts and reading program, kindergarten through the
 twelfth grade.

Incentive Publications
Box 12522
Nashville, TN 37212

Offers reading-readiness kits. Free "Kids' Stuff" catalog on request.

Instructor Publications, Inc.
Box 6099
Duluth, MN 55806

Publishes *Instructor Magazine,* a well-known, colorful magazine for elementary school teachers. It offers articles, advertisements, and coupons for free and inexpensive promotional materials offered by manufacturers. They also offer ditto masters, pictures and guides.

Judy Company
250 James Street
Morristown, NJ 07960

Offers toys and materials, including a fine selection of wooden puzzles, and distributes Invicta Educational Aids. Catalog on request.

Lakeshore Equipment Company
1144 Montague Avenue
San Leandro, CA 94577
and
5369 W. Pico Boulevard
Los Angeles, CA 90019
and
16463 Phoebe Avenue
La Mirada, CA 90637

Carries a complete line of quality learning materials for preschool through elementary, including special-education items. Large, well-organized catalog on request. Lists prices.

The Macmillan Publishing Company
866 Third Avenue
New York, NY 10022

Publishers for the Bank Street prereading material and the Bank Street reading primers. Bank Street is used in many Headstart programs and public schools.

Montessori Educational Environments
Fernhaven Studio
8655 S. Main Street
Los Angeles, CA 90003

Manufactures the full range of Montessori materials and recent innovations by Montessorians. The materials come with instructions for their use. Also offered are consultant help, workshops, demonstrations, and teacher training with credit through the California State College at Los Angeles. Montessori schools qualify for a ten percent discount on their expensive line. A catalog, which explains the purpose of each item, and a price list are available on request.

Niehuis B.V.
Industriepark 14, Box 16
Zelhem (Gld), Holland
    and
Mr. Monte Kenison
Niehuis Montessori Branch Office
3171 Moorpark Way
Mountain View, CA 94041

Manufacturers of authentic, high-quality, expensive Montessori materials and other preschool and kindergarten equipment. Niehuis also is a center for information regarding Montessori education. Nonprofit schools can qualify for duty-free shipments. The U.S. office does not have a warehouse at this time, but they speed orders to Holland via Telex, and they also provide help and information needed when ordering from a company abroad. Large, full-color catalog and price list sold by the U.S. branch office.

179

Ohaus Scale Corporation
29 Hanover Road
Florham Park, NJ 07932
   Offers metric teaching aids—balances, cubes, rulers, measurement kits, etc.

Open Court Publishing Company
1039 Eighth Street
LaSalle, IL 61301
   Offers the very structured kindergarten readiness curriculum program, "Open Court," and reading seminars. This program is used in many public schools.

Playground Corporation of America
29-24 Fortieth Avenue
Long Island City, NY 11101
   and
2298 Grissom Drive
St. Louis, MO 63141
   Makers of expensive, high-quality physical education and playground equipment. Divisions include: SportsPlay Products, PlayLearn Products, Modular AquaSystems, Salsich Recreation, and TheraPlay Products. Catalogs on request. Prices listed.

Practical Drawing Company
Box 5388
Dallas, TX 75222
   This company carries items from many major firms which produce educational equipment: Judy, Tumble Forms, Little Tikes, Playskool, Instructo, Creative Playthings, Lauri, Milton Bradley, and Holbrook. Truly a comprehensive selection—from audio-visual to furniture. Especially noteworthy is their large selection of wooden puzzles of all types. Materials in their large catalog are listed by manufacturers. Prices included.

PTL Publications
Box 1277
Tustin, CA 92680

Does a line of photo-posters featuring the unlikely combination of animals and scripture texts. However, the animal poses just fit the scripture messages! Available at most Christian bookstores and from the publisher.

Questor Educational Products, Child Guidance, Platt & Munk, Tinkertoy
1055 Bronx River Avenue
Bronx, NY 10472

Makers of safe, reasonably priced, mostly flexible plastic toys for babies through childhood. Among their items are the famous wooden tinkertoys, magnetic boards, Sesame Street toys, and a fine line of books from Platt & Munk, including their Perma Life Series of inexpensive, wipe-clean books for children ages one through four. Full-color catalog, no prices listed.

S & S Arts and Crafts
Division of S & S Leather Company
Colchester, CT 06415

Offers material for a host of craft projects, various types of kits, and Lauri crepe foam rubber educational products. (Many of the Lauri items use Montessorian principles to develop sensorial awareness and academic skills. They are excellent, safe, and reasonably priced.) Some of S & S's supplies include many kinds of beads (useful in teaching math as well as crafts), colored pipe cleaners, leather, lacing, felt, wood-burning equipment, wire, cellulite, waxes, candle-making equipment, looms, yarns, colored sand, loops, etc. Full-color catalog which lists prices and also some project costs per person is available on request.

Saint Nicholas Training Centre
23 Princes Gates
London SW 7, England

> Offers a complete line of Montessori materials (generally a bit less expensive than other European and American manufacturers) and a Montessori teacher correspondence course with exams and two-week seminars in the States.

Science Research Associates
57 W. Grand Avenue
Chicago, IL 60610

> Publishes inexpensive pamphlets on dealing with children, tests, and reading programs and materials. Their materials are used in many public schools.

SDE Company (Skill Development Company),
Division of Ampro Corporation
1340 N. Jefferson
Anaheim, CA 92807

> This company pioneered inflatable and foam-filled equipment for physical education and therapy. Their unique line of equipment opens many more safe ways to promote muscular development and coordination. Since their material is so distinctive, they have two books—one for regular physical education and one for special education—to assist the teacher in the use of their equipment. They also make gym mats and foam furniture, busy blocks, plastic blocks, trampolines, and bean bag furniture. Full-color catalog lists prices.

SVE (Society for Visual Education, Inc.)
Singer Education Division
1345 Diversey Parkway
Chicago, IL 60614

> Produces filmstrips, films, records, cassettes, and study prints in a wide range of subject areas for

preschool through elementary levels. The large, full-color, laminated study prints with information on the back are most useful for preschoolers. The children especially respond to the magnified pictures of insects, fruit, land, sea, clouds and animals. Eight different prints of one subject area make a set, and must be purchased as such. Many public schools use items from SVE. Catalog on request.

Teacher
One Fawcett Place
Greenwich, CT 06830
    Teacher, the "professional magazine of the elementary grades," is one of Macmillan's publications and incorporates *American Childhood* and *Early Education*. It features articles, advertisements, announcements, and a coupon service whereby manufacturers offer teachers free samples and information.

Teachers College Bureau of Publications
525 W. 120th Street
New York, NY 10027
    Publishes, among other things, inexpensive pamphlets on understanding children, parenthood, family life, etc.

Things from Bell
Box 26 30 N. Main Street
Homer, NY 13077
    Offers parachutes, cargo nets, stretch ropes (Chinese Jump Ropes) and individual gymnastic mats, among other items.

U.S. Government Printing Office
Washington, DC 20402
    Offers inexpensive, informative booklets and books on many subjects. The office carries publications by the

U.S. Department of Health, Education and Welfare, as well as other governmental agencies. A few of their listings:

Outdoor Classrooms on School Sites, 1972, #0100–1458. Includes photos. *Aids to Media Selection for Students and Teachers,* compiled by Yvonne Carter et al., 1971, #1730–0810. Basically an extensive annotated bibliography of books and sources of audio-visual and multi-media materials. *Directory of 16-Millimeter Film Libraries,* published bi-annually. Some of their publications are in public and school libraries, but write to them to get on their mailing list so as to keep up with current offerings—of which there are thousands!

Wayne Adams
15701 Blackhawk Street
Granada Hills, CA 91344
Maker of plywood, 5" x 5" grid, sanded and sealed geoboards.

Record Companies

Most libraries have sound-effect records under "miscellaneous" in their record sections. The following companies produce sound-effect records suitable for sound identification and other activities.

Audio Fidelity
Audiofidelity Enterprises, Inc.
221 W. 57th Street
New York, NY 10019

Electra
15 Columbus Circle
New York, NY 10023

Folksways/Scholastic
701 Seventh Avenue
New York, NY 10036

RCA Records
1133 Avenue of the Americas
New York, NY 10036
   Offers many records for children and their activities,
   and cassettes of the Dr. Seuss books.

Screening Tests
   Most of the following tests are for professional use, and
   must be ordered on institutional letterheads.

The Frostig Developmental Test of Visual Perception
   (ages 4½-7; no reading required)
   Follett Educational Corporation
   Box 5705
   Chicago, IL 60680

Goodenough-Harris Drawing Test
   Harcourt, Brace, and Jovanovich, Inc.
   757 Third Avenue
   New York, NY 10017

Jordon Left-Right Reversal Test
   (ages 6-10)
   Academic Therapy Publications
   1539 Fourth Street
   San Rafael, CA 94901

The Motor-Free Visual Perception Test (MVPT)
   (ages 4-8)
   Academic Therapy Publications
   1539 Fourth Street
   San Rafael, CA 94901

The Peabody Picture Vocabulary Test
(ages 2½-18; no reading required)
American Guidance Service, Inc.
Publishers' Building
Circle Pines, MN 55014

Slingerland Screening Test
(ages 6-12; for identification of dyslexic children)
Educators Publishing Service
75 Moulton Street
Cambridge, MA 02138

SRA Primary Mental Abilities Test
(no reading required)
Science Research Associates, Inc.
259 E. Erie Street
Chicago, IL 60611

The 3-D Test for Visualization Skill
(ages 3-8)
Academic Therapy Publications
1539 Fourth Street
San Rafael, CA 94901

Utah Test of Language Development (UTLD)
(ages 5-7)
Communication Research Associates
Box 11012
Salt Lake City, UT 84101

Wechsler Intelligence Scale for Children (WISC)
(correlates well with the Stanford-Binet I.Q. test)
Psychological Corporation
304 E. 45th Street
New York, NY 10017

Wepman Test of Auditory Discrimination
  (no reading required)
    Language Research Associates
    950 E. 59th Street
    Chicago, IL 60605

Associations

American Library Association
50 E. Huron Street
Chicago, IL 60611

American Montessori Society
175 Fifth Avenue
New York, NY 10010 (attention: Ms. Cleo Monson)
  A teacher- and school-certifying bureau. Clearing
  house for information, i.e., lists schools offering
  approved Montessori courses (including universities
  offering Montessori graduate and undergraduate
  programs), and firms producing Montessori material.
  Publications available. Information on request.

American Personnel & Guidance Association
16 New Hampshire Avenue N.W.
Washington, DC 20009

American Psychiatric Association
850 Third Avenue
New York, NY 10022

Association for Childhood Education International
3615 Wisconsin Avenue N.W.
Washington, DC 20016
  Publishes *Childhood Education*, a professional journal
  devoted to the varied problems of children from two to
  twelve years. Also publishes articles, pamphlets,
  bulletins and books on subjects relevant to childhood
  education. List of publications on request.

Association for Children with Learning Disabilities
95 Madison Avenue
New York, NY 10016

Association for Family
28 E. Jackson Street
Chicago, IL

Association Montessori International
Koninginneweg 161
Amsterdam, Holland

California Association for Neurologically Handicapped
Children
Box 4088
Los Angeles, CA 90051

Child Study Association of America
132 E. 74th Street
New York, NY
    Publishes *Child Study*, a quarterly journal of parent
    education.

The Children's Book Council
175 Fifth Avenue
New York, NY 10010
    Headquarters for *Book Week*. Gives year-round
    promotion and information on books for children. Most
    libraries have free pamphlets from this source.

Christian Librarians Fellowship, Inc.
    Publishes *Christian Periodical Index* and the
    Christian Librarian. Write to Mr. Wayne Woodward,
    President CLF, Library, Asbury College, Wilmore,
    KY 40390.

Council for Exceptional Children
1920 Association Drive
Reston, VA 22091

Health Publications Institute
216 N. Dawson Street
Raleigh, NC

International Association of Progressive Montessorians
Box 28164
San Diego, CA 92127
    Offers teacher-training programs with college credit, a
    reading program and a twenty-five-minute film on
    Montessori education. Brochures on request.

Montessori Institute of America
Box 265
Delmar, NY 10054

National Association for Mental Health
1790 Broadway
New York, NY

National Association for the Education of Young Children
1834 Connecticut Avenue N.W.
Washington, DC 20009
    Publishers of *Young Children* and other works. List of
    publications on request.

National Association of Christian Schools
Box 550
Wheaton, IL 60187
    Offers many services including: a bi-monthly magazine,
    Christian Teacher's Magazine; placement service;
    teacher certification programs; accreditation; insurance
    and retirement programs; curriculum guides; some
    teaching materials; and representation in Washington.
    Sponsors the Christian Children's Literature award.

Membership in the nonsectarian organization is open to individuals and schools which subscribe to NACS's doctrinal statement. Write to them for their free literature and material guide sheet.

The National Council of Teachers of English
1111 Kenyon Road
Urbana, IL 61801
Publishes the journal, *Elementary English;* various papers and reports; and offers teaching sets and kits.

The National Council of Teachers of Mathematics
1201 Sixteenth Street N.W.
Washington, DC 20036
Publishes *The Arithmetic Teacher*, a magazine for elementary teachers of math.

The National Educators Fellowship, Inc.
1410 West Colorado Boulevard
Pasadena, CA 91105
Publishes *Vision*, the helpful, small bi-monthly official organ of the Fellowship. Founded in 1953 by Dr. Clyde M. Narramore and Benjamin S. Weiss, the current president. Prospective members must be Christian, adhere to the Fellowship's doctrinal statement, and be career educators. Their purpose is to project a Christian influence in education.

National School Boards Association
State National Bank Plaza, #12
Evanston, IL 60201
Publishes *The American School Board Journal* monthly. Offers: cassettes which give information regarding legal responsibilities of board members, curriculum and organization; workshops; films; and other services. Its purpose is to advance quality education and to preserve and strengthen lay control of public education. Information on request.

National Union of Christian Schools
865 Twenty-eighth Street S.E.
Grand Rapids, MI 49508
   Publishes a free catalog of Christian school curriculum
   materials offered through NUCS. The catalog,
   covering grades kindergarten through twelfth, gives
   helpful summaries of the contents of each reference
   book listed and a description of subject-area teaching
   programs and materials offered. Included are source
   books for administrators. Also offered are curriculum
   guides, written by NUCS consultants, for the
   development of Christian curricula in art, Bible,
   language, music, physical education, science, and social
   studies.

Office of Child Development
Box 1182
Washington, DC 20013
   Publishes *Children Today*.

The Orton Society
8415 Bellona, suite 206
Towson, MD 21204
   Publishes bulletins, information, and technical papers on
   dyslexia. List of publications and reprints on request.

Public Affairs Committee
22 E. 38th Street
New York, NY 10016

The Sierra Club
1050 Mills Tower
San Francisco, CA 94104
   Devoted to the study and protection of the nation's
   ecological resources. Publishes (through trade

publishers) books and calendars filled with some of the most beautiful pictures of nature seen anywhere. These pictures are useful in teaching programs. Write to them for information. (Many of their publications are available in bookstores.)

Society for Research in Child Development
University of Chicago
5801 Ellis Avenue
Chicago, IL 60637
  Publishes *Child Development*, a professional journal concerned with research and theory in the growth and development of children.

U.S. Children's Bureau
% Superintendent of Documents
Washington, DC
  Publishes many inexpensive pamphlets, and *Children*, an interdisciplinary journal for the professions serving children.

Institutions, Libraries, and other Sources

R.R. Bowker Company
A Xerox Educational Company
1180 Avenue of the Americas
New York, NY 10036
  Publishes, yearly, *Books in Print* (volumes 1-2 *Authors*, volumes 3-4, *Titles*). These volumes, available at most libraries and bookstores for reference, list all the general books currently in print (old and new), their prices, type and publisher. (Vol. 4 includes a directory of publishers in the United States.) One caution: *Books in Print* is not infallible. This company also does small pamphlets regarding books, including annotated bibliographies such as "Growing up with Books." These are available at most libraries.

Educator's Progress Service
208 Center Street
Randolph, WI 53956
   Publishes several different guides to free materials for schools, libraries and teachers. The comprehensive guides can be purchased on a thirty-day approval basis. Write to them for a description of the guides and prices.

Institutions—public and private

   When seeking help or information, universities, colleges, trade schools, government agencies (like the Welfare Department) can be of service. Some groups offer free training in nursery care programs. Sympathetic faculty members can direct you to sources of information and may give you copies of "handouts" used in their courses. When calling a college for information on early childhood education ask for that department, although the human development and home economics departments may be able to serve you too. It is a good idea to go to your library first and look up the school's catalog to get the correct name of the particular department and its faculty members. It is also good to ask for a specific faculty member, otherwise you run the risk of never getting beyond the operator for lack of definite information. There is a wealth of opportunities around if one is willing to dig to find them!

International Institute
Box 99
Park Ridge, IL 60068
   This Christian company offers approved elementary correspondence courses for children in grades kindergarten through eighth, and an advisory service to parents monitoring and teaching the courses to their children. Full-time Christian workers qualify for a twenty percent discount. Also, for each additional child

in the family who is enrolled in a course from I.I. the price is reduced. Textbooks required for the courses are available at wholesale prices through the company. Brochure on request.

Libraries

Modern libraries can help you find addresses of organizations, firms, schools, publishers, etc. Many carry telephone directories for other cities. They carry free literature and bibliographies on many topics. In some libraries one may borrow posters, records, tapes, audio-visual equipment (such as film projectors), science exhibits, puzzles, magazines and journals as well as books. Libraries will frequently arrange programs (and possibly a movie, too) for your class visits. The secret to getting the most out of any library is to look and to ask.

Moody Literature Mission
Mark O. Sweeney
820 N. LaSalle Street
Chicago, IL 60610
Furnishes free, on request, a set of Christian literature books for classroom use.

Public Schools

In some public school systems, when textbooks are changed, the used books, as well as the new unissued ones, are recalled. These are then stored in warehouses until authorized teachers and principals take their pick. The remainder are burned! Perhaps if you have a need for such textbooks, and have a friend who works for a public school system, you might ask the friend if he or she could obtain permission to salvage some for you. Or perhaps you could call on your local school adminstrators to find out if there is a way for you to go to the warehouse yourself.

Rental Libraries

Many educational films are available for rental through state universities. Films can usually be previewed in the library prior to rental. Below is a list of some universities which have film rental services:

University of Arizona
Bureau of Audiovisual Services
Tucson, AZ 85721

Arizona State University
Audio-Visual Center
Tempe, AZ 85281

Boston University
Abraham Krasker Memorial Film Library School of Education
765 Commonwealth Avenue
Boston, MA 02215

Buffalo State College
Film Rental Library
1300 Elmwood Avenue
Buffalo, NY 14222

University of Colorado
Bureau of Audiovisual Instruction University Extension Division
Boulder, CO 80302

Florida State University
Educational Media Center
Tallahassee, FL 32306

University of South Florida
Film Library
4202 Fowler Avenue
Tampa, FL 33620

University of Georgia
Centers for Continuing Education
Athens, GA 30601

University of Illinois
Visual Aids Service
1325 S. Oak Street
Champaign, IL 61820

Indiana University
Audio-Visual Center
Bloomington, IN 47401

University of Iowa
Audiovisual Center
Iowa City, IO 52240

Kent State University
Audio-Visual Services
221 Education Building
Kent, OH 44240

University of Maine
Film Rental Library
Shibles Hall
Orono, ME 04473

University of Michigan
Audio-Visual Educational Center
416 S. Fourth Street
Ann Arbor, MI 48103

University of Minnesota
Audio-Visual Extension Service General Extension
Division
2037 University Avenue S.E.
Minneapolis, MN 55455

University of Mississippi
Audio-Visual Education
School of Education
University, MS 38677

University of Missouri
University Extension Division
119 Whitten Hall
Columbia, MO 65201

Eastern New Mexico University
Film Library
Portales, NM 88130

Northern Illinois University
Audio-Visual Center
DeKalb, IL 60115

University of Oklahoma
Extension Division
Educational Materials Services
Audio-Visual Education
Norman, OK 73069

Oklahoma State University
Audio-Visual Center
Stillwater, OK 74074

Oregon State University
Audiovisual Services
Corvallis, OR 97331

Pennsylvania State University
Audio-Visual Aids Library
University Park, PA 16802

University of South Carolina
College of General Studies and Extension
Audio-Visual Division
Columbia, SC 29208

Southern Illinois University
Learning Resources Service
Carbondale, IL 62901

Syracuse University
Film Library, Collendale Campus
1455 E. Colvin Street
Syracuse, NY 13210

University of Texas
Visual Instruction Bureau
Division of Extension
Austin, TX 78712

University of Utah
Film Library
Salt Lake City, UT 84112

University of Washington
Audio-Visual Center
Seattle, WA 98195

University of Wisconsin
Bureau of Audio-Visual Instruction
137 University Avenue
Madison, WI 53701

III. REFERENCE WORKS

Books classified as "theory" include the reactions of real children to various experiments and activities. These revealing portions will help you gauge a child's thinking and responses realistically—knowing what or what not to expect from a child in any activity is a must. For this reason the activity books in any subject area will be far more advantageous if the theory books are read first.

For example, under the heading "Activities" you will find arts and crafts books with many attractive suggestions. It is important to be aware that, in all art and manipulative activities, the process is far more important than the product.

In a few of the books listed, children are held to be either innately good or neutral in moral character and, as a result, discipline is underemphasized. This, of course, is contrary to the clear teaching of Scripture on the inheritance of an unregenerate nature and the need for discipline that stems from love. These books have been included because of their value in other areas, and their shortcoming is not harmful so long as the Christian teacher is aware of the erroneous basic premise. Therefore, such bias has been noted in the comments.

Much of teaching theory has been influenced by two giants in child study, Jean Piaget and Maria Montessori. Both emphasize sensitive learning periods or developmental stages in a child, the creation of environments which encourage a child to learn, and the necessity for a young child to participate physically in his own learning rather than to memorize by rote facts which are not part of his concrete experience. But the two are sufficiently different to warrant reading both. Montessori deals with the child as a whole, whereas Piaget emphasizes the process of cognitive development. Montessori applies her observations to teaching methods, while Piaget leaves teaching methods to others.

Although Piaget's books are fascinating, they may prove to be laborious reading. Starting directly with Piaget's own writing is a bit like starting the Bible at Genesis—one soon gets bogged down in the "begats." Other authors, cited below, ably summarize his work for you.

Conversely, when reading Montessori it is most helpful to delve into her own works yourself. Many people who are skeptical of Montessori have based their opinions on hearsay, misinformation, and some of the so-called

"Montessori schools." She has been criticized for results that came from misapplying her methods, and has been denied credit for her work that has influenced modern education for the good. But she remains one of the foremost educators of all time, and anyone working with young children should be personally acquainted with her work. Also, she is the only early-childhood educator of renown who has recognized a spiritual component in child development.

It is indeed a privilege for a teacher to watch children grow into the unique persons God has created. The books listed here will help you to understand, guide, and inspire your students in this beautiful process.

THEORY

Teaching approaches

Ashton-Warner, Sylvia. *Teacher.* New York: Bantam Books, 1971;

Candid comments by a New Zealand teacher in a Maori school. Describes the author's methods and philosophy. "Organic reading" proved successful for this teacher who is also the author of several well-known novels. Passionately written. Illustrated. Soft-cover. (Hardcover available from Simon & Schuster.)

Haystead, Wesley. *Ways to Plan and Organize Your Sunday School: Early Childhood, Birth to Five Years.* Glendale, CA: Regal Books, 1971.

Covers the Sunday School hour and church hour schedules. Equipment, materials, teacher selection, and building Christian homes discussed. Details on how to make unit blocks and furnishings for class. Floor plans included. Illustrated, bibliography. Soft-cover.

Mayers, Marvin K., Ph.D.; Lawrence Richards, Ph.D.; and Robert Weber, Ph.D. *Reshaping Evangelical Higher Education.* Grand Rapids: Zondervan Publishing House, 1972.

One should not be misled by the word "higher" in the title, as the principles discussed in this book apply to all levels of education. Especially helpful is the examination of relative cultural values as they apply to modes of teaching. This topic, concisely treated, aids the teacher in determining both his own value bias and that of his students—not for criticism, but to enable him to set up a program which will be effective in the students' lives. An important book. Scholarly but clear. Bibliography, index. Hardcover.

Maynard, Fredelle, Ph.D. *Guiding Your Child to a More Creative Life: How to Help a Child Discover His Own Best Self and Develop His Natural Creative Powers.* New York:

Doubleday & Co., 1973.

Because the author is a talented writer as well as an authority in child development, this book is a delight to read. Dr. Maynard presents an overview of the methods in education for children from two through ten years. Much information concisely given. Various aspects of art, dance, music, literature, child development, creativity, family activities, and play. Specific children's books discussed. A major portion of the book is devoted to bibliographies of the subjects discussed. Lists publishers' addresses. A valuable resource book. Bibliographies. Hardcover.

Richards, Lawrence O., Ph.D. *Creative Bible Teaching*. Chicago: Moody Press, 1970.

Part One, "The Bible We Teach," discusses theology and Bible teaching; Part Two, "Teaching the Bible Creatively," discusses an approach which Dr. Richards finds consistent with the nature and purpose of the Bible; and Part Three, "Guidelines to Creative Teaching," applies to learning situations for different age levels the educational philosophy already presented. Illustrated, bibliography. Hardcover.

Winn, Marie, and Mary Ann Porcher. *The Playgroup Book*. New York: Macmillan Publishing Co., 1967.

What you need to know and what you need to do to start your own cooperative mini preschool. Topics range from child development to how to select members for your project. The host of activities listed includes a few finger plays and recipes for food children can make. Much information. Practical. Illustrated, bibliography of children's books and records, index. Hardcover.

Montessori works

Montessori, Maria, M.D. *The Advanced Montessori Method. Vol. 2: The Montessori Elementary Material*. Cambridge, MA: Robert Bentley, 1964.

A detailed account of Dr. Montessori's method and

teaching materials for teaching grammar, reading, math, design, poetry, music, and interpretative movement. She advances the idea of reading with bodily interpretation, and of the teacher reading literature (even adult material and Bible stories) to children while their hands are occupied drawing geometric designs with the aid of insets (similar to single stencils). Also unique to this book is her definitive discussion of introducing children to poetry and her extraordinary vocabulary building and language awareness exercises. (Volume 1 is entitled: *Spontaneous Activity in Education.*) Illustrated, appendix. Hardcover. (Soft-cover available from Schocken Books.)

————*The Discovery of the Child.* New York: Ballantine Books, 1972.
One of Dr. Montessori's later books. Among other things, religious education is discussed. Exciting reading. Illustrated. Soft-cover.

————*Doctor Montessori's Own Handbook.* New York: Schocken Books, 1965.
This book describes the prepared environment of "children's houses," and discusses, in depth, didactic material for preschoolers. Illustrated. Hardcover, soft-cover.

————*The Montessori Method.* Cambridge, MA: Robert Bentley, 1964.
Dr. Montessori describes her method, materials, observations, and experience with children. Theoretical, practical, helpful, fascinating, effusive. I highly recommend this book. Sensitively written: "But let us seek to implant in the soul the self sacrificing spirit of the scientist with the reverent love of the disciple of Christ, and we shall have prepared the *spirit* of the teacher" (p. 13). Excellent. Illustrated. Hardcover. (Soft-cover, available from Schocken Books, contains no photographs.)

Piaget-influenced works:
Brearley, Molly, ed. *The Teaching of Young Children*. New York: Schocken Books, 1970.

The contributors to this book draw on their Piaget-influenced teaching methods in infant schools in England, presenting ways to cause children to learn in depth. Chapters on the teaching of math, art, music, science, literature, morality and movement (which includes kinesthetic dance). Concerning the chapter on morality, the Christian should be aware that this teaching is not specifically Christian. Apart from Christ and a belief in God, the teaching of morality is lame and essentially irrelevant. However the book is valuable for its other information, including children's observations of life about them. Practical ideas. Illustrated, bibliography. Hardcover.

Furth, Hans G. *Piaget for Teachers*. Englewood Cliffs, NJ: Prentice-Hall, 1970.

Piaget cites Furth, well known for his work with deaf children, as correctly interpreting his theories into practical applications. Chapters are written as informal letters to teachers and clarify many terms and concepts of Piaget. Suggests various ways of adapting Piaget's findings to practical teaching methods. Good background reading, but mainly concerned with school-age children's learning. Another new book on the same subject is: *Thinking Goes to School: Piaget's Theory in Practice*, by Hans G. Furth and Harry Wachs. Illustrated. Hardcover, soft-cover.

Child development
Beadle, Muriel. *A Child's Mind*. New York: Doubleday & Co., 1971.

Capsulized explanations of differing theories of development and learning in children from birth to age five. Finds from many sources of research are discussed. Fascinating reading. Illustrated. Soft-cover.

Beard, Ruth M. *An Outline of Piaget's Developmental Psychology for Students and Teachers*. New York: New American Library, 1972.

Introduction to Piaget's research. Simple and brief explanations aptly distill Piaget's investigations. The author makes broad suggestions for modifying learning situations to accommodate Piaget's findings. Glossary, bibliography, index. Soft-cover. (Hardcover available from Basic Books.)

Gesell, Arnold, M.D. et. al. *The First Five Years of Life: A Guide to the Study of the Preschool Child*. New York: Harper & Row Pubs., 1940.

Timetable of child development. Regarded as a standard work in its field. Major topics include: adaptive behavior; motor, language and social development. Illustrated, index. Hardcover.

Pulaski, Mary A. Ph.D. *Understanding Piaget*. New York: Harper & Row Pubs., 1971.

Introduction to children's cognitive development, from birth through adolescence. Gives three stages of Piaget's writing, his books for each period, and what he based his observations on during each period. (*Thinking Is Child's Play*, listed under activities, is more valuable if this book is read first.) Illustrated, glossary, bibliography. Hardcover.

Rowen, Dolores. *Ways to Help Them Learn: Early Childhood, Birth to Five Years*. Glendale, CA: Regal Books, 1972.

Divided into three parts. The first concerned with child development, the second with the teacher, and the third with teaching methods. Contains Bible thoughts for conversation as the day goes by. Illustrated, bibliography. Soft-cover.

Spiritual guidance and values
Dobson, James. *Hide or Seek*. Old Tappan, NJ: Fleming H.

Revell Co., 1974.

Dr. Dobson exposes common pitfalls which can undermine a person's self-concept, and also gives strategies for avoiding them which, at the same time, build self-respect. Examines false and damaging values of our society so that we—especially as Christians—may be free of them. Extremely valuable. Captivating style of writing. Hardcover.

Haystead, Wesley. *You Can't Begin Too Soon*. Glendale, CA: Regal Books, 1974.

Practical guidance for parents and teachers on educating a child for Christian living. Based on sound scriptural advice and educational insights. This well-organized book includes many examples of thought-provoking conversations with children which give the reader a new look at a child trying to formulate his concepts of God. Excellent. Illustrated, bibliography. Soft-cover.

Montessori, Maria, M.D. *The Child in the Family*. Translated by Nancy Circillo. Chicago: Henry Regnery Co., 1970.

Dr. Montessori continues her campaign to sensitize adults to the needs of children. This book offers, besides a distillation of her basic methods, advice on when to interfere with a child's activities and when to respect them, and gives insights into a child's cycle of activity—orderly and disorderly. Hardcover. (Soft-cover available from Avon Books.)

Mow, Anna B. *Your Child from Birth to Rebirth*. Grand Rapids, MI: Zondervan Publishing House, 1963.

The purpose of this book is to help a parent or teacher learn how to prepare children for a personal experience with Christ. Mrs. Mow explains an adult's part in a child's response to God. Warm, personal, and scriptural. Bibliography. Soft-cover.

Narramore, Clyde M., Ed.D. *Young Children and Their Problems*. The Christian Psychology Series. Grand Rapids, MI: Zondervan Publishing House, 1961.

This little booklet deals with four common problems of young children: thumbsucking, bedwetting, temper tantrums, and speech problems. Other helpful booklets in this series by the same author are:*Is Your Child Gifted?* and *How to Help Your Child Develop Faith in God*. Illustrated. Soft-cover.

Narramore, S. Bruce, Ph.D. *An Ounce of Prevention: A Parent's Guide to Moral and Spiritual Growth in Children*. Grand Rapids, MI: Zondervan Publishing House, 1973.

Why do children of sincere, dedicated Christians sometimes go wrong? Dr. Narramore attempts to answer this question by showing how values take shape, how the conscience develops, and how parents' attitudes and life style affect children. He also suggests fifteen succinct guidelines for moral and spiritual growth. A large portion of the book is devoted to workbook-type exercises to give parents an opportunity to keep a record of their methods of dealing with their children. The style is very much like the workbook, *A Guide to Child Rearing*, by the same author. Illustrated. Soft-cover.

Discipline
Dobson, James, Ph.D. *Dare to Discipline*. Wheaton, IL: Tyndale House Pubs., 1970.

A psychologist discusses the need for discipline in raising healthy, well-balanced children. Helpful suggestions and insights. Includes scriptural references as the bases of opinions given. Hardcover, soft-cover.

Narramore, S. Bruce, Ph.D. *Help! I'm a Parent*. Grand Rapids, MI: Zondervan Publishing House, 1972.

A Christian psychologist examines common vexations of parenthood and gives suggestions as to how to deal with them. Various types of approaches to discipline explained. Helpful tables summarize the differences (with scriptural references) between punishment vs. discipline, types of discipline, and righteous indignation vs. carnal hostility. Practical. A workbook for parents, *A Guide to Child Rearing*, is available to accompany this text. Illustrated, brief bibliography, index. Hardcover, soft-cover.

Communication

Axline, Virginia M., M.D. *Play Therapy*. Rev. ed. New York: Ballantine Books, 1974.

Non-directive play therapy, a technique for helping troubled children through play, is explained and illustrated by many case histories. Lessons gained from this book can be helpful in learning how to listen to children and let them discover their own feelings and motivations. Illustrated. Soft-cover.

Ginott, Haim G., M.D. *Between Parent and Child*. New York: Macmillan Publishing Co., 1965.

Dr. Ginott feels that parents and children frequently have a communication gap. He humorously explores common pitfalls adults fall into very early in their children's lives, which weaken and sometimes even prevent communication in later years. Very helpful in learning how to become a sensitive listener so that parents may build a close relationship with their offspring. As in most non-Christian books, discipline is under-emphasized. Social agencies also listed. Bibliography, index. Hardcover. (Soft-cover available from Avon.)

Art

Boeve, Edgar, M.S.D. *Children's Art and the Christian Teacher*. Text ed. St. Louis: Concordia Publishing House, 1966.

Written for teachers of kindergarten through eighth grade. Discusses how to have a meaningful,

Christian-oriented art program. Chapters include information on the use of art in expressing oneself about God, art displays, storing art supplies, problems in teaching art, evaluating art, art appreciation, sequence in art activities, design, use of craft materials, drawing, painting and printing. Some illustrations are in full color. Illustrated, annotated bibliography, index. Hardcover.

Di Leo, Joseph H. M.D. *Young Children and Their Drawings*. New York: Brunner/Mazel, 1970.
Explores the development of a child's expression of himself in art. Defines six progressive stages of drawing. A great help to understanding the child and his art. Normal and abnormal states of development as reflected in art. This is not an art instruction book. Many illustrations. Bibliography. Hardcover.

Canner, Norma. *And a Time to Dance*. New ed. Boston: Plays, 1975.
This book contains photographs of children and teacher engaged in a movement program. The text illustrates how movement can be used to teach basic concepts as well as aid in self-discovery and in exploring God's world about us. Contains suggestions on how to begin and how to teach movement. Written for teachers—especially those of retarded children—but this type of program has been used with normal kindergarten children with profitable results. Parents could benefit from this book also. Illustrated. Hardcover.

Lowndes, Betty. *Movement and Creative Drama for Children*. Boston: Plays, 1971.
Chapters include movement and drama, teacher and child, sensory awareness, body awareness, locomotion, creative movement, mime, and verbal drama improvisations. Black-and-white photos. Illustrated, bibliography, index. Hardcover.

Creative movement

Barlin, Anne and Paul. *The Art of Learning through Movement: A Teachers' Manual of Movement for Students of All Ages*. (From the film "Learning Through Movement.") Photos by David Alexander. Pasadena, CA: Ward Ritchie Press, 1971.

How to begin a creative movement program. Suggestions for: 1)establishing technique, 2)using movement in various curriculum areas, 3)using movement to release emotions, and 4)developing concepts of space, etc. Chapters include movement as related to stories, fantasy, self discovery; vigorous movement; and moving with others. Applicable ages for various levels of difficulty given. With this book come two records which have music for various types of movement—but you must request the free records when ordering the book. The authors have also done a series of story books and records for kinesthetic interpretation, "Dance-a-Story" by RCA, listed under "Activities, Creative Movement," in this bibliography. Illustrated. Hardcover.

Play

Caplan, Frank and Theresa. *The Power of Play*. New York: Doubleday & Co., 1973.

The authors, founders of Creative Playthings, maintain that play is the child's most powerful learning tool. Aspects of play include body building, personality and social development, creativity, and culture. Programs and toys for various maturation levels are discussed. A history of educators' contributions and programs based on play are given. Illustrated, bibliography, index. Hardcover, soft-cover.

Learning Disability—Dyslexia

Carpenter, Robert D., M.D. *Why Can't I Learn?* Glendale, CA: Regal Books, 1973.

Faces learning problems from Christian and medical

points of view. Many types and aspects of dyslexia presented. The author, a former medical missionary, draws on the experience of colleagues as well as his own experience of the past eight years of specializing in children with learning problems. His active patient load of 500 children gives him a rich source to research. The book ministers to parents. Good witness; faith building. Very informative. Illustrated, glossary, bibliography, author and subject indexes. Hardcover, soft-cover.

Clarke, Louise. *Can't Read, Can't Write, Can't Talk Too Good Either: How to Recognize and Overcome Dyslexia in Your Child.* New York: Walker & Co., 1973.
A mother shares her son's case history in which he overcomes his problem and becomes a doctoral candidate. Sources of information and help given state by state. Possible causes and cures discussed. Signs and symptoms noted. Most of the cures involve a multi-sensory approach (such as Montessori uses for preschoolers) and a highly structured environment. Very readable and informative. Illustrated, bibliography, index. Hardcover. (Soft-cover available from Penguin Books.)

Teacher-enrichment books
Arbuthnot, May H., compiled by. *The Arbuthnot Anthology of Children's Literature.* New 4th ed. New York: Lothrop, Lee & Shepard Co., 1976.
A source book of children's literature, covering ages 2-14 approximately. The books reviewed are good literature, but they are not selected with a Christian bias. Some full-color plates. Illustrated, music, indexes. Hardcover.

Dodson, Fitzhugh. *How to Parent.* New York: New American Library, 1973.
A practical, interesting book. The text does not reflect Christian thought, so watch out when reading some portions on certain subjects like television. Children's books are

mentioned in the bibliography. Appendix, bibliography. Soft-cover. (Hardcover available from Nash Publishing Corp.)

Emberley, Ed. *Ed Emberley's Drawing Book of Animals*. Boston: Little, Brown & Co., 1970.

A simple drawing technique that reduces animals to a series of geometric forms. Little text. Step-by-step pictures. Helpful for teachers with limited art experience. Written for children ages seven and up, it may be used to reinforce geometric shape concepts as well as art. I have used this technique with children in kindergarten in the States, and with children and adults in Mexico, and found it profitable. However, do not limit yourself to one technique; there is no one "right" way to draw. (The author has another hardcover book by the same publisher, entitled: *Ed Emberley's Drawing Book: Make a World*, 1972.) Illustrated. Hardcover.

Hunt, Gladys. *Honey for a Child's Heart*. Grand Rapids, MI: Zondervan Publishing House, 1969.

Imaginative use of books in the family. Approaches to introducing your child to a world of good literature. Value of picture books discussed. Bibliography is a categorized listing of suggested books for children through teen years. Illustrated, bibliography. Hardcover.

O'Gorman, Ned. *The Wilderness and the Laurel Tree*. New York: Harper & Row Pubs., 1972.

The diary of a teacher telling of his frustrating experiences in a Harlem storefront day-care center. In spite of the fact that Mr. O'Gorman gets a bit carried away with his own writing and that he idealizes children, the book gives valuable insights that can challenge Christian teachers! On the whole, sensitively written although not specifically Christian oriented. Illustrated. Hardcover.

Salisbury, Gordon. *Catalog of Free Teaching Materials*. 8th ed. Ventura, CA: Gordon Salisbury, n.d.

Lists companies and agencies which offer teachers, schools, and other teaching agencies free materials. It is available in some public libraries. When ordering from the companies and agencies given in the catalog, use letterhead stationery from school or church. Soft-cover.

Schaeffer, Edith. *Hidden Art*. Wheaton, IL: Tyndale House Pubs., 1975.

This book can be a great help in fostering creativity in Christian wives and mothers. The suggestions and experiences related by Mrs. Schaeffer, cofounder of L'Abri Fellowship, are conducive to the establishment of a positive home environment. The environment she created for her own family is an example of the type of atmosphere other authors hint at but do not explain. Many ideas, practical, inspiring. Illustrated. Soft-cover.

Schaeffer, Francis and Edith. *Everybody Can Know*. Wheaton, IL: Tyndale House Pubs. 1975.

The founders of L'Abri Fellowship in Switzerland explore the gospel of Luke. To be read as a family. Difficult Biblical concepts explained. Much descriptive detail may be tedious to adults but enjoyable to children. The Schaeffers make the reader aware of the differences between modern day liberal and conservative positions by comparing them to different groups in Jesus' time on earth. Illustrated. Hardcover.

Weisheit, E. *Sixty-one Worship Talks for Children*. Rev. ed. St. Louis: Concordia Publishing House, 1975.

"Parables" for children written by a Lutheran pastor. Clear object lessons. Chidren are not "talked down to." The three to five minute action talks, which use familiar references, are presented by the scripture text. Although the talks themselves are geared to older children, they can help give the reader ideas on how to clarify concepts for little children. (The author has another soft-cover book by the same publisher, entitled: *Sixty-one Gospel Talks for Children*, 1969.) Soft-cover.

ACTIVITIES

Arts and Crafts
Card and Cardboard. Color Crafts Series. New York: Franklin Watts, 1971.

Full color throughout. Large print, large photos. Very clear directions. Ideas categorized from easy through difficult. Although projects are given which preschoolers or kindergarten children could accomplish, projects are also given for older children or adults—like mat picture-framing. Written specifically for children grades one to four. The best paper craft book I've seen. Illustrated. Hardcover.

Hollender, H. Cornelia. *Creative Opportunities for the Retarded Child at Home and in School*. New York: Doubleday & Co., 1971. Booklets one to six come as a set:

"Getting Started," "Finger Painting and Single Print Making," "Drawing and Painting," "Clay and Other Dimensional Media," "Stitchery," "Woodworking and Odds and Ends." Although these booklets are specifically written for parents of retarded children, any parent could profit from them. Contain excellent tips for working with children which could be used for normal preschoolers and children a little older. Explain how to make materials for silk-screen printing, clay, tone boards, painting, etc. Many activities. Illustrated. Soft-cover.

Kampmann, Lothar. *Creating with Colored Paper*. Art Media Series. New York: Van Nostrand Reinhold Co., 1968.

For children ages six through fourteen. Fine background for a parent or teacher. Paper techniques in collage, lamination, decoupage, weaving, and three dimensional relief, using construction, tag board, tissue, newsprint, and wrapping papers. The illustrations (which are lessons in themselves) make this book, like the other in this series, a joyous learning adventure. Skill level chart. Excellent. Illustrations, index. Hardcover.

————. *Creating with Crayons*. Art Media Series. New York: Van Nostrand Reinhold Co., 1968.
Pictorial survey of wax crayon techniques using scraping, shaving, wax color etching, abrasion, covering with wax, painting with turpentine, paper batik, and encaustic painting. The rich illustrations, many student done, are an inspiration. Most of the techniques are too advanced for little children, but this is an excellent source book for parents and teachers. Skill level chart for grades one through nine. Illustrations, index. Hardcover.

————. *Creating with Poster Paints*. Art Media Series. New York: Van Nostrand Reinhold Co., 1968.
A comprehensive yet tersely written book explaining various techniques used with ordinary tempera from wet paper to mixed media. The illustrations, many student done, do much of the teaching. Skill level chart for children ages 6-14. Excellent source book for parents and teachers. Illustrations, index. Hardcover.

Sunset Editors. *Crafts for Children*. Menlo Park, CA: Lane Publishing Co., 1968.
Many good and easy ideas for various types of media. However, the suggestions for doing batik are highly simplistic. Read further on this craft before attempting it. Illustrated. Soft-cover.

Bible-related activities
White, Marian. *More Bible Finger Plays*. Grand Rapids, MI: Baker Book House, 1974.
Young children are fascinated by finger plays, which are

rhymes with finger and hand actions. This book features 150 Bible finger plays to entertain and teach. Illustrated. Soft-cover.

Creative movement

Barlin, Anne and Paul. *The Magic Mountain.* Illustrated by Louis Zener. Dance-a-Story Series. Cherry Hill, NJ: RCA, 1967.

The Magic Mountain is just one of several delightful record-book combinations (listed below) for creative movement. The record features an instrumental side for free dance, and a story side in which the story in the book is narrated with appropriate action-cuing music. The long-playing record is a little over eight and one-half minutes per side. The book is a short story about a child who goes to the mountain and pretends, through dance, to become what he sees on the mountain. The books in this series feature young, multi-racial dancers of both sexes in full color, with background sketches generally in black and white. To use this or any of the books in this series, read the story to the children, explain any unfamiliar words, then play the record and express the narrated story in movement. It is good to have the class do a bit of "warming up" before reading the story. Other record-books in this series are: *Little Duck, Noah's Ark, Balloons, Brave Hunter, Flappy and Floppy, Toy Tree* and *At the Beach. Flappy and Floppy* is perhaps the easiest and can be used with very young children, while *Brave Hunter* is perhaps the most advanced. The age range for use is 3 to 9.

Field trips

Wurman, Richard S., ed. *Yellow Pages of Learning Resources*. Washington, DC: Day Care & Child Development Council of America, 1972.

Suggestions on how to make field trips meaningful. Some schools base almost their entire teaching on such out-of-school activities. The book is organized by questions:

"What can you learn from a locksmith?", "What can you learn at the post office?", etc. Under each place of interest is found information, illustrations, sample questions and discussion topics to provide direction in learning from firsthand observation. The philosophy is, the city is the teacher. A list of schools which agree with this philosophy is also given. Illustrated. Soft-cover.

Music

Overholtzer, Ruth, compiler. *Salvation Songs for Children*. Nos. 1, 2, 3, & 4. Grand Rapids, MI: Child Evangelism Fellowship Press, 1966.

A collection of well-known Christian music for children. Book One: 100 songs. Book Two, 105 songs. Book Three: 100 songs. Book Four: 96 songs. Index. Soft-cover.

Rejoice in Jesus Always. Costa Mesa, CA: Maranatha Evangelical Assn., 1973.

From Calvary Chapel of Costa Mesa, California, songs of worship and praise. Songs like "Banner of the Lord" are especially adaptable for accompanying actions and for inventing new verses. Music symbols explained. Cartoon illustrations and scripture versus punctuate this lively contemporary hymn book. Guitar chords given and illustrated. Illustrated, index. Soft-cover.

Structured/Academic

Hainstock, Elizabeth G. *Teaching Montessori in the Home*. New York: Random House, 1968.

Montessori theory and technique briefly explained. How to make your own Montessori "school" at home for your own children. Directions for making materials. Activities clearly detailed with appropriate ages, goals, and procedures. Learning activities categorized by specific skill areas: motor, sensory, perception, math, and language. Written especially for parents of preschool children. Information on where to purchase materials and what kind to buy (brands included). Excellent. (The author has a sequel to this book: *Teaching Montessori in the Home: The School Years.*) Illustrated, glossary, bibliography. Hardcover.

Lorton, Mary B. *Workjobs*. Reading, MA: Addison-Wesley Publishing Co., 1972.
   A comprehensive activity book with many large, clear photographs. Materials, many of which are common household items, are listed. Skill index. Activities to aid perception, matching, classification, sounds and letters, sets, number sequences and other mathematical and language skills. Practical. (A new, smaller edition for parents is available from the same publisher.) Illustrated. Hardcover.

Shakesby, Paul. *Child's Work: A Learning Guide to Joyful Play*. Philadelphia: Running Press, 1974.
   How to make materials, adapted from Montessori, for sensorial awareness, manual dexterity, size, shape, form, math, and language concepts. The materials have suggested ages for their use, and the book covers a range of from 2½ to 8 years. Illustrated. Soft-cover.

Sharp, Evelyn. *Thinking Is Child's Play*. New York: E.P. Dutton & Co., 1969.
   Geared to parents of children ages 2 through 7. Briefly discusses Piaget's work with children and gives forty "games" derived from Piaget's research. Directions for everything from making simple materials for the activities to how to guide your child through the experiences. The activities are designed to give the child a concrete base from which problem-solving abilities emerge. Excellent. Illustrated, bibliography, index. Hardcover. (Soft-cover available from Avon Books.)

MAKE YOUR OWN EQUIPMENT
Doan, Eleanor L., compiler. *Make-It-Yourself Equipment Encyclopedia*. Glendale, CA: Gospel Light Pubs., 1962.

Complete directions for 200 useful projects including basic equipment such as shelves, bookracks, chairs, tables, toys, unit blocks, rhythm band instruments, costumes, dividers, storage units, book ends, and chalk and flannel boards. Illustrated. Soft-cover.

Farrow, Elvira C., and Hill, Carol. *Montessori on a Limited Budget: A Manual for the Amateur Craftsman*. Rev. ed. Ithaca, NY: Montessori Workshop, 1975.
Step-by-step directions for making your own Montessori and Montessori-like materials. Illustrated, bibliography, indexes. Soft-cover.

Haystead, Wesley. *Ways to Plan and Organize Your Sunday School: Early Childhood, Birth to Five Years*. See "Theory, Teaching Approaches."

Sunset Editors. *Children's Rooms and Play Yards*. Rev. ed. Menlo Park, CA: Lane Publishing Co., 1970.
A do-it-yourself book crammed with ideas for furniture, storage, indoor and outdoor play equipment, sandboxes, geometric toys, playhouses and park equipment. Many of the ideas presented use natural materials and settings. Playscapes are beautiful, neat and safe. Illustrated, index. Soft-cover.

IV. PICTURE BOOKS LITTLE CHILDREN LIKE

This bibliography is unique in three ways: 1) it is confined to picture books for preschoolers, 2) it presents books selected with a Christian bias, and 3) it lists picture books from Christian publishing houses as well as from secular houses.

Most of the books listed here can be found in public libraries, generally in the children's picture-book section, although some are from other areas. Many of the books from

Christian publishing houses will not be found in public libraries, but rather in Christian bookstores. All books are hardcover unless otherwise noted, but many now have soft-cover editions.

The address of each publisher mentioned is in section five, "Publisher Directory." For helpful notes on children's literature, see chapter eight of Part One, "Materials and Books."

This list is meant to be comprehensive, but it is far from exhaustive, for "of making many books there is no end . . ." (Ecclesiastes 12:12 KJV).

BIBLE THEMES AND THE CHRISTIAN LIFE
Arch Books Aloud. Books Aloud Series. St. Louis: Concordia Publishing House, 1974.

This series has new titles added every year. The rhyming texts and full-color illustrations are based on Bible Stories and Christian concepts. Some books, however, are fantasies, such as the story which explains the first Christmas as seen from a mouse's perspective. I prefer not to mix fantasy with Biblical truth, so I choose only those Arch Books which are faithful to Biblical stories. A letter to parents with further information is included in each book. Some titles:

Old Testament
The World God Made (Creation)
The Story of Noah's Ark
The Silly Skyscraper (Tower of Babel)
The Great Promise (Abraham and Sarah)
The Wicked Trick (Rebekah and Jacob)
The Boy Who Saved His Family (Joseph and his brothers)
The Princess and the Baby (Moses)
The Great Escape (Moses and the Exodus)
The Walls Came Tumbling Down (Joshua and Jericho)
The Man Who Won Without Fighting (Gideon)
The Man Who Took Seven Baths (Naaman)
The Boy with the Sling (David)

The Secret of the Arrows (David and Jonathan)
The Water That Caught on Fire (Elijah)
A Ring of Fiery Horses (Elisha)
The Man Caught by a Fish (Jonah)
The Queen Who Saved Her People (Esther)
Three Men Who Walked in Fire (Shadrach, Meshach, and
    Abednego)
Daniel in the Lions' Den
The Braggy King of Babylon (Nebuchadnezzar)

New Testament

Mary's Story
The Baby Born in a Stable
The Secret of the Star (Wise Men)
The Happiest Search (Wise Men)
The Secret Journey (Flight into Egypt)
The Boy Who Was Lost (Jesus at twelve years)
The Strange Young Man in the Desert (John the Baptist)
The Feast That Almost Flopped (The wedding in Cana)
The Little Sleeping Beauty (Jairus' daughter)
The Beggar's Greatest Wish (Blind Bartimaeus)
The Lame Man Who Walked Again (The man let down
    through the roof)
The Boy Who Gave His Lunch Away (The miracle of the
    loaves and fishes)
The Great Surprise (Zacchaeus)
The Little Boat That Almost Sank (Jesus walks on water)
The Fishermen's Surprise (Jesus and His disciples,
    including post-resurrection)
The Most Wonderful King (crucifixion, resurrection)
The Man Who Couldn't Wait (Peter)
The Man Who Changed His Name (Saul/Paul)
He Didn't Mind Getting Wet (Philip and the Ethiopian)
The Jailer Who Changed His Mind (Paul and Silas)

New Testament Parables and
Examples by Jesus

Jon and the Little Lost Lamb
The House on the Rock
The Boy Who Ran Away (Prodigal Son)

The Rich Fool
The Unforgiving Servant
Two Men in the Temple
Ages 6-10. Laminated paper covers.

Baby's First Christmas Book, illustrated by Jim Roberts. St. Louis: Concordia Publishing House, n.d.
Semi-slick cardboard pages. Bold, full color. Large print. Text simply names the people and objects in the Christmas story. Ages 3 and under.

Ballard, Joan Kadey. *I Saw a Mother Chicken*. Chicago: Moody Press, 1963.
Jesus cares for children as a hen cares for her chicks. Pleasant rhyming text and fragile drawings of a boy and girl on a farm. Some pages in full pastel color, others in line sketch only. (The line sketches may be colored in if desired.) Slick paper cover. Ages 3-6.

The Bible Visualized Series. Standard Publishing Co., 1970.
This series features Bible stories told in full-color comic book form. Ages 8-12.

Braga, Meg. Illustrated by Gordon Stowell. See and Say Book #1, Standard Publishing Co., 1972.
An unusual technique—Bible stories are combined to complete a picture. Each story adds one thing to the bright, bold picture which is completed by the end of the book. The book should be read part by part, rather than all at one sitting, which would present too many complex ideas. It also can be adapted for flannel board use. Biblical references given. Book #2, *Build*, is also good. Ages 2½-6. Also, *Count*.

The Creation. Illustrated by Jo Spier. New York: Doubleday & Co., 1970.
The handwritten text by Joseph P. Ascherl is taken from Genesis, Jerusalem Bible Version. Beautiful watercolor and

ink illustrations in full color. Ages 3-6. Hardcover.

Duitsman, Betty. *It Is So!* The Christmas Story. Illustrated by Vera Gohman. Standard Publishing Co., n.d.
A modern-day girl and boy raise questions about Christmas and Jesus relative to their lives. The questions and answers in rhyme tell the Christmas story and stress the inerrancy of the Word of God. Scripture text and references, full-color illustrations. Paper. Inexpensive. Ages 3½-6.

Field, Rachel. *Prayer for a Child*. See "Bedtime Books."

Fletcher, Sarah. *My Bible Story Book*. Illustrated by Don Kueker. St. Louis: Concordia Publishing House, 1974.
Tales from the Old and New Testaments. Stories on one page, large, full-color beautiful illustrations on the facing page. Ages 6½-11. Hardcover.

————. *Prayers for Little People*. Illustrated by Don Kueker. St. Louis: Concordia Publishing House, 1974.
Full-color pictures recall Biblical scenes which relate to the adjacent short prayer. Thoughts and prayers on forgiveness, illness, fear, praying, praise, table grace, grownups, friends, etc. Excellent. Ages 3-6. Laminated paper cover. Inexpensive.

Gibson, C.R., Company has several small, inexpensive plastic-coated paper books which can be cleaned with a damp cloth. Full-color, cheery illustrations and stitched bindings are features of each book. Unfortunately, most are not multi-racial. Some titles: *Our Lovely World* (1958), *When I Talk to God* (1968), *Our Happy Family* (1968), *Noah's Ark* (1968), *My Nighttime Book* (1970), *My Sunday Book* (1971), *God Made a Time* (1969), *Father, We Thank Thee* (1971), *My Happiness Book* (1972), *God's Loving Care* (1972), and *Thank You, God* (1973). Age 2 and under.

Gibson, Joyce L., and Eleanor Hance. *Who's Got the Answers?*, illustrated by Richard Mlodock. Discovery Book, Scripture Press, Publications, Inc., 1971.

The story of the Bible—why God gave us the Bible, who wrote it, how it was written, its format and books, the time it took to write it, etc. Verses quoted in smaller print, text in larger print. Children (and adults) enjoy this succinct, informative little book. Full-color, cartoon style. Excellent. Ages 7-10. Soft-cover. Inexpensive.

Hance, Eleanor. *Man Alive*, illustrated by Richard Mlodock. Scripture Press, Publications, Inc., 1970.

This small, tract-like book tells the salvation story in an easy conversational style. Children enjoy this clear presentation. Full-color cartoon art. Verses quoted. Thirty-one pages. Paper. Ages 7-12.

———. *Me—a Phony?*, illustrated by Richard Mlodock. Discovery Book. Scripture Press, Publications, Inc., 1971.

A clear message about the Christian walk. Medium-sized, hand-lettered print, except for verse quotations which are in small print. Full-color cartoon art. Thirty-one small pages. Inexpensive. Excellent. Ages 7-12. Soft-cover.

Hayes, Wanda. *Jesus and Me*. Illustrated by Ron Lowry. Cincinnati: Standard Publishing Co., n.d.

A child talks to Jesus remembering things about Him. Scriptural text and references given. Full-color, modern streamlined illustrations. Ages 2½-6. Semi-slick paper cover. Inexpensive. Other similar books by this author are: *When I Go to Church*, *God and Me*, *Who Is Jesus?*, *Who Is God?*

———. *My Book of Bible Stories*. Illustrated by Frances Hook. Cincinnati: Standard Publishing Co., 1974.

Old or New Testament Bible stories appear on one page; soft, full-color large illustrations on the facing page. Ages

6-10. Also: *My Jesus Book* and *My Thank-You Book*.

Hook, Martha, and Tinka Boren. *Little Ones Listen to God*.
Grand Rapids, MI: Zondervan Publishing House, 1971.
    Bible stories with a few questions at the end of each page.
Full-color, bold cartoon-style happy pictures on one side,
text with offset paragraph format on the opposite page. A
visually charming book. Scripture references. Ages 6-10.
Hardcover.

How to Become God's Child and Live in His Family.
Visualized for primaries and juniors. Wheaton, IL:
Scripture Press, Publications, Inc., 1970.
    A fifteen-page salvation tract for children. Clear and
effective. Scripture references cited. Two-color photos of
children. Excellent. Ages 7-12. Soft-cover. Inexpensive.

Jones, Mary Alice. *My First Book About Jesus*. Illustrated
by Robert Hatch. Rand, McNally and Co., 1953.
    Gospel stories told in a simple, summary fashion. Nicely
done. Full-color. Ages 3-6.

Little Big Books. Waco, TX: Word Books, 1971.
    A series of inexpensive, small, slick, hardcover books with
few pages, and bright, bold collage illustrations. Scripture
references given for the Bible stories. Generally the pictures
take one page each, and large print appears on the facing
page. Even though the books are small, their uncluttered,
streamlined format permits use with small groups. Some
titles: *Jesus Helps the Little Girl, The Boy Who Shared, God
Made the World, The Loving Shepherd, The Wedding Party,
The Man Up a Tree, The Loving Father, The First
Christmas*. Ages 3-6.

LeBar, Mary E. *Sh-h-h-h*. Pattibook, A Christian Education
Book for two- and three-year-olds. Illustrated by Faith M.
Lowell. Scripture Press, Publications, Inc., 1965.

Respect for another's quiet time with God is the message of this little paper book. Full-color pastel illustrations with large bold-printed text appearing on the opposite page from the illustrations. Other titles by the author: *Joe's Strong* (1965), *Who Loves the Children?* (1965), and *I'm Giving* (1965). Ages 2-4. Inexpensive.

Lexau, Joan M. *More Beautiful Than Flowers*. Illustrated by Don Bolognese. J.B. Lippincott Co., 1966.
Fresh, lively, and delicate full-color illustrations highlight this love poem to God from a child. A sampling of the text, which covers more than one page:
I love you, God, for when I am sorry for being bad,
Your forgiveness is like sunshine after the rain.
You are more certain than that night follows day,
Larger than the universe,
Closer to me than the air I breathe.
You know me better than I know myself.
Ages 4-9.

Marxhausen, Joanne. *Three in One: A Picture of God*. Illustrated by Benjamin Marxhausen. St. Louis: Concordia Publishing House, 1973.
An apple is used to illustrate the concept of the Trinity. Full-color, bold illustrations. Large print. Ages 3-7. Hardcover.

Mueller, A.C. *My Good Shepherd Bible Story Book*. Illustrated by Richard Hook. St. Louis: Concordia Publishing House, 1969.
Old or New Testament Bible stories on one page, large full-color illustrations on the other. Scripture references. Ages 6-10. Hardcover.

Mullan, Carol. *Bible Picture Stories*. Illustrated by Gordon Laite. New York: Western Publishing Co., 1974.
Capsulized Biblical events. The book is beautiful,

although the text says that while Jesus was praying, Peter, James, and John slept "peacefully," whereas the Bible says that they were sleeping "from sorrow" (Luke 22:45). Full-color, culturally authentic illustrations. Inexpensive. Ages 2½-6.

Petersham, Maud and Miska. *The Christ Child*. New York: Doubleday & Co., 1931.

The text is taken from the gospels according to Matthew and Luke, King James Version. The book is divided into seven parts: Prophecy, The Babe, The Shepherds, In the Temple, The Wise Men, The Flight into Egypt, and The Child. Every other page is in full color, the text in bold, medium-sized print. Very beautifully done. These award-winning illustrators also have other Biblical books for older children. Ages 3-6. Hardcover.

Prayers for Everyday. Dean & Son, 1971.

A collection of prayers authored by various people, plus the 23rd psalm. Full color. Ages 6-10. Inexpensive.

Prince, Merle. *God Made You, Me, and Everything*. Illustrated by Dan Devlin. Standard Publishing Company, 1972.

Full-color story of creation. Ages 2½-6. Semi-slick paper cover. Inexpensive.

———. *Sometimes I Lie Awake at Night*. Standard Publishing Company, 1968.

A boy recounts thoughts about God, His greatness, and His creation. Black, grey and white silhouettes. Large print. Ages 3-7. Semi-slick paper cover. Inexpensive.

Richards, Dorothy Fay. *The Happy Day*. Illustrated by Ann Esher. Standard Publishing Company, 1962.

The children are happy because this is the day their mothers take them to see Jesus. Full-color illustrations. Not multi-racial. Ages 2½-5. Laminated paper cover. Inexpensive.

Rubow, Carol. *God Made You Somebody Special.* Concordia Publishing House, 1968.
Capsulized doctrines of God's omniscience, the creation, God's love, and Jesus as Savior. Personal salvation still needs to be explained. Lovely full-color illustrations. Ages 5-7.

Summer, Joan. *A Gift for Jesus.* Moody Press, 1963.
A little boy thinks about what he'd give Jesus if he were a farmer, a cowboy, a king, etc. Some pages are in full pastel color, others are in fragile sketch form which could be colored in if desired. Rhyming text. Ages 3-6. Slick paper cover. Inexpensive.

————. *I Wonder Why.* Moody Press, 1963.
Various children wonder about the universe, themselves, and God. Some pictures are in full pastel color, others in sketch form which may be colored in to permit racial balance, if desired. Rhyming text. Ages 4-7. Slick paper cover. Inexpensive.

Taylor, Kenneth N. *The Bible in Pictures for Little Eyes.* Chicago: Moody Press, 1956.
One full-color picture and Bible story per page. The illustrations are traditional "old master" in style. The more compressed format makes this selection better for individual reading than for group presentation. Scriptural references. Ages 5-10. Hardcover.

Tester, Sylvia. *Gifts for Baby Jesus.* Illustrated by Jane March. David C. Cook Publishing Company, 1973.
The story of the wise men's visit. Full pastel color sketches. Ages 3-6. Soft-cover. Inexpensive.

————. *Jesus and the Children.* Illustrated by Jack Gehring. Standard Publishing Company, 1964.
Full color. Repetitive phrases. Not multi-racial. Wipe-clean, plastic-coated paper. Stapled. Ages 1½-4. Inexpensive. Also, *A New Coat for Samuel* (1964).

Wilkin, Eloise. *Song of Praise.* New York: McGraw-Hill Book Co., 1970.
Softly realistic full-color illustrations of little children in home and natural settings. Text written in the style of the Psalms, using King James English. Ages 5-7. Hardcover.

DISCOVERY BOOKS: THE WORLD AROUND US.
The animal kingdom
Allen, Robert. *The Zoo Book.* Photos by Peter Sahula. Platt & Munk Publishers, 1966.
Full-color photographs of zoo animals. Ages 3-7.

Anderson, Clarence W. *Lonesome Little Colt.* New York: Macmillan Co., 1961.
An orphaned colt is shunned by the other ponies. Her owners team up a mare, who has just lost her foal, with the colt. Illustrates the closeness of the mother-offspring relationship. The author, who is acquainted with ponies and their ways, writes sensitively. Soft, black-and-white, realistic pencil sketches. Ages 4-7. Hardcover, soft-cover.

Barker, Carol. *Carol Barker's Birds and Beasts.* New York: Franklin Watts, 1972.
This minimal-text book uses well-chosen words. The delightful artwork has a bombastic quality that assaults one's vision through the exaggeration of much geometric detail found in nature. A good book to use to bring attention to the focus of the artist's eye. Full color. Ages 2½-6. Hardcover.

Brown, Margaret Wise. *The Duck.*

See "Fantasy Literature."

————. *Home for a Bunny*.
See "Fantasy Literature."

————.*The Sleepy Little Lion*.
See "Fantasy Literature."

Carle, Eric. *The Very Hungry Caterpillar*. Cleveland: Collins, William, World Publishing Co., 1970.

A caterpillar with a voracious appetite eats holes through the pages of this book and, on the last page, emerges as a beautiful butterfly. The book features half pages and smaller, as well as full-size sheets. Fresh, bright, rich, full-color illustrations. One of the most popular children's picture books. Ages 2-6. Hardcover.

Cole, Joanna. *My Puppy Is Born*. Photos by Jerome Wexler. New York: William Morrow & Co., 1973.

Stunning black-and-white photos of the birth of dachshund puppies, and their growth over the next eight weeks. Excellent. All ages. Hardcover.

Crume, Marion W. *I Like Cats*, photos by Harvey Mandlin. Bowmar Early Childhood Series, Bowmar Publishing Company, 1968.

Various kinds of cats and their behavior are discussed by a little girl, who finds her own cat just right for her tastes. Full-color, uncluttered photographs on the right page, brief text on the left. Ages 2½-6.

D'Aulaire, Ingri, and Edgar Parin. *Animals Everywhere*. New York: Doubleday & Co., 1954.

Children will investigate every inch of the large pictures to find each animal mentioned in the text. The expertly crafted illustrations, some in full color, display unusual use of color and composition. Ages 2½-6. Hardcover, soft-cover.

Disney, Walt. *Bambi*.
   See "Fantasy Literature."

Dugan, William. *The Bug Book*. A Golden Shape book, Western Publishing Co., Inc., 1965. Library edition only.
   Enlarged, well illustrated insects. There are many other informative paper books in this inexpensive "Golden Shape" series. Full color. Ages 2 (and under)-6.

Elzbieta. *Little Mops and the Butterfly*.
   See "Fantasy Literature."

Freschet, Berniece. *The Web in the Grass*. Illustrated by Roger Duvoisin. New York: Charles Scribner's Sons, 1972.
   The story of a spider, beautifully and interestingly told. Full-color, multi-media illustrations. Ages 5½-8. Hardcover.

Garelick, May. *What's Inside? The Story of an Egg That Hatched*. Photos by Rena Jakobsen. New York: Scholastic Book Services, 1970.
   Records the hatching and first day of a gosling with closeup, black-and-white photographs. The text aims at getting children to analyze what type of bird is hatching. The text is on one page, the photo on the facing page. Ages 3½-7. Soft-cover.

———. *Where Does The Butterfly Go When It Rains?*
   See "Poetry and Nursery Rhymes."

Ginsburg, Mirra. *The Chick and the Duckling*.
   See "Fantasy Literature."

Grabianski, Janusz. *Grabianski's Wild Animals*. New York: Franklin Watts, 1969.
   Beautiful, rich, full-color paintings of wild animals in their

natural habitats. The natural, flowing, concise text is refreshing. Ages 4-6. Hardcover.

Hall, Bill (William Norman). *Whatever Happened to Baby Animals?* Illustrated by Virginia Parsons. Western Publishing Co., Inc., 1965. Library edition only.
   Puppies, kittens, and bear cubs. Full-color pictures.

Hamberger, John. *The Lazy Dog.* New York: Scholastic Book Services, 1973.
   A shaggy dog stretches himself awake and begins to chase after a ball. As it defies being caught, the early morning chase takes the pooch all over the farm. Finally, he claims the ball and comes home exhausted—just when the little boy wakes up and wants to play! The story is told without one word—just tremendous, action-packed, two-color pictures. Children enjoy the change of pace wordless books offer. They like to form their own story. Ages 4-6. Soft-cover.

Hazen, Barbara S. *Where Do Bears Sleep?.* Illustrated by Ian E. Staunton. Reading, MA: Addison-Wesley Publishing Co., 1970.
   Beautiful, full-color pictures with colorful, handprinted text which tells in rhyme the names of animals and the places where they sleep. Excellent. Ages 2-5. Hardcover.

Heyduck-Huth, Hilde. *The Three Birds.* New York: Harcourt Brace Jovanovich, 1971.
   A terse story of three birds hatching. An added feature: one very basic map. Sturdy, laminated cardboard pages, extra large print, full-color on much white space. Nicely done. Ages 2-5. Hardcover.

Keats, Ezra J. *Kitten for a Day.*
   See "Fantasy Literature."

Keith, Eros. *Rrra-ah.* Scarsdale, NY: Bradbury Press, 1969.

Lavish, sun-drenched watercolor illustrations make you want to join "Rrra-ah," the toad, in his pond. But, alas, inquisitive children take Rrra-ah prisoner. Later they take him back to his pond and free him because, they discover, their home is not like his home. Full color. Ages 4½-8. Hardcover.

Krauss, Ruth. *The Happy Day.*
See "Fantasy Literature."

The Life Picture Book of Animals, Time Life Books, distributed by Little, Brown and Company, 1969.
Magnificent, full-color large photos of various types of animals including some birds and fish. Only the name of the animal appears with the photo, but the back of the book gives more information and an index. All ages. Excellent.

National Georgraphic Society, ed. *Lion Cubs.* Books for Young Explorers, 4 vols., set 1. Washington, DC: National Geographic Society, 1972.
Superb, full-color photo essay. The text, which is brief, can be further shortened when reading to very small children. Excellent. All ages.

Lionni, Leo. *Fish Is Fish.*
See "Fantasy Literature."

Mari, Iela and Enzo. *Chicken and the Egg.* Illustrated by Iela and Enzo Mari. New York: Pantheon Books, 1970.
This delightful, wordless book with crisp illustrations traces an egg from being laid to hatching and on to the early growth of a chick. The illustrations show the development of the embryo within the egg. Color. Excellent. Ages 3½-6. Hardcover.

Miles, Miska. *Rabbit Garden.* Illustrated by John

Schoenherr. Boston: Little, Brown & Co., 1967.

A sensitive story of an uprooted rabbit adjusting to his new garden environment. Soft, realistic pencil sketches. Color. Ages 6-9. Hardcover.

Moremen, Grace. *No, No, Natalie.* Photos by Geoffrey P. Fulton. Chicago: Childrens Press, 1973.

Through black-and-white photos and a few words Natalie, a preschool's uncaged pet rabbit, describes her day. Ages 3-6. Hardcover.

Munari, Bruno. *Bruno Munari's Zoo.* Cleveland: Collins, William, & World Publishing Co., 1963.

Clear, full-color illustrations of zoo animals with a tongue-in-cheek statement about each one, such as: "A kangaroo is all legs, but he does not know it." Ages 2-6. Hardcover.

Pfloog, Jan. *Wild Animals and Their Babies.* New York: Western Publishing Co., 1971.

This large-size book features full-color double-page illustrations of wild animal families, one kind at a time, in their natural environments. Notes at the back for parents give a bit more information than the brief text throughout the body of the book. Ages 3-7. Hardcover.

Reit, Seymour V. *Animals Around My Block.* Photos by AlexV. Sobolewski. My World Series for Early Childhood. New York: McGraw-Hill Book Co., 1970.

Follow a boy as he shows you the animals around his block. The text is on the left-hand pages, the full-color photos on the right. Ages 3-6. Hardcover.

Risom, Ole. *I Am a Kitten.* Illustrated by Jan Pfloog. New York: Western Publishing Co., 1970.

The story of a kitten from the kitten's viewpoint.

Full-color. Slick cardboard pages. Also: *I Am a Puppy, I Am a Bear, I Am a Mouse,* and *I Am a Bunny.* Ages 2 (and under)-5. Hardcover.

Selsam, Millicent E. *How Puppies Grow.* Photos by Esther Bubley. New York: Scholastic Book Services, 1972.
Black-and-white photos of puppies from one day after birth through eight weeks. Ages 3½-7. Hardcover.

Stevens, Carla. *The Birth of Sunset's Kittens.* Photos by Leonard Stevens. Reading, MA: Addison-Wesley Publishing Co., 1969.
Splendid black-and-white photos and text record the actual birth of Sunset's four kittens. Excellent. Ages 3-10. Hardcover.

————. *Catch a Cricket.* Photos by Martin Iger. Reading, MA: Addison-Wesley Publishing Co., 1961.
Great black-and-white photos of little boys and bugs. Text holds the attitude that little girls do not like worms, bugs, etc., but that boys do. Other than this, it is an excellent, two-color book. Ages 3½-8. Hardcover.

Sugano, Yoshikatsu. *The Kitten's Adventure.* New York: McGraw-Hill Book Co., 1971.
No words, but so beautifully done it positively tickles one's senses. Exquisite paper, color, and photography. Full color. Excellent. All ages. Hardcover.

Ward, Lynd. *The Biggest Bear.* Boston: Houghton Mifflin Co., 1952.
A boy finds an orphaned bear cub and adopts it, but when the cub grows up he becomes a problem to everyone but the boy. After the bear's narrow escape from death, he ends up in a zoo. The powerful brown-and-white sketches won the Caldecott award. Ages 5-9. Hardcover, soft-cover.

Watson, Jane Werner. *Birds: A Child's First Book about Our Most Familiar Birds*. Illustrated by Eloise Wilkin. New York: Western Publishing Co., Inc., 1958. Library edition only.

Each season very young children discover different birds, their resting places, young, habits, and food. Unfortunately not multi-racial. Rhyming text. Full color. Large print. Ages 3-6.

Welch, Martha M. *Just Like Puppies*. New York: Coward, McCann & Geoghegan, 1969.

Black-and-white photo essay of a mother poodle who adopts a litter of orphaned raccoons. Ages 3-7. Hardcover.

Wiest, Robert and Claire. *Down the River Without a Paddle*.

See "Fantasy Literature."

Wildsmith, Brian. *Brian Wildsmith's Wild Animals*. New York: Franklin Watts, 1967.

Impressionistic, free illustrations in blazing colors. The often playful, one-line texts use a generic name for each set of animals, e.g. "a pride of lions." Other books done in this same style are: *Brian Wildsmith's Birds* (1967), and *Brian Wildsmith's Fishes* (1968). The children enjoy these very much. Ages 2½-7. Hardcover.

Williams, Garth. *Baby Farm Animals*. New York: Western Publishing Co., 1959.

Soft, beautiful full-color action illustrations of young animals. Large print, large illustrations. Excellent. Ages 2-6. Hardcover.

―――. *The Chicken Book: A Traditional Rhyme*. New York: Delacorte Press, 1970.

Five little chicks mope about the different types of food

240

they wish they had, until the mother hen comes along and tells them to scratch! Told in brief rhyme which reinforces ordinal counting. Full color. Excellent. Ages 2½-5. Hardcover.

Wright, Betty R. *Good Morning Farm*. Illustrated by Fred Weinman. New York: Western Publishing Co., 1971.
  A mixture of illustrations and photography of farm animals. Very cheery text written in rhyme. For example:
  Good morning kittens,
  You're looking perky,
  Don't gobble your
  breakfast, Mr. Turkey.
Full color, large print. Ages 2-6. Hardcover.

Ylla. *The Little Elephant*.
  See "Fantasy Literature."

Zoll, Max A. *Animal Babies*. Translated by Violetta Castillo. New York: Hill & Wang, 1971.
  The author personally escorts the reader through his magnificent photograph collection of animals in their natural environments. Some are in black and white; some are in full color. The text is natural and informative. This book offers an exceptional experience for children. Excellent. Ages 5-9. Hardcover.

General nature
Atwood, Ann. *Haiku: The Mood of the Earth*.
  See "Poetry and Nursery Rhymes."

————. *The Wild Young Desert*. New York: Charles Scribner's Sons, 1970.
  Beautiful, full-color photos illustrate the story of a desert's slow cycle of change. Not a preschool book, but young children will enjoy the pictures and your own brief comments. All ages. Hardcover.

Caudill, Rebecca. *Come Along!* See "Poetry and Nursery Rhymes."

Elwart, Joan P. *What Hides Inside?* Illustrated by Marie Michal. Chicago: Rand McNally & Co., 1972.
Go exploring with two children as they discover nature's mysteries. Rhyming text: "Outsides—thorny, barbed, and prickly—can hold insides all warm and tickly." Full-color, delicate pen and watercolor illustrations on white with some fuzzy applications for the tactile pleasure of small children. Ages 3½-6. Hardcover.

Freeman, Don. *The Seal and the Slick*. New York: Viking Press, 1974.
Ecological theme tells the story of a seal pup caught in an oil slick, but rescued and scrubbed by a young girl and boy. Soft, full-color watercolor pictures. Ages 4-7. Hardcover.

Heyduck-Huth, Hilde. *In the Forest*. New York: Harcourt Brace Jovanovich, 1971.
A short journal of life in the forest. Sturdy, laminated, cardboard pages, rich full color, large print. Ages 2 (and under)-5. Hardcover.

Krauss, Ruth. *The Carrot Seed*. See Fantasy Literature."

Krieger, David. *Too Many Stones*. Reading, MA: Addison-Wesley Publishing Co., 1970.
An uncommon book about a common pastime of children: collecting rocks. Color. Ages 4½-8. Hardcover.

Tresselt, Alvin. *The Dead Tree*. Illustrated by Charles Robinson. New York: Parents Magazine Press, 1972.
The life and death of a tall, proud oak is told by a skilled writer. The multiple causes of the tree's death are shown. Children especially enjoy the enlarged picture inserts of

bugs which invade the tree. Exquisite, full-color watercolor illustrations done in muted forest hues. Excellent. Ages 4½-9. Hardcover.

Udry, Janis M. *A Tree Is Nice*. Illustrated by Marc Simont. New York: Harper & Row Pubs., 1956.
Shows reasons why trees are nice—some from a child's point of view and some from an adult's. Simple, childlike style of writing. Most pages are brilliantly colored. A Caldecott winner. Ages 4½-7. Hardcover.

Cycles—time, seasons, water
Birnbaum, A. *Green Eyes*. See "Fantasy Literature."

Brown, Margaret W. *Home for a Bunny*. See "Fantasy Literature."

Burningham, John. *Seasons*. New York: Bobbs-Merrill Co., 1970.
A treasury of extravagant seasonal scenes and simple text in large print. Full color. Very popular. Ages 4-7. Hardcover.

Kessler, Ethel. *Splish Splash!* Illustrated by Leonard Kessler. New York: Parents Magazine Press, 1973.
A beautifully illustrated book in full color about the coming of spring. *Slush, Slush!*, a book about winter, is available from the same publisher. Ages 4-6. Hardcover.

Krauss, Ruth. *The Happy Day*. See "Fantasy Literature."

MacDonald, Golden. (Brown, Margaret Wise) *Red Light, Green Light*. See "Basic Academic Concepts."

Russell, Solveig P. *Spring, Fall and in Between*. Illustrated by Don Pallarito. St. Louis: Concordia Publishing House, 1968.

A book describing the seasons in rhyme:
        Sometimes in the summer
        God sends us His showers
        To cool the warm air
        And freshen the flowers.
Beautiful, full-color illustrations. Ages 3½-6. Hardcover.

Shulevitz, Uri. *Rain, Rain, Rivers*. New York: Farrar, Straus & Giroux, 1969.

Pictures in blues and yellows mingling into greens, some with double-page landscapes, tell the story of the water cycle and more. Because of the muted colors, small print, and detailed pictures, this book is better used with individual children or very small groups. Ages 4½-7. Hardcover.

Tresselt, Alvin. *It's Time Now!* Illustrated by Roger Duvoisin. New York: Lothrop, Lee & Shephard Co., 1969.

Animated, full-color illustrations capture the hum and change of each season as it comes to the city. Ages 4½-7. Hardcover.

Tudor, Tasha. *First Delights: A Book About the Five Senses*. See "Discovery Books: The World Around Us, The five senses."

Zolotow, Charlotte. *Wake Up and Good Night*. Illustrated by Leonard Weisgard. New York: Harper & Row Pubs., 1971.

Full-color pictures interpret the words of early morning and nighttime experiences. Ages 3½-6. Hardcover.

Weather, sky, astronomy
De Regniers, Beatrice S., and Isabel Gordon. *The Shadow Book*. Photos by Isabel Gordon. New York: Harcourt Brace Jovanovich, 1960.

Go through the day with a little boy as he traces his

shadow and the shadows of others. A fine photo essay in black and white. Ages 3-7. Hardcover.

Field, Enid. *I Wondered . . . About the Sky*. Photos by Florence Harrison. Chicago: Childrens Press, 1973.
   Black-and-white photos with rhyming text:
       How birds can fly
       and not bump others in the sky
       with no signs to let them know
       when to STOP and when to GO?
Ages 4-7. Hardcover.

Freeman, Don. *A Rainbow of My Own*. New York: Viking Press, 1966.
   Out in a storm, a little boy finds rainbows beautiful and perplexing. When the real rainbow disappears, he imagines one. Then, awed by the splendor of the sun bursting through the storm-spent clouds, he hurrys home to find a rainbow on his wall! Full-color, watercolor illustrations. Ages 3½-7. Hardcover.

Hutchins, Pat. *The Wind Blew*. See "Fantasy Literature."

Keats, Ezra, J. *The Snowy Day*. See "Social Themes, Self."

Ringi, Kjell. *The Sun and the Cloud*. See "Fantasy Literature."

Shaw, Charles G. *It Looked Like Spilt Milk*. New York: Harper & Row Pubs., 1947.
   Royal blue paper with white print comprises one page, and a white silhouette, which assumes many forms, is on the facing page. What is it? The last page gives the answer. Ages 2½-6. Hardcover.

The five senses
Brenner, Barbara. *Faces*. Photos by George Ancona. New

York: E.P. Dutton & Co., 1970.
Black-and-white photos of the face, some very close up, explore the senses by monitoring facial expressions. Ages 3-7. Hardcover.

Seuss, Dr. (Theodor Geisel). *Mister Brown Can Moo! Can You?* See "Fantasy Literature."

Tudor, Tasha. *First Delights: A Book About the Five Senses*. Bronx, NY: Platt & Munk Pubs., 1966.
Each season brings delightful new sensations to Sally which are perceived through her five senses. The cheerful, full-color pastel illustrations of a little girl in a rural setting carry a quaint, old-fashioned, greeting-card flavor. Ages 5-7. Hardcover.

Human physiology
Baer, Edith. *The Wonder of Hands*. See "Social Themes, Self."

McGuire, Leslie. *You: How Your Body Works*. Illustrated by Susan Perl. Bronx, NY: Platt & Munk Pubs., 1974.
Bands of energetic children romp across the pages of this book illustrating and testing the various properties of their bodies described by the text. External observations mentioned first, then internal hows and whys, and processes of breathing, digestion, and sleeping. Explains why it is important to treat the body kindly. It is too long (forty-eight pages) to be read in one sitting, but can be easily divided into small sections. Full color. Ages 4½-8. Hardcover.

Teeth. Illustrated by Michael Ricketts. Giant Starters Series. New York: Grosset & Dunlap, 1974.
Story of a boy's teeth and their care. Animals and their teeth are also shown. Word-list index with pictures. Uninspired but clear, controlled vocabulary. Large print.

Full color. Ages 4½-7. Hardcover.

Construction, origins of everyday products

Beskow, Elsa. *Pelle's New Suit*. Translated by Marion L. Woodburn. New York: Harper & Row Pubs., 1929.

A story from turn-of-the-century rural Sweden with framed illustrations done in soft, full color. Pelle, a very resourceful young boy, needs a new suit. What he can do—shearing the sheep and dying the wool—he does. What he cannot do—carding, spinning, weaving, and tailoring—he asks others to do for him in exchange for labor. Although an informative book, the information is secondary to the plot and its social implications, making this a doubly valuable work. Ages 4-7. Hardcover.

Carle, Eric. *Pancakes, Pancakes!* New York: Alfred A. Knopf, 1970.

In earlier days, wanting a pancake and getting it were two different things. Follow the step-by-step sequence of getting and preparing the necessary ingredients. Full-color, printed collage pictures. Ages 4½-8. Hardcover. (Soft-cover available from Pantheon Books.)

DePaola, Thomas A. *Charlie Needs a Cloak*. Englewood Cliffs, NJ: Prentice-Hall, 1974.

Simple, humorous, color illustrations tell the straightforward story of a shepherd who shears his sheep, cards and spins the wool, weaves and dyes the cloth, and sews a warm new cloak. Large print. Ages 3-6. Hardcover.

Hildebrandt, Greg and Tim. *How Do They Build It?* See "Fantasy Literature."

Lebar, Mary. *How God Gives Us Peanut Butter*. Illustrated by Vera Gohman. Cincinnati: Standard Publishing Company, n.d.

An action book which shows the steps in peanut butter

production. Also by the same author, *How God Gives Us bread*, . . . *Apples*, . . . *Jelly*, . . . *Ice Cream*, etc. Slick paper cover. Full color. Ages 4-7. Inexpensive.

Rockwell, Anne. *Machines*. Illustrated by Harlow Rockwell. New York: Macmillan Co. 1972.

With an amazing economy of words, various basic concepts about machines are described: eggbeaters, sewing machines, airplanes, pulleys, bicycles, etc. Similar to this book is *The Toolbox*, which describes the treasures to be found in a toolbox. Fresh, watercolor illustrations and large hand lettered text against white space. Excellent. Ages 2½-6. Hardcover.

Watson, Aldren. *Where Everyday Things Come From*. See "Fantasy Literature."

SOCIAL THEMES
Self
Baer, Edith. *The Wonder of Hands*. Photos by Tana Hoban. New York: Parents Magazine Press, 1970.

Rhyming, simple one-line texts headline the marvelous photographs. The subjects, mostly children, are shown working, playing, rejoicing, loving. Black and white. Excellent. Ages 3-7.

Cunningham, Aline. *Who Am I?* St. Louis: Concordia Publishing House, 1973.

A child discusses who he is in terms of his unique life and relationship to God. Full-color illustrations on white space. Ages 2-6. Soft-cover.

Gill, Bob. *I Keep Changing*. New York: Scroll Press, 1971.

A book of comparisons. A boy compares himself from various perspectives. To an ant he is a giant, to an elephant he is quite small. In the tub his voice is like thunder, but at the band concert he can hardly hear himself. Bold printing and bold pictures. Color. Ages 3-6. Hardcover.

Green, Mary M. *Is It Hard? Is It Easy?*. Photos, illustrations by Len Gittleman. Reading, MA: Addison-Wesley Publishing Co., 1960.
Four friends have different skills, types of muscular coordination, and maturity. Strikingly simple, almost complete silhouette-type photography. Children find this book very interesting. Large print. Ages 3-6. Hardcover.

Keats, Ezra J. *Dreams*. New York: Macmillan Co., 1974.
Roberto brings home a paper mouse that he made in school. His friend asks, "Does it do anything?" Read the book and find out! Full-color collages and marble-like acrylics illustrate this sweet little story. Hardcover.

————. *The Snowy Day*. New York: Viking Press, 1962.
This Caldecott Award winning book pictures a little boy in his solitude delighting in the deep, fresh-fallen snow. Full-color collage illustrations. Excellent. Ages 3½-7. Hardcover.

Lund, Doris H. *Did You Ever Dream?*. Illustrated by Franklin Luke. New York: Parents Magazine Press, 1969.
Feathery, soft, full-color pastel pictures add a dream-like quality to this book about dreams and some of their origins. Ages 2½-6. Hardcover.

Rand, Ann and Paul. *I Know a Lot of Things*. New York: Harcourt Brace & World, 1956.
A small, satisfied child inventories his current knowledge, yet realizes his knowledge will continue to grow as he gets bigger. Color. Ages 3-5. Hardcover.

Rogers, Fred. *Mister Rogers Talks About: The New Baby, Fighting, A Trip to The Doctor, Going to School, Haircuts, Moving*. Photos by Myron Papiz. Bronx, NY: Platt & Munk

249

Pubs., 1974.

The subjects are those which interest small children especially if they are presented when applicable. Many full-color photos with a sensitive text. The ninety-three page book can be read chapter by chapter. Hardcover.

Simon, Norma. *How Do I Feel?* Illustrated by Joe Lasker. Chicago: Albert Whitman & Co., 1970.

A boy describes his feelings in different situations and notes that they are often different from his twin brother's. Also shown is the effect of people's remarks and feelings on others—a very important concept for everyone to learn. About half of the illustrations are in full color, the other half are in black and white. Ages 3½-7. Hardcover.

————. *I Know What I Like.* Illustrated by Dora Leder. Chicago: Albert Whitman & Co., 1971.

Children discuss many everyday things they like—and a few things they don't like. Two color. Ages 3½-7. Hardcover.

Tymms, Jean. *The Me Book.* See "Fantasy Literature."

Yashima, Taro. *Umbrella.* New York: Viking Press, 1958.

A little girl can't wait to use her birthday rain boots and umbrella, but the weather doesn't cooperate. When it finally does rain she proudly wears her presents, and also passes into a new maturity. Full color. Ages 7-9. Hardcover.

Zolotow, Charlotte. *William's Doll.* Illustrated by William Pene Du Bois. New York: Harper & Row Pubs., 1972.

William, who is all boy, wants a doll. He is laughed at until his grandmother comes for a visit and understands his need to learn to play a father's role as well as to learn to play ball. Full-color watercolor illustrations. Ages 4-8. Hardcover.

Family

Alexander, Martha. *The Story Grandmother Told*. New York: Dial Press, 1969.

A book about a small girl who asks her grandmother to tell her a story. To make sure grandmother tells the right one, the little girl tells her the whole story first! Soft, realistic sketches. To color. Ages 4-7. Hardcover.

Anderson, Clarence W. *Lonesome Little Colt*. See "Discovery Books: The World Around Us, The animal kingdom."

Buckley, Helen E. *Josie and the Snow*. i.t.a. ed. Illustrated by Evaline Ness. New York: Lothrop, Lee & Shepard Co. 1964.

A family has a spontaneous time of snow fun and then retreats inside to curl up "rosy and red" by the fire. A perfect finish for a perfect day. Poetic text. Color. Ages 4-7. Hardcover.

Caines, Jeannette. *Abby*. Illustrated by Steven Kellogg. New York: Harper & Row Pubs., 1973.

A very warm, natural, home dialogue between a mother, her preschool adopted daughter, and her school-age natural son. Beautiful black-and-white sketches. Ages 4-8. Hardcover.

Holland, Vicki. *We Are Having a Baby*. New York: Charles Scribner's Sons, 1972.

An extremely well-done black-and-white essay of a little girl's experiences before, during, and after the birth of her brother. The beautiful pictures are natural and in good taste. They express tenderness and insight into the little girl's bewilderments, and adjustment to a new situation. Excellent. Ages 3-7. Hardcover.

Keith, Eros. *Rrra-ah*. See "Discovery Books: The World

Around Us, The animal kingdom."

Krauss, Ruth. *The Bundle Book*. Illustrated by Helen Stone. New York: Harper Row Pubs., 1951.
A mother plays a guessing game with her small child who is under the covers of his bed. Really delightful. Dreamlike, sketchy illustrations. Color. Ages 2 (and under)-5. Hardcover.

Lasker, Joe. *Mothers Can Do Anything*. Chicago: Albert Whitman & Co., 1972.
A book which keeps pace with the changing status of working mothers. Many interesting nonstereotyped kinds of work that mothers do. Illustrated half in full color, half in black and white. Ages 3-6.

Mannheim, Grete. *The Two Friends*. See "Social Themes, Friends, occupations."

Moss, Jeffrey. *People in My Family*. See "Fantasy Literature."

Reich, Hanns, ed. *Children and Their Fathers*. Text by Eugen Roth. New York: Hill & Wang, 1962.
The five introductory pages of text are intended for adults. The balance of this book is a wordless, black-and-white photo commentary on children—here and around the world—and their fathers. This book captivates young children but should, because of its length, be presented in two or three sessions. Other books of interest in this Terra Magica Series are: *Children and Their Mothers*, *Children of Many Lands*, *Baby Animals and Their Mothers*, *The World from Above*, *Cats*. Excellent. All ages. Hardcover.

Scott, Ann H. *On Mother's Lap*. Illustrated by Glo Coalson. New York: McGraw-Hill Book Co., 1972.
A little Eskimo boy finds his mother's lap is a very cozy place, with room for everyone. Two color. Ages 2½-5. Hardcover.

Seuss, Dr. (Geisel Theodor). *And to Think That I Saw It on Mulberry Street.* Chippewa Falls, WI: E.M. Hale & Co., 1937.

A little boy with a talent for embellishing stories fantasizes a real whopper which melts under the stern gaze of his father. Another imaginative book by Dr. Seuss. Full color Ages 5-8. Hardcover.

Shecter, Ben. *If I Had a Ship.* New York: Doubleday & Co., 1971.

A small boy and his mother converse as he shares his daydreams—the places he'd sail and the presents he'd bring her. Full-color well-executed artwork. Ages 2½-6. Hardcover.

Welber, Robert. *The Winter Picnic.* Illustrated by Deborah Ray. New York: Pantheon Books, 1970.

Happy, bright, snow-covered pictures of a boy and his mother having an unlikely winter picnic in the city. Full color. Ages 4-6. Hardcover.

Zolotow, Charlotte. *Big Sister and Little Sister.* Illustrated by Martha Alexander. New York: Harper & Row Pub., 1966.

A younger sister learns about love from her thoughtful older sister. A charming story, with pink and spring-green illustrations. Ages 4-7. Hardcover.

———. *Do You Know What I'll Do?* Illustrated by Garth Williams. New York: Harper & Row Pubs., 1958.

A little girl expresses love for her smaller brother through the many things she plans to do for him. Two color. Ages 3¼-7. Hardcover.

———. *The Sky Was Blue.* Illustrated by Garth Williams. New York: Harper & Row Pubs., 1963.

A family keepsake album opens a little girl's

understanding to the fact that, although styles and times change, human nature is the same. Color. Ages 5-7. Hardcover.

Friends, occupations

Balian, Lorna. *The Aminal*. Nashville: Abingdon Press, 1972.

A little boy finds a small "aminal" and decides to keep it as his very own pet-friend. In describing this animal, verbal communication provides an imprecise vehicle; hence, the story becomes more and more wild as it travels from friend to friend. Fragile, warm, full-color pastel illustrations lend an ethereal quality to this work. Ages 4-7. Hardcover.

Bemelmans, Ludwig. *Madeline*. New York: Viking Press, 1939.

The well-loved story of Madeline, the littlest girl in a Paris boarding school, and her bout with an appendectomy. The brief story, told in rhyme, captures the warmth, humor and empathy in the lives of the girls and the teacher. Some full-color and some two-color illustrations. Excellent. Ages 3-7. Hardcover. (Soft-cover available, same publisher.)

Cunningham, Aline. *New Friends*. St. Louis: Concordia Publishing House, 1973.

God makes many "friends" for children, including plants and animals. Full-color, outlined illustrations in watercolor on white space. Ages 2-6. Laminated paper cover.

Gergely, Tibor. *Busy Day, Busy People*. New York: Random House, 1973.

A story of various occupations. Busy, busy, full-color pictures of activities at construction sites, supermarkets, farms, restaurants, etc. Ages 3-7. Slick paper cover.

Kaufman, Joe. *Busy People*. New York: Western Publishing Co., 1973.

Modern, information-packed book about common and not-so-common occupations. Follow Trudy Teacher, Doris Doctor, Fred Fireman, Carlo Clown, Zeke Zookeeper, Irma Installer (telephone), and others through their work routines. Clear, large, dynamic, full-color illustrations. A must for schools. Ninety-three pages with a table of contents. Excellent. Ages 3½-7. Hardcover.

Keats, Ezra J. *A Letter to Amy*. New York: Harper & Row Pubs., 1968.
Peter writes a birthday party invitation to Amy and goes out in the storm to mail it. The storm blows the letter out of Peter's hand, and who catches it? Amy! But she mustn't know the letter is for her—at least not in Peter's presence! A story of mixed emotions with full-color, luminous illustrations which look so wet, one almost catches the rain. Ages 4½-9. Hardcover.

————. *Pet Show!* New York: Macmillan Publishing Co., 1972.
All gather round for the neighborhood pet show, where everyone is a winner. In full-color thick acrylics. Ages 3½-7. Hardcover, soft-cover.

Lasker, Joe. *Mothers Can Do Anything*.
See "Social Themes, Family."

Look at Me! Photos by Bob McCown. "Look at Me!" Project. Dallas, TX: Dallas Public Library, 1973.
Little children like to see pictures of people—older children do especially—and peer into their mysterious world. This book is a commentary by older children from a low socio-economic group. If read—or just looked at—in stages, this book can be well received by young children. Black-and-white photos. Written for children ages 8-12, can be used by ages 3-12.

Mallett, Anne. *Here Comes Tagalong*. Illustrated by Steven Kellogg. New York: Parents Magazine Press, 1971.

Cheery full-color pictures and text of a little boy and his big friends—and his new smaller friends and their activities. Treats the adjustment of children to a new neighborhood, new friends. Ages 3½-6. Hardcover.

Mannheim, Grete. *The Two Friends*. New York: Alfred A. Knopf, 1968.

Two special days in the life of a little girl are recorded by black-and-white photographs which reveal her family, their activities, her new friends, and their first day at school together. Ages 4½-6. Hardcover.

Oppenheim, Joanne. *On the Other Side of the River*. See "Fantasy Literature."

Peterson, Glen and Barbie. *Let's Visit the Fire Department*. New York: Western Publishing Co., 1974.

The fire chief escorts a little girl and boy on a tour of his station and equipment. Also, *Let's Visit the Policemen*. Full-color photos. Cardboard pages. Excellent. Ages 3-6. Hardcover.

Weil, Lisl. *Fat Ernest*. New York: Parents Magazine Press, 1973.

Set in a housing project, a delightful story of friends and neighbors and a pet gerbil, Ernest, who turns out to be Ernestine. Color. Ages 3-6. Hardcover.

Wilkinson, Jean and Ned. *Come to Work with Us in a Television Station*. Chicago: Childrens Press, 1970.

Full-color photos of children representing adult workers with rhyming descriptive text. The English is a bit strained to make it rhyme. Some others in series: *Come to Work with Us in a Toy Factory, . . . in Aerospace, . . . in House Construction*. Large print. Ages 5-8. Hardcover.

Far away places, people of other lands

Adoff, Arnold. *Ma nDa la*. Illustrated by Emily A. McCully. New York: Harper & Row Pubs., 1971.

The sounds Ma, nDa, La, Ha, Ra, Na and Ah represent, respectively, mother, father, singing, laughing, cheering, sighing, and contentment. The sounds form a chant sung while an African family plants and harvests corn; they are the only words in the book. Warm, rich, true-to-culture artwork conveys a feeling of family closeness and happiness. Full color. Ages 4-7. Hardcover.

Balet, Jan. *The Fence: A Mexican Tale*. New York: Delacorte Press, 1969.

The story of a stingy rich family who lived next door to a poor family. Much food for thought charmingly and humorously presented. Neat, detailed, true-to-culture watercolor pictures as colorful as Mexico. Ages 7-9. Hardcover.

————. *Joanjo: A Portuguese Tale*. New York: Delacorte Press, 1967.

A discontented little boy dreams of bigger things than his life provides. But, in his dream, his constant seeking for ego gratification proves to be his downfall. He wakes a much more accepting and grateful person. Vivid, full-color, outlined figures in Portuguese style make this book memorable. Ages 7-9. Hardcover.

Bemelmans, Ludwig. *Madeline*.
See "Social Themes: Friends, occupations."

Bernheim, Marc and Evelyne. *The Drums Speak: The Story of Kofi, a Boy of West Africa*. New York: Harcourt Brace Jovanovich, 1972.

Through the magic of full-color photography we spend two weeks with a young West African. During this time important changes take place in his life. The adult should read the text to himself and then use the book as a picture book, supplying comments as the children wish. (Used in this way, conflicting values are also avoided.) A favorite of children. Written for ages 9-12, but can be adapted for children 4-9. Hardcover.

Beskow, Elsa. *Pelle's New Suit.*
See "Discovery Books: The World Around Us, Construction, origins of everyday things."

Carle, Eric. *Have You Seen My Cat?*
See "Fantasy Literature."

Feelings, Muriel. *Moja Means One: The Swahili Counting Book.* Illustrated by Tom Feelings. New York: Dial Press, 1971.
For each set of double pages the text consists of a numeral, its name in Swahili (with pronunciation guide), and a sentence about East African culture. The magnificent illustrations convey a feeling of African heat—one almost feels a part of Africa. Lush, misty-soft, two-tone illustrations. Excellent. Ages 4-9. Hardcover.

Scott, Ann H. *On Mother's Lap.*
See "Social Themes, Family."

Smith, Marion H., and Carol S. Prescott. *Families Around the World.* Rev. ed. Man and Communities Series. Grand Rapids, MI: Fideler Co., 1976.
The text asks questions and you and your children provide the answers and the values! Photos of the earth from space introduce the concept of location on our planet which is used throughout the book. Many of the photographs are in full color. Word-list index. Ages 4-8. Hardcover.

Tolstoy, Leo. *Little Stories.* Nashville: Aurora Publishers, 1971.

Stories about children from the Russian culture reflect a serious, studied approach to life. One story blends into another without fanfare or markers. Ordinary events of life are seen through the eyes of young and old, who try to give warmth and find comfort. A unique reading experience—thought provoking. Full-color, rich illustrations set in a turn-of-the-century motif capture the mood. Ages 6-9.

Yashima, Taro. *Crow Boy*. New York: Viking Press, 1955.

A sensitively told story, set in Japan, of a rejected boy who finally wins acceptance from his peers as they come to know him and recognize his talents. Full-color crayon and ink illustrations. Ages 6-9. Hardcover.

School.
Bowmar Early Childhood Series. Los Angeles: Bowmar Publishing Company.

Bowmar has fine full-color photo-stories dealing with young children in preschool or kindergarten environment. Records accompany all the books in this early childhood series, including others mentioned elsewhere in this bibliography. Some titles:
Furry Boy. Children take care of a pet rabbit at school. *Funny Mr. Clown*. A clown visits the classroom. *Do You Suppose Miss Riley Knows?* A boy wonders if his teacher will remember his birthday. *A Beautiful Day for a Picnic*. The class goes to the park for a picnic. *What Is a Birthday Child?* A birthday girl tells of all the privileges she enjoys in school on her birthday. *A Box Tied with a Red Ribbon*. Children try to guess what Nancy brought to school. *Watch Me Outdoors*. A little boy explores the sand at his school. *My Tricycle and I*. Two rides, one real, one pretend. *Friends! Friends! Friends!* Classroom friendships explored. These books help children to develop a greater awareness of everyday life about them. Ages 3-6.

259

Mannheim, Grete. *The Two Friends*.
See "Social Themes, Friends, occupations."

Moremen, Grace. *No, No, Natalie*.
See "Discovery Books: The World Around Us, The animal kingdom."

Speiser, Jean. *Schools Are Where You Find Them*. New York: John Day Co., 1971.
Black-and-white photos of children learning all over the world. The book is geared to youngsters ages 7-12, yet is valuable and interesting to five-year-olds if the text is paraphrased and thereby shortened. Ages 5-12. Hardcover.

Whitney, Alma M. *Just Awful*. Illustrated by Lillian Hoban. Reading, MA: Addison-Wesley Publishing Co., 1971.
A refreshingly written story of a boy's first trip to the school nurse. Restricted use of full color. Very likeable characters. Ages 5-7. Hardcover.

Transportation
Fuchs, Erich. *Journey to the Moon*. New York: Delacorte Press, 1970.
The story of the historic flight to the moon in full-color illustrations. All the text is given in two pages before the pictures begin. Ages 4-7. Hardcover.

Lippman, Peter. *Busy Wheels*. New York: Random House, 1973.
Full-color, action-packed, detailed cartoon illustrations about vehicles at work. Brief text. Ages 4-6. Laminated paper cover.

Pope, Billy N. *Let's Take an Airplane Trip*. San Angelo, TX: Taylor Publishing Co., 1975.

A full-color photo essay taken with children at an airport and aboard a 727. Glossary for children. Well done. Ages 3-6. Hardcover.

Zaffo, George. *The Giant Nursery Book of Things That Go: Fire Engines, Trains, Boats, Trucks, Airplanes.* New York: Doubleday & Co., 1959.

One hundred and sixty-nine pages make this book too long to be read at one sitting, but it can easily be divided into more manageable chunks. Half of the exciting, streamlined illustrations are in full color. Simple text. This book is a must for schools. Excellent. Ages 2-6. Hardcover.

Recreation, fine arts

Baylor, Byrd. *Sometimes I Dance Mountains.* Illustrated by Ken Longtemps, photos by Bill Sears. New York: Charles Scribner's Sons, 1973.

Follow the movements of a child as she dances whirlwinds, bubbles, bugs, sad things, explosive things, anything. She invites you to say things with dance, too. The artwork captures the quality of the movement and adds a fluid element. The book is helpful to parents and teachers in understanding kinesthetic movement and its place in a young child's life. Two color. Ages 4-9. Hardcover.

Mendoza, George, with Prasanna Rao. *Shadowplay.* Photos by Marc Mainguy. New York: Holt, Rinehart & Winston, 1974.

Mr. Rao displays the ancient art of shadowplay in black-and-white photos. His hands and the name of the object he is making appear on the left page, the silhouette on the right page. Helps children to identify objects by their shapes as well as to interpret pictures for their own attempts at the skill. Excellent. All ages. Hardcover.

Merriam, Eve. *What Can You Do with a Pocket?* Illustrated by Harriet Simon. New York: Alfred A. Knopf, 1964.

Different objects serve as symbols for imaginative role play. "If you have a string in your pocket, you can be a fisherman." Helps young children expand their thinking, placing objects in larger conceptual contexts. Color. Ages 4-7. Hardcover.

Radlauer, Ruth. *What Can You Do with a Box?* Illustrated by Jay Rivkin. Chicago: Childrens Press, 1973.
    Imaginative uses for boxes. Black and white. Ages 4-6. Hardcover.

Spilka, Arnold. *Paint All Kinds of Pictures*. New York: Henry Z. Walck, 1963.
    A picture can be large or small. It can have many colors or just one. It can be anything you want it to be—happy or sad, pretty or scary. It tells a little bit about its artist. Full-color illustrations and some black and white serve as examples. Ages 5-9. Hardcover.

Wildsmith, Brian. *Brian Wildsmith's Circus*. New York: Franklin Watts, 1970.
    The entire text of this book is: "The circus comes to town . . . the circus goes on to the next town." In between the two parts of the text is a collection of dazzling full-color circus illustrations. Children enjoy supplying their own "ooooohs" and "aahhhs" for comments. Ages 2½-7. Hardcover.

BASIC ACADEMIC CONCEPTS
Mathematics
Allen, Robert. *Numbers*. Photos by Mottke Weissman. Bronx, NY: Platt & Munk Pubs., 1968.
    Full-color photographs of familiar objects for children to count from one to ten. Ages 3-7.

Berenstain, Stanley and Janice. *Bears on Wheels*.
    See "Fantasy Literature."

Budney, Blossom. *A Kiss Is Round*. New York: Lothrop, Lee & Shepard, Co., 1954.

The concept "round" is discussed in rhyme and color. Ages 2½-5. Hardcover.

Carle, Eric. *One, Two, Three to the Zoo*. Cleveland: Collins, William, & World Publishing Co., 1968.

Count full-color zoo animals from one to ten, and after that take a tour of the zoo on the last page. Painted paper collage. Ages 2¼-6. Hardcover.

———. *The Rooster Who Set Out to See the World*. See "Fantasy Literature."

Cunningham, Aline. *My Counting Book*. St. Louis: Concordia Publishing House, 1973.

Children enjoy counting their arms, buttons, pockets, and fingers, but only God can count the stars. Full-color sketches on white space. Text on yellow below the pictures. Ages 3-6. Laminated paper cover.

Emberley, Ed. *The Wing on a Flea: A Book About Shapes*. Boston: Little, Brown & Co., 1961.

Children enjoy recognizing the shapes on each page. The text is in rhyme:

It's a sail for a sailor
Who sails on the sea,
A teepee or a tree
If you'll just look and see.

Color. Ages 3-6. Hardcover.

Hoban, Tana. *Count and See*. New York: Macmillan Publishing Co., 1972.

Unique black-and-white photos of everyday objects illustrate numbers one to fifteen, twenty, thirty, forty, fifty and one hundred. On the left pages are the numeral, the number word, and the corresponding numbers of dots in white on black. On the right pages are the photos of the objects. Extremely clear. Excellent. Ages 3-6. Hardcover.

————. *Shapes and Things*. New York: Macmillan Publishing Co., 1970.
Skillful use of the camera brings fresh insights into basic concepts. White silhouettes of ordinary objects are projected on black space to create an awareness of form and shape. Very precise, interesting use of space. No test. Ages 2 (and under)-5. Hardcover.

Kruss, James. *Three by Three*. See "Fantasy Literature."

Le Sieg, Theodore. *Ten Apples Up on Top*. See "Fantasy Literature."

Mendoza, George. *The Marcel Marceau Counting Book*. Photos by Milton H. Greene. New York: Doubleday & Co., 1971.
In this inventive book Marcel Marceau portrays a series of occupations, wearing a hat appropriate to each—from astronaut to cowboy. The growing collection of hats, tastefully displayed, reinforces counting from one to twenty. Full color. Ages 3-7. Hardcover.

Moss, Jeffrey. *People in My Family*. See "Fantasy Literature."

Rowan, Dick. *Everybody in! A Counting Book*. New York: Bradbury Press, 1968.
Count the children as they plunge, one by one, into the swimming pool. Black-and-white photos. Ages 3-6. Hardcover.

Russel, Solveig P. *One, Two, Three, and More*. Illustrated by Don Pallarito. St. Louis: Concordia Publishing House, 1966.

A counting book with numerals, animals, and verses. Example:

> One little bird sits
> High on a limb
> Enjoying God's world
> And singing to Him.

Full-color, beautiful illustrations. Ages 3-6.

Sesame Street Book of Numbers. Ed. by Children's TV Workshop. New York: New American Library, 1971.

Gives number sequence and concepts one to ten. Very motivating and exciting for children. Partly full color and partly black and white. Excellent. Ages 3-7. Soft-cover.

Wildsmith, Brian. *Brian Wildsmith's One, Two, Threes.* New York: Franklin Watts, n.d.

Colorful geometric designs form basic shapes which illustrate the designated numeral. As these shapes grow in number they are combined to form recognizable objects, and soon the reader must count the parts to supply the correct numeral. Helpful for distinguishing part-whole relationships, recognition of basic shapes, and counting practice. This creative approach lets the children see that mathematics can be beautiful from the very beginning. Ages 2½-6. Hardcover.

Williams, Garth. *The Chicken Book.* See "Discovery Books: The World Around Us, The animal kingdom."

Part-whole relationships, logic, observation
Anno, Mitsumasa. *Topsy-Turvies: Pictures to Stretch the Imagination.* See "Fantasy Literature."

Brown, Margaret W. *The Important Book.* Illustrated by Leonard Weisgard. New York: Harper & Row Pubs., 1949.

The uses of various objects are analyzed and one outstanding quality is repeated. "But the important thing about a shoe is that you put your foot in it." Half the illustrations are in full color. The text is printed in different type faces and script to heighten the interest. Ages 4-6. Hardcover.

Hoban, Tana. *Look Again!* New York: Macmillan Publishing Co., 1971.
Very cleverly done, wordless, black-and-white photo studies are first seen in part (by the aid of a black page with a center square cut out), then a bit more, and finally, as you turn the last page, the whole object is revealed in perspective. An exciting book. Excellent. Ages 3½-7. Hardcover.

James, Albert. *Wet and Dry*. Illustrated by Anne Knight. Starter-Science Series. London: Macdonald & Co., 1973.
Concepts relating to wetness and dryness are discovered as the text moves from general to more specific notions. Participation in the experiments shown is encouraged. Although the word content is controlled, it does build vocabulary and clearly states the concepts. Full color, aptly illustrated. Numbered pages. Picture-word index. Notes for parents and teachers. Large print. (This book is one of almost 100 titles available in the valuable "Starter Series.") Ages 6-8.

Loss, Joan. *What Is It?* New York: Doubleday & Co., 1974.
Marvelous, large black-and-white photos of greatly magnified parts of various objects. Text on one page, picture—artistically presented—on the other. Excellent. Ages 4½-8. Hardcover.

Milgrom, Harry. *ABC Science Experiments*. Illustrated by Donald Crews. New York: Macmillan Publishing Co., 1970.
Through the alphabet with simple experiments in science. The experiments have to do with the properties of things and changes in those properties, and are shown in simple, full-color illustrations. The experiments are given in three

parts: (1) directions, (2) questions, (3) answers (which are in the back of the book and designed as a guide for parents or teachers). Ages 2½-6. Hardcover, soft-cover.

Peppe, Rodney. *Odd One Out*. New York: Viking Press, 1974.

Follow Peter through his busy day as he goes to school, on a bus, visits the zoo, the toy shop, and the farm. In each picture there is one thing which doesn't fit. Finding it makes this book a game as well as a story. Dazzling full-color on white space. Large print. Excellent. Ages 3-6. Hardcover, soft-cover.

Selsam, Millicent E. *Is This a Baby Dinosaur and Other Science Puzzles*. New York: Scholastic Book Services, 1972.

Black-and-white photos and brief text examine, from different perspectives, the characteristics of various plants and animals. Ages 4-8. Soft-cover.

Wildsmith, Brian. *Brian Wildsmith's Puzzles*. New York: Franklin Watts, 1971.

Questions whose answers can be found by exploring the colorful illustrations. Ages 4-7. Hardcover.

ABC's
ABC: An Alphabet Book. Illustrated by Thomas Matthiesen. Bronx, NY: Platt & Munk Pubs., 1968.

The letter (presented in upper-and lower-case forms), an object using the letter initial, and a brief text concerning the object are on the left-hand page. On the right-hand page is a full-color photo of the object. Beautiful in its simplicity. Excellent. Ages 2½-6. Hardcover.

Anglund, Joan W. *In a Pumpkin Shell: A Mother Goose ABC*. See "Poetry and Nursery Rhymes."

Barton, Byron. *Applebet Story*. See "Fantasy Literature."

Gag, Wanda. *The ABC Bunny*. See "Fantasy Literature."

Hayes, Wanda. *Standard ABC Book* (series) *Bible People*. Illustrated by Olga Psyche Packard. Standard Publishing Co., 1972.
> Capital letters highlighted with scriptural illustrations:
> R is for Rhoda
> Who raced across the floor
> And left poor Peter standing
> Knock, knock, knocking at the door.

References given. Full-color, large illustrations. Slick paper cover. Ages 3½-6. Also, *Life of Jesus*.

Milgrom, Harry. *ABC Science Experiments*. See "Basic Academic Concepts, Part-whole relationships, logic, observation."

Peppe, Rodney. *The Alphabet Book*. New York: Scholastic Book Service, 1968.
> Full-color, well-executed, uncluttered, interesting pictures and lower-case letters. The words, used to highlight the letters, represent concepts generally related to each other: "This is the *a*nchor . . . that holds the *b*oat." Ages 4-6.

Wildsmith, Brian. *Brian Wildsmith's ABC*. New York: Franklin Watts, 1963.
> Brightly colored objects representing initial-letter sounds appear on colored paper, one per page. On the facing page the letter is shown in upper- and lower-case forms along with the object's name. Winner of Britain's Kate Greenaway award. Color. (A set of Wildsmith's alphabet picture cards for classroom display is also available from the publisher.) Ages 2-6. Hardcover.

Vocabulary basics

Balian, Lorna. *Where in the World Is Henry?* New York:

Bradbury Press, 1972.

Order and location concepts. A boy and his big sister look for their pet. The search relates things to their places, each within a larger framework.

> Where is the bedroom? The bedroom is in the house.
> *Where is the house? The house in on the street. . . .*

Soft, simple, outlined figures. Two colors. Ages 3½-6. Hardcover.

Berenstain, Stanley and Janice. *Inside, Outside, Upside down.* See "Fantasy Literature."

————. *Old Hat, New Hat.* See "Fantasy Literature."

Hanson, Joan. *More Antonyms: Wild and Tame and Other Words That Are As Different in Meaning As Work and Play.* Minneapolis: Lerner Pubs. Co., 1973.

A simple black-and-white sketch (except for our hero's red hat) illustrates the concept behind a word. One word and illustration per page, facing its antonym. Also by the same author: *Antonyms* (1972) *Homographs* (1972), *More Synonyms* (1973), and *British-American Synonyms* (1972). Ages 3½-6. Hardcover.

Hoban, Tana. *Push Pull, Empty Full: A Book of Opposites.* New York: Macmillan Publishing Co., 1972.

Extremely simple yet interesting black-and-white photo studies illustrate the large-print words—just one per page, with its opposite on the facing page. Excellent. Ages 2 (and under)-5. Hardcover, soft-cover.

Kaufman, Joe. *Words.* New York: Western Publishing Co., 1968.

Illustrations of objects arranged by categories, and their individual names under generic terms. Major categories include: body parts, furniture, vehicles, clothes, family, domestic animals, playthings, and food. Slick cardboard pages. Full color. Excellent. Ages 2-6. Hardcover.

Kohn, Bernice. *How High Is Up?* Illustrated by Jan Pyk. New York: G.P. Putnam's Sons, 1971.

A book to help clarify basic concepts: cold, high, down, big, etc. "How small is small? Small is as small as a newborn puppy/One grape when you're hungry/An ant." Simple, color illustrations. Ages 3-6. Hardcover.

MacDonald, Golden (Brown, Margaret W.). *Red Light, Green Light*. Illustrated by Leonard Weisgard. New York: Doubleday & Co.,1944.

Children enjoy the repetitive phrase "red light, green light" which reinforces the stop-go concept throughout the book. Daytime and nighttime activities are also reinforced. In white and browns with touches of red and green. Ages 3-6. Hardcover, soft-cover.

Pulet, Virginia. *Blue Bug's Vegetable Garden*. Illustrated by Donald Charles. Chicago: Childrens Press, 1973.

Basic direction words are reinforced as blue bug hunts for his favorite food. The bug-size perspective makes this book especially nice for group reading. This book includes a vegetable classification table at the end, similar to an appendix. Vivid full color. Ages 2½-5. Hardcover.

Seuss, Dr. (Geisel, Theodor). *The Foot Book*. See "Fantasy Literature."

Taylor, Talus and Annette Tison. *The Adventures of the Three Colors*. Cleveland: Collins, William, & World Publishing Co., 1971.

Transparent overlays show the effect of mixing combinations of color. The text reinforces color names and invites child participation and exploration. A fun way to learn about color effects. One caution—use this book only after children already know their color names. Excellent. Ages 4-7. Hardcover.

Wiest, Robert and Claire. *Down the River Without a Paddle*. See "Fantasy Literature."

BEDTIME BOOKS

Brown, Margaret W. *Child's Goodnight Book*. Illustrated by Jean Charlot. Reading, MA: Addison-Wesley Publishing Co., 1950.

The slow rhythm of a world drifting off into sleep is echoed through this book. Full-color crayon illustrations. Ages 2 (and under)-4. Hardcover.

————.*Home for a Bunny*. See "Fantasy Literature."

————. *The Little Fur Family*. See Fantasy Literature."

Field, Eugene. *Wynken, Blynken and Nod*. See "Poetry and Nursery Rhymes."

Field, Rachel. *Prayer for a Child*. Illustrated by Elizabeth O. Jones. New York: Macmillan Publishing Co., 1944.

A little girl and those mentioned in her prayer are pictured. Sweet but not saccharin. A Caldecott award winner. Half of the soft pictures are full color, half are two-color. Ages 3½-6. Hardcover.

Hazen, Barbara S. *Where Do Bears Sleep?* See "Discovery Books: The World Around Us. The animal kingdom."

Memling, Carl. *What's in the Dark?* Illustrated by John E. Johnson. New York: Parents Magazine Press, 1971.

A reassuring glimpse of household items in the dark, and activities of the night. Full color. Ages 2½-5. Hardcover.

Seuss, Dr. (Geisel, Theodor). *Dr. Seuss's Sleep Book*. See "Fantasy Literature."

Warburg, Sandol. *Curl Up Small*. See "Poetry and Nursery Rhymes."

Ylla, photos by. *The Sleepy Little Lion*. See "Fantasy Literature."

POETRY AND NURSERY RHYMES

Abisch, Roz, and Boche Kaplan. *Sweet Betsy from Pike*. New York: E. P. Dutton & Co., 1970.

An historical poem about a gold rush couple who actually find gold! The unusual illustrations, beautiful examples of precise cloth collage and stitchery, are an inspiration for cloth crafting. Music for the song "Sweet Betsy from Pike" is included. Full color. Ages 5-8. Hardcover.

Adoff, Arnold. *Black Is Brown Is Tan*. Illustrated by Emily A. McCully. New York: Harper & Row Pubs., 1973.

Splendid, full-color watercolors of everyday family scenes radiate the happiness this interracial family shares. The theme of the sophisticated poem is how the various family members view themselves and their assorted relatives.

. . . And my face gets tomato red
when I puff and yell you into bed.
This is the way it is for us
this is the way we are. . . .

"There is granny white and grandma black/kissing both your cheeks and hugging back." Ages 6-7. Hardcover.

Anglund, Joan. *In a Pumpkin Shell: A Mother Goose ABC*. New York: Harcourt Brace Jovanovich, 1960.

Going through the alphabet with corresponding nursery rhymes. Fanciful, quaint, ink sketches—some in full color. Ages 4-6. Hardcover.

————.*Morning Is a Little Child.* New York: Harcourt Brace Jovanovich, 1969.
Fanciful pen and ink sketches in full color pastels.
The work of water is bubbles!
Day is the job of the sun.
Green is the business of gardens,
And the duty of children is fun!
Ages 6-9. Hardcover.

Atwood, Ann. *Haiku: The Mood of the Earth.* New York: Charles Scribner's Sons, 1971.
Two absolutely breathtaking, rich full-color photographs of nature accompany each three-line Haiku poem. One may choose to skip some of the poetry with young children. This book is beautiful just for sitting in silence with the children and admiring the pictures. Excellent. All ages. Hardcover.

Caudill, Rebecca. *Come Along!* Illustrated by Ellen Raskin. New York: Holt, Rinehart & Winston, 1969.
A poem about the joys of nature. Full-color illustrations by the award winning artist. Ages 4½-8. Hardcover, soft-cover.

Emberley, Barbara. *Drummer Hoff.* Illustrated by Ed Emberley. Englewood Cliffs, NJ: Prentice-Hall, 1967.
A lively folk tale with bouncy verses about the building of a cannon. Each soldier has a part:
Sergeant Chowder
brought the powder,
Corporal Farrell
brought the barrel.
The bright, ornate, full-color woodcut illustrations won this book the Caldecott award. Excellent. Ages 3-7. Hardcover, soft-cover.

Field, Eugene. *Wynken, Blynken and Nod.* Illustrated by

Barbara Cooney. New York: Hastings House Pubs., 1970.

A classic in children's poetry, well-mirrored in ethereal illustrations which capture the dream-like imagery. White, which looks more like silver, fades into dark blue. Heavy, textured paper. Ages 5-9. Hardcover.

Fisher, Aileen. *Do Bears Have Mothers Too?* Illustrations by Eric Carle. New York: Thomas Y. Crowell Co., 1973.

Fairly long poems appear on the left-hand pages, pictures appear mostly on the right-hand pages:

... But elephant calf,
You're much more grand—
You've a flexible trunk
like a flexible hand. ...

Multi-media full-color illustrations. Ages 6-8. Hardcover.

Garelick, May. *Where Does the Butterfly Go When It Rains?* Illustrated by Leonard Weisgard. Reading, MA: Addison-Wesley Publishing Co., 1961.

Various animals are mentioned as they seek—or don't seek—cover from the rain. But a child wonders where the butterfly goes in a storm. A few pictures are two-color, but most are in rainy shades of blue. Ages 4-7. Hardcover. (Soft-cover available from Scholastic Book Services.)

MacDonald, Golden (Margaret W. Brown,). *The Little Island*.

See "Fantasy Literature."

Martin, Bill, Jr. *America, I Know You*. Illustrated by Ted Rand. Freedom Book Series. Bowmar Publishing Co., 1970.

Luminescent, crisp, full-color paintings of life in America highlight the sparingly used one liners. "You (America) are a spoonful of honey on a slice of bread." The subject matter is above the experience of young children, but they enjoy the understandable pictures and rhythm of the words. Ages 4-9. Hardcover.

————. *I Reach Out to the Morning*. Illustrated by Henry Markowitz. Freedom Book Series. Bowmar Publishing Co., 1970.

The person speaking through the poem is a prisoner of his own prejudices and fears, from which he longs to be set free. Offers a good chance to discuss the changes that occur when one is born again.

> . . . her skin looks strange to me,
> so I cut myself off from the noon time
> I cut myself out of the day
> and I pull back into my snug little world
> where nobody looks that way.
>
> . . . O, I want to reach out to the morning
> friendly, open and free,
> so that strangeness doesn't estrange me
> and newness won't frighten me.

Full, bright colors. Ages 7-10. Hardcover.

Mendoza, George. *And I Must Hurry for the Sea Is Coming In*. Photos by DeWayne Dalrymple. Englewood Cliffs, NJ: Prentice-Hall, 1969.

Photographs of the sea, a boy, and a boat. The social message is above most children under nine years old, but the hope of the little boy's dream and the photos will enchant young children. Full color. Excellent. Ages 4-11.

O'Neill, Mary. *Hailstones and Halibut Bones*. Illustrated by Leonard Weisgard. New York: Doubleday & Co., 1961.

Poetry about color, with illustrations in black and the particular color being described.

> What is Brown?
> Brown is the color of a country road
> Back of a turtle

Back of a toad
Brown is cinnamon
And morning Toast
And the smell of
The Sunday roast. . . .
Ages 4½-9. Hardcover, soft-cover.

Parsons, Virginia. *Rainbow Rhymes*. New York: Western Publishing Co., 1974.

Each page offers one picture of children and one rhyme. The little children are attired in eighteenth century clothing. Colored double-page borders set the tone for the color scheme used in the illustrations—an aesthetically pleasing technique. Unfortunately, not multi-racial. Large print, extra-large, clear full-color pictures. Ages 2-6. Hardcover.

Petersham, Maud and Miska. *The Rooster Crows*. New York: Macmillan Publishing Co., 1945.

Familiar rhymes include "Ladybug, ladybug" and "Roses are red, violets are blue." The illustrations—some in full color, some in two colors—won the Caldecott award. Ages 4-7. Hardcover. (Soft-cover abridged edition available.)

Scarry, Richard, Illustrations. *Best Mother Goose Ever*. New York: Western Publishing Co., 1970.

It should be remembered that some Mother Goose rhymes are not edifying. Full-color, large illustrations, less print per page than most Mother Goose books. First line index. Ages 2 (and under)-6. Hardcover.

Warburg, Sandol. *Curl Up Small*. Illustrated by Trina S. Hyman. Boston: Houghton Mifflin Co., 1964.

Excellent poetry that tickles one's ears and entices wee ones to:
. . . curl up small
In the dark in the warm

In the soft in the safe
In the lap of the world
And dream and dream
And sleep and sleep. . . .

Soft, warm color illustrations. Absolutely charming. Ages 3-6. Hardcover.

Wildsmith, Brian. *Brian Wildsmith's Mother Goose: A Collection of Nursery Rhymes*. New York: Franklin Watts, 1965.

Mother Goose lives again through the free, impressionistic artwork of Mr. Wildsmith. (Remember, not all of Mother Goose is edifying!) Full color. Ages 2 (and under)-6.

Wright, Blanche F. *The Real Mother Goose*. Chicago: Rand McNally & Co., 1944.

Old fashioned, delicate, full-color illustrations. The rhymes are printed in two columns with larger print than most Mother Goose books. It should be noted that not all Mother Goose themes are edifying. First-line index and list of rhymes. Ages 2 (and under)-6. Hardcover.

FANTASY LITERATURE

Alexander, Lloyd, *The King's Fountain*. Illustrated by Ezra J. Keats. New York: E. P. Dutton & Co., 1971.

A piece of literature in the form, flavor and setting of Hebrew parables. As a father is forced into action to save his family and neighbors, he discovers resources he never suspected were his. A skillfully written story rich in imagery, e.g. ". . . the merchants whose words were smooth as pearls and who could string them together endlessly." The illustrations, reproduced from the original acrylics on canvas, convey a surprising degree of texture. Full color. Ages 7-9. Hardcover.

Anno, Mitsumasa. *Topsy-Turvies: Pictures to Stretch the Imagination*. New York: John Weatherhill, 1970.

This wordless wonder mildly jars one's sensibilities through optical illusions and mind-boggling scenes. Great fun for children to study and inject their own meanings. The author has a new book, *Upside-Downers*, with more pictures to ponder and text—some of which is written right side up and some upside down. Full color. Ages 4-9. Hardcover.

Barrett, Judith. *Animals Should Definitely Not Wear Clothing*. Illustrated by Ron Barrett. New York: Atheneum Pubs., 1970.

Simple, humorous illustrations show why each particular animal should not wear clothing. The littlest children enjoy this imaginative spoof. Color. Ages 2-5. Hardcover, soft-cover.

Barton, Byron. *Applebet Story*. New York: Viking Press, 1973.

An amazing sequence of improbable events caused by an apple's being blown off a tree and bouncing through the city—and bouncing through the alphabet! Clever. No text—just one word, in lower case, for each highlighted capital letter. Black and white except for the red apple. Action figures. Ages 4-6. Hardcover, soft-cover.

———. *Buzz, Buzz, Buzz*. New York: Macmillan Publishing Co., 1973.

The stupidity of displaced anger rings loud and clear in this hilarious tale of an ill-will cycle, starting with a bee who stings a bull. Super funny. Bold, bring full color. Excellent. Ages 3-6. Hardcover.

Berenstain, Stanley and Janice. *Bears on Wheels*. New York: Random House, 1969.

Zany fantasy figures and rhyming words teach number and ratio concepts. Children really enjoy this funny book.

Full color. Ages 4-7. Hardcover.

———.*Inside, Outside, Upside Down*. New York: Random House, 1968.
Fantasy figures on white space illustrate basic concepts of "in," "out," and other direction words. Funny rhyming text. Full color. Ages 2½-6. Hardcover.

———. *Old Hat, New Hat*. New York: Random House, 1970.
Many different qualities of hats are described in the rhyming tale of a choosy customer. Another child-pleasing book from this Bright & Early Series. (This book and the two above by the same authors are done in a style similar to the Dr. Seuss books, which are also in the Bright & Early Series.) Fantasy figures on white space. Full color. Ages 2½-6.

Birnbaum, A. *Green Eyes*. New York: Western Publishing Co., 1973.
Through the seasons as seen from a cat's perspective. Large and bold, bright and simple, full-color illustrations. Ages 3½-6. Hardcover.

Blue Eagle, Acee. *Echogee*. Palmco Investment Corporation, 1971.
An Indian folk tale of a little deer who believes that he is ready for the big world. Exquisite art work in American Indian form, with an uncluttered simplicity reminiscent of Japanese flower arrangements. Soft, restrained use of full color conveys a feeling of tenderness. Printed on rich, thick paper. Ages 6-8.

Brown, Margaret W. *Home for a Bunny*. Illustrated by Garth Williams. New York: Western Publishing Co., 1972.
It is springtime when bunny goes looking for a home. As he searches he finds many animal friends and investigates their habitats. Ms. Brown weaves words to roll off the

reader's tongue. Large, soft and simple full-color pictures. Large print. Excellent. Ages 2½-6. Hardcover.

————. *The Little Fur Family*. Illustrated by Garth Williams. New York: Harper & Row Pubs., 1968.

Poetic form weaves the warm cozy tale of an animal family's everyday routine and their offspring's adventures discovering, but not harming, nature. Full-color, rather dainty pictures. Ages 2-6. Hardcover.

Burningham, John. *Mr. Gumpy's Outing*. New York: Holt, Rinehart & Winston, 1971.

Mr. Gumpy agrees to let children and creatures ride with him in his boat if they comply with certain restrictions—to which they all readily assent. But their resolutions do not last the journey, and they accidentally capsize the boat. The happy result is unexpected. Crosshatched colored lines with much white space peeking out and the subdued use of full color also make this book memorable. Large print. Ages 3-6. Hardcover.

Burroway, Janet. *The Truck on the Track*. Illustrated by John Vernon Lord. New York: Bobbs-Merrill Co., 1970.

An outrageous story of a sheik and his odd assortment of passengers who try in vain to urge and tug their stuck truck off a railroad track. The tongue-twisting words add to the confusion of this misadventure. The exquisitely detailed, wildly imaginative, hilariously funny full-color illustrations keep children (and adults!) happily fascinated. Excellent. Ages 4½-9. Hardcover.

Cameron, Polly. *"I Can't" Said the Ant: A Second Book of Nonsense*. New York: Coward, McCann & Geoghegan, 1961.

Our hero, the ant, was taking a walk when he spied the teapot lying broken on the floor. The teapot's explanation of the accident is attended by the occupants of the kitchen:

"Teapot fell," said the dinner bell.
"Teapot broke," said the artichoke.
"She went kerplop!" said the mop.
"Is she dead?" asked the bread.
"Just a break," said the steak.
For the climactic details of the dramatic rescue, read the book! Besides pure entertainment, this text increases children's awareness of the individual phoneme sounds. The text is punctuated by small red line drawings and occasional full-page red line illustrations on white space. Ages 4-8. Hardcover.

Carle, Eric. *Do You Want to Be My Friend?* New York: Thomas Y. Crowell Co., 1971.
The hero of the story is an engaging little mouse who looks for and finally finds a friend. A book with words on only the first and last pages. Bright, full-color, painted collage illustrations lead the pre-reader to supply his own text as he moves from left to right. *A Very Long Tail: A Folding Book* (soft-cover), by the same author, is based on this work. Ages 2 (and under)-5. Hardcover.

————. *Have You Seen My Cat?* New York: Franklin Watts, 1973.
A boy goes on a worldwide search looking for his cat (which he finally finds) and encounters cats of other types—like leopards and tigers! Full color, painted paper collage. Ages 2-6. Hardcover.

————. *The Rooster Who Set Out to See the World*. New York: Franklin Watts, 1972.
As the rooster talks up his travel plans, he gathers other creatures to join him on his trip. But as night falls they desert him, one kind at a time. Reinforces number concepts one to five. One of the children's all time favorites. Full-color brilliant pictures. Ages 3-6. Hardcover.

Dennis, Wesley. *Flip and the Morning*. New York: Viking Press, 1951.

The dramatic use of line makes the crisp, black-and-white realistic pencil sketches an excellent vehicle for projecting the reader into a colt's early morning adventure. Ages 4-6. Hardcover, soft-cover.

Disney, Walt. *Bambi*. Based on an original story by Felix Salten. A Golden Press Book, Western Publishing Company, 1965.

A sensitive story of a young fawn and his life in the woods. More text than most books in this bibliography. Large size pages with many full page pictures. Full color. Beautiful! Ages 4½-8.

Elzbieta. *Little Mops and the Butterfly*. New York: Doubleday & Co., 1974.

Whimsical outlines dramatically set on white space tell, without words, the humorous story of a traveling bear-like creature who learns the secret of the butterfly. A rich experience for the child as he enters into the magical, fleeting mood of this wonder of nature. Also by Elzbieta, more wordless books: *Little Mops and the Moon* (1974), and *Little Mops at the Seashore* (1974). Ages 4-6. Hardcover.

Ets, Marie H. *Play with Me*. New York: Viking Press, 1955.

A little girl tells of a special early morning experience when she learned to sit so still that the shy animals finally came to her. Ages 2 (and under)-6. Hardcover, soft-cover.

Flack, Marjorie. *The Story About Ping*. Illustrated by Kurt Wiese. New York: Viking Press, 1933.

Ping is a duck who lives with his large family on a Chinese junk on the Yangtze River. Every time the ducks board their boat for the night, the last duck on gets a spank. To avoid the spank, Ping trys very hard to be punctual.

However one day, to his horror, he sees he can't avoid being last—what can he do? Ping's decision leads to a scary adventure, an important lesson, and a happy ending. Full-color chalk illustrations. Ages 3-5. Hardcover, softcover.

Gag, Wanda. *The A B C Bunny*. New York: Coward-McCann, 1933.
Follow a bunny in rhyme through the alphabet. This Newberry Award winning book is actually a story. Lithographs and hand lettering in black and white, except for the capital letter being highlighted. Music included. Ages 2 (and under)-4. Hardcover.

————. *Millions of Cats*. New York: Coward-McCann, 1938.
An old man tries to find a cat to keep him and his wife company. He can't decide which one to choose and ends up, for a short time at least, with millions of cats! Children readily identify with the difficulty in making choices. Black and white. Ages 2½-5. Hardcover.

Ginsburg, Mirra. *The Chick and the Duckling*. Illustrated by Jose Aruego. New York: Macmillan Publishing Co., 1972.
The traditional story of the look-alike yellow fuzzies and their discovery of their different abilities. The light-hearted artwork has a joyous springtime flavor. Large print. Full color. Ages 2½-5. Hardcover.

Hildebrandt, Greg and Tim. *How Do They Build It?* Bronx, NY: Platt & Munk Pubs., 1974.
Animal crews construct ships, buildings, airplanes, dams, etc. Full color. Ninety-six large pages. Ages 4½-8. Hardcover.

Hutchins, Pat. *Changes, Changes*. New York: Macmillan Publishing Co., 1971.

A wordless, full-color book about two wooden dolls who continually rearrange their unit blocks to form different items. Interesting. Ages 2-6. Hardcover.

————.*The Surprise Party*. New York: Macmillan Publishing Co., 1969.
A rabbit invites a friend to a party and tells him to pass the invitation on but the message is, alas, continually distorted. Color. Ages 3½-6. Hardcover.

————. *The Wind Blew*. New York: Macmillan Publishing Co., 1974.
A witty tale of a wind which whips up objects on its way through town. But happily, before it blows out to sea it drops all the objects on the ruffled, wind-chasing crowd below. Illustrated with lively people and a bit of the town. Full color. Ages 4-7. Hardcover.

Keats, Ezra J. *Kitten for a Day*. New York: Franklin Watts, 1974.
This delightful, almost wordless book describes a puppy's experiences with a litter of friendly kittens. The full-color artwork is very warm and simple—just right for wee ones. Large print. Excellent. Ages 2½-5. Hardcover.

Kraus, Robert. *Herman the Helper*. Illustrated by Jose Aruego and Ariane Dewey. New York: E.P. Dutton & Co., 1974.
Herman, the green octopus, spends his time and superabundant energy helping absolutely everyone under the psychedelic sea. Very full color. Ages 4½-7. Hardcover.

————. *Leo the Late Bloomer*. Illustrated by Aruego, Jose. New York: E.P. Dutton & Co., 1973.
The almost psychedelic artwork lightens the anxious

theme: "Will Leo (pictured as a lion) *ever* bloom?" (Everyone else can read, write, talk, and eat properly.) His father is anxious; his mother, calm. Leo is sad—very sad. But one day he blooms! His first relieved words are: "I made it!" Ages 4-6. Soft-cover.

―――. *Milton the Early Riser*. Illustrated by Jose Aruego and Ariane Aruego. New York: E.P. Dutton & Co., 1972.
An early rising panda seeks company, but everyone else is asleep. Then a fantastic wind blows an unexpected twist into the story. Bright, cheery, full-color illustrations. Ages 5-6. Hardcover.

Krauss, Ruth. *Bears*. Illustrated by Phyllis Rowand. New York: Harper & Row Pubs., 1948.
Bears, bears, bears everywhere, doing many unbearlike things. Short, rhyming text in large cursive script. Two-color. Ages 2 (and under)-4. Hardcover.

―――. *The Carrot Seed*. Illustrated by Crockett Johnson. New York: Harper & Row Pubs., 1945.
This little book, about a boy who plants a carrot seed and faithfully tends it and waits for the carrot to grow, is a real child-pleaser. Clear, simple, mostly two-color pictures. Excellent. Ages 2 (and under)-6. Hardcover.

―――. *The Happy Day*. Illustrated by Marc Simont. New York: Harper & Row Pubs., 1949.
It is a snowy, wintry kind of day in the forest and the animals are all curled up asleep. Suddenly a fresh aroma fills the air and stirs them into action. One by one, the animals awake and follow the scent to its source—the first flower of spring. In soft greys and white except for a single yellow flower. Ages 2½-6. Hardcover.

Kruss, James. *Three by Three*. Illustrated by Eva J. Rubin;

translated by Geoffrey Strachan. New York: Macmillan Publishing Co., 1965.

One day in the life of three foxes, three chickens, three mice, three cats, three dogs, and three men. Full color. Ages 2½-5. Hardcover, soft-cover.

Leaf, Munro. *The Story of Ferdinand*. Illustrated by Robert Lawson. New York: Viking Press, 1964.

The old favorite story of the peaceful, flower-sniffing bull has been republished. Marvelously funny black-and-white sketches. Also by Leaf and Lawson: *Wee Gillis*. Ages 4½-8. Hardcover, soft-cover.

Le Sieg, Theodore. *Ten Apples Up on Top*. Illustrated by Roy McKie. New York: Beginner Books, 1961.

A zany, rhythmic text with madcap animals trying to balance more and more apples on their heads. Similar to the Dr. Seuss books. A real child-pleaser. Color. Ages 3-6. Hardcover.

Lionni, Leo. *The Biggest House in the World*. New York: Pantheon Books, 1968.

A snail, not satisfied with the normal-size house on his back, puts his whole life into enlarging and embellishing his shell. When it comes time to find more food he tries to move but finds his house is so large that he cannot. Thus he dies and his proud house crumples away. Full color. Large illustrations. Ages 4½-7. Hardcover.

———. *Fish Is Fish*. New York: Pantheon Books, 1970.

A friendship between a tadpole and a fish is interrupted when the tadpole changes into a frog. But the frog returns to the pond to tell his fish friend of all the terrestial wonders he has observed. The fish, astonished by these words, must see for himself. But as he nearly dies trying, he concludes such knowledge is not for him, for "fish is fish." Exquisitely done full-color illustrations. Ages 5-7. Hardcover, soft-cover.

————. *Frederick*. New York: Pantheon Books, 1966.
All the mice work hard gathering physical supplies for the coming winter. All except Frederick, who explains: "I gather colors . . . for winter is gray." Later, when things do indeed become winter dull, the family huddles around Frederick who recites original poetry to refresh their souls. Full-color illustrations. Ages 5-7. Hardcover.

————. *Swimmy*. New York: Pantheon Books, 1963.
An underwater tale of one little black fish who organizes his friends, the little red fishes, for protection against the larger fish. Whimsical text: "An eel whose tail was almost too far away to remember. . . ." Done with multilayered, full-color pastel prints and other techniques. Also by Lionni: *Inch by Inch* (1962) and *The Greentail Mouse* (1973). Ages 4½-7. Hardcover.

MacDonald, Golden (Margaret W. Brown). *The Little Island*. Illustrated by Leonard Weisgard. New York: Doubleday & Co., 1971.
A Caldecott Award-winning picture-story of an island personified, and a kitten who visits it. Elegantly written.
> Winter came
> and the snow fell softly
> like a great quiet secret in the night
> cold and still.

Children love it! Full-color illustrations. Excellent. Ages 4½-8. Hardcover, soft-cover.

————. *Little Lost Lamb*. Illustrated by Leonard Weisgard. New York: Doubleday & Co., 1945.
The story is based on the Biblical parable of the shepherd and the lost lamb. In this book the shepherd is a conscientious young boy. Full color. Ages 5-9. Hardcover.

Mahy, Margaret. *Rooms for Rent*. Illustrated by Jenny Williams. New York: Franklin Watts, 1974.

A delightfully written tale of a man "bitter as medicine" who rents rooms to an odd array of unlikely tenants. Their love and compatibility break through to the old man and he finds he wants to share in their happiness. Beautiful full-color illustrations on heavy, textured paper. Excellent. Ages 5-9. Hardcover.

Moss, Jeffrey. *People in My Family*. Illustrated by Leon Jason Studios. New York: Western Publishing Co., 1976.

Two families—one of five "normal" people and one of five friendly monsters—romp through this book designed to reinforce counting skills. Full color. Ages 2½-6. Hardcover.

Munari, Bruno. *The Circus in the Mist*. Cleveland: Collins, William, & World Publishing Co., 1975.

Before we get to the circus we must go through the mist. After we arrive, our visit is narrated by the very coy artist-author. Then it is back out into the mist again. Colored and semitransparent paper make reading this book an unusual experience. Ages 3½-7. Hardcover.

Oppenheim, Joanne. *On the Other Side of the River*. Illustrated by Aliki. New York: Franklin Watts, 1972.

Villagers from two villages separated by a river do not get along. The bridge breaks and everyone is relieved! But it's not long before they realize their need for one another and rebuild the bridge and live happily ever after. Fun artwork. Full color. Ages 3½-7. Hardcover.

Oxenbury, Helen. *Helen Oxenbury's ABC of Things*. New York: Franklin Watts, 1972.

Humorous, unlikely matches of animals and familiar things illustrate initial-letter sounds. No text, just words. Large print. Upper- and lower-case letters. Full-color pastel and ink illustrations. Ages 3½-6. Hardcover.

Peppe, Rodney. *The House That Jack Built*. Illustrated by Rodney Peppe. New York: Delacorte Press, 1970.
   An old favorite from Mother Goose all dressed up in colorful collage. Ages 3½-6. Hardcover.

Piper, Watty. *The Little Engine That Could*. New ed. Bronx, NY: Platt & Munk Pubs., 1976.
   An age-old tale illustrating the "good Samaritan" and "positive thinking" approaches to problems. Happy, bright full-color pictures. Ages 3-6. Hardcover.

Potter, Marian. *The Little Red Caboose*. Illustrated by Tibor Gergely. New York: Western Publishing Co., 1953.
   The little red caboose puts on its brakes and saves the train. Large action-packed panoramic pictures. A longtime favorite. Full color. Ages 3-6. Hardcover.

Ringi, Kjell. *The Sun and the Cloud*. New York: Harper & Row Pubs., 1971.
   The sun states its claims to fame only to be covered by a cloud who states his own claims. The argument that ensues is stopped by a tiny plant who declares that he needs them both, and then proceeds to grow into a gigantic bouquet. Charmingly simple, abstract designs in full color. Ages 2½-6. Hardcover.

Ryan, Cheli D. *Hildilid's Night*. Illustrated by Arnold Lobel. New York: Macmillan Publishing Co., 1971.
   Hildilid is an old lady who hates the night and spends all night trying to wipe it away. Day comes but she is too tired to enjoy it, and must rest up for her recurring battle with the dark. A rather subtle moral for little ones, but could be useful. Black and white are used for the night pictures, and two colors for the day pictures. Ages 4-7. Hardcover, soft-cover.

Sandburg, Carl. *The Wedding Procession of the Rag Doll and the Broom Handle and Who Was in It*. Illustrated by Harriett Pincus. New York: Harcourt Brace Jovanovich, 1967.

This tale of outlandish nonsense is irresistible because of its rich imagery, repetitive lines, and superb use of the English language. Some full-color, some two-color illustrations. Ages 4-7.

Seuss, Dr. (Geisel, Theodor). *Dr. Seuss's Sleep Book*. New York: Random House, 1962.

A "still of the night" sleep report on all the creatures who are asleep, and their sleeping habits. An invitation for children to join the "ninety-nine zillion, nine trillion and two creatures" who are already asleep. Full color. Ages 4-8. Hardcover.

———. *The Foot Book*. New York: Random House, 1968.

The bouncy, rhyming text (considerably simpler than other books by Dr. Seuss listed in this bibliography) is designed to illustrate basic directional words and to encourage a bit of reading. Full color. Ages 2½-6. Hardcover.

———. *Green Eggs and Ham*. New York: Beginner Books, 1960.

Lively, but not lovely, fantasy characters romp across the pages of another of Dr. Seuss's child-pleasing books. Dr. Seuss has a distinctive writing style which has kept him on the best-selling children's list for years. Color. Ages 4-7. Hardcover.

———. *The Lorax*. New York: Random House, 1971. A fantasy with an ecological message written in Dr. Seuss's inimitable style:

I am the Lorax. I speak for the trees.
I speak for the trees for the trees

have no tongues.
And I'm asking you, sir, at the top
of my lungs— . . .
Full color. Excellent. Ages 6-9. Hardcover.

————. *Mister Brown Can Moo! Can You?* New York:
Ramdom House, 1970.
Clever Mr. Brown makes and imitates common sounds—
like knocking on a door, and imaginative sounds—like a
hippopotamus chewing gum. A very exciting participation
book for little children. Full color. Ages 3-6. Hardcover.

Smith, Kay. *Parakeets and Peach Pies*. Illustrated by Jose
Aruego. New York: Parents Magazine Press, 1970.
Feminists may not enjoy this book but children certainly
do. The story is about a boy who wants to ask his mother a
question, but first his mother has one for him. It seems his
uncaged pets caused quite an uproar at the ladies' luncheon.
For the outcome of this hilarious tale, read the book! Full
color. Ages 2½-6. Hardcover.

Tolstoy, Alexei. *The Great Big Enormous Turnip*.
Illustrated by Helen Oxenbury. New York: Franklin Watts,
1969.
A turnip grows so large that it takes the old man, his wife,
their granddaughter, the dog, cat, and mouse all pulling
together to unearth it. Helen Oxenbury's detailed full-color
illustrations embellish this zany tale. Ages 2½-6.
Hardcover.

Tymms, Jean. *The Me Book*. Illustrated by Tibor Gergely.
New York: Western Publishing Co., 1974.
The functions of various parts of the body, and children's
activities, are shown with cartoon animals. Full color. Slick
cardboard pages. Ages 2-6. Hardcover.

Wagner, Ken. *The One Word Storybook*. New York:

Western Publishing Co., 1968, Library edition only.

Clever stories of animals told in pictures, with only one word of text per picture. All the words in each story rhyme. Good for teaching picture reading and rhyming words. Large print. Large pages. Bold, bright full color. Ages 3-6.

Watson, Aldren. *Where Everyday Things Come From*. Bronx, NY: Platt & Munk Pubs., 1974.

Various creatures operate machines which produce household articles. This ninety-six-page full-color book is best read to children individually, one chapter at a time. Ages 4½-8. Hardcover.

Wiest, Robert and Claire. *Down the River Without a Paddle*. Chicago: Childrens Press, 1973.

A wonderfully simple text about a caterpillar who, when swept off his breakfast leaf and into the river, becomes disoriented but lives to become a butterfly. Large print. Exquisite, soft, shimmering full-color pictures done on wet paper with paint and ink. Ages 3-7. Hardcover.

Wildsmith, Brian. *The Owl and the Woodpecker*. New York: Franklin Watts, 1972.

The owl and the woodpecker annoy each other until a storm comes and one finds himself helping the other. More of Brian Wildsmith's fabulous full-color artwork. Ages 3-6. Hardcover.

Ylla. *The Little Elephant*. Photos by Ylla. New York: Harper & Row Pubs., 1956.

Pictorial essay of a baby elephant and its mother in their natural habitat. Eventually the elephant and its family are chosen for a royal procession. The text is a bit long and may need to be given free oral interpretation rather than be read word for word to young children. The black-and-white photos are very interesting to youngsters. Ages 3½-7. Hardcover.

Ylla, photos by. *The Duck*. Margaret W. Brown. New York: Harper & Row Pubs., 1953.

Children are intrigued by the black-and-white photos of a duck and various other animals met by the duck at the zoo. The story is too long for small children; perhaps a modified oral interpretation could be given instead. Ages 3½-7. Hardcover.

————. photos by. *The Sleepy Little Lion*. Margaret W. Brown. New York: Harper & Row Pubs., 1947.

Another black-and-white photo essay of animals by Ylla. This one's about a lion cub who can't seem to stay awake. The text is simple and printed in fairly large size. Other books by Ylla, which have more advanced text but whose photographs delight children, are: *Animal Babies*, *Listen*, *Listen*, and *Two Little Bears*. Ages 2½-7. Hardcover.

OTHER

Brown, Margaret W. *The Dead Bird*. Illustrated by Remy Charlip. New York: Addison-Wesley Publishing Co., 1958.

Children confront death in a realistic manner. After they bury the bird and give it a proper funeral, they pass on to other things and leave death to itself. Vivid, full color. The hues are restricted to carry the mood. Ages 4-7. Hardcover.

Carle, Eric. *The Secret Birthday Message*. New York: Thomas Y. Crowell Co., 1972.

A boy receives a birthday message which he must decode and obey to find his gift. Cleverly done with half pages that let the reader hunt along with the boy. In the end, the boy finds his gift and the reader finds a map which gets the cryptic code together. Lively color collage. Ages 4-7. Hardcover.

Cunningham, Aline. *My House*. St. Louis: Concordia Publishing House, 1973.

Different types of housing discussed—for God, for

humans, and for creatures. Full-color illustrations on white space. Ages 2-6. Soft-cover.

Dunn, Judy. *Things*. Photos by Phoebe and Tris Dunn. New York: Doubleday & Co., 1968.

Exquisite, full-color photographs of young children exploring the world about them. Accompanied by rhyming text:

> Trees hide lots of secret homes
> Way inside their bark;
> But every time I look inside—
> All I see is dark.

Excellent. Ages 2-6. Hardcover.

Hautzig, Esther. *In the Park: An Excursion in Four Languages*. Illustrated by Ezra J. Keats. New York: Macmillan Publishing Co., 1968.

For a change of pace that children enjoy, this book offers words for familiar park objects and activities in English, French, Spanish, and Russian, with additional words and the Russian alphabet at the back. Full color. There is a series of these books, but this one is more suited to young children than are the others. Ages 4½-8. Hardcover.

Klein, Gerda. *The Blue Rose*. Photos by Norma Holt. Westport, CT: Lawrence Hill & Co., 1974.

Though not necessarily written for smaller children, this book can help a child understand and have compassion for mentally handicapped youngsters. Black-and-white photos of a little girl. Age 7-up. Hardcover, soft-cover.

Martin, Dick. *The Sand Pail Book*. New York: Western Publishing Co., Inc., 1964. Library edition only.

A book about the various types of containers and their uses. Full color. Ages 2 (and under)-5.

Parker, Bertha M. *The New Golden Dictionary*. Illustrated

by Aurelius Battaglia. New York: Western Publishing Co., 1972.

An excellent first picture-word dictionary in full color. Both forms of a letter appear at the top of each page with the full alphabet in gray at the bottom. The letter, with which the words on any given page start, is highlighted by red in the all-gray alphabet. This device provides auto-instruction in sequencing. Verb roots and verb derivations are given. Over seventeen hundred entries and two thousand pictures. With subtle help from an enthusiastic adult, children can be taught to enjoy dictionary researching. Ages 5-8 (depending on prior reading instruction). Hardcover.

Rothman, Joel. *Night Lights*. Illustrated by Joe Lasker. Chicago: Albert Whitman & Co., 1972.

Night lights shimmer, glare, glitter, pierce, dazzle, flash, burst, flicker, and shine as they help, assist, follow, signal, brighten, decorate, mark, and direct people through the night. Half of the fine illustrations are in full color. Ages 3½-7. Hardcover.

Wright, Betty R. *I Want to Read!* Illustrated by Aliki. New York: Western Publishing Co.,1965.

Motivation to want to read is encouraged by this book's enticing comments and effective use of signs, cards, and everyday events. Full color. Ages 4-7. Hardcover.

V. PUBLISHER DIRECTORY

The addresses of publishers mentioned here are correct as reported in *Books in Print 1976* and *Children's Books in Print 1975*. Publishers frequently change names and addresses, merge, and go in and out of business. Therefore, when trying to locate a book it is sometimes easier to deal with a book distributor (jobber), for they keep pace with the changing status of publishers. One such distributor is Melton Book Company, 111 Leslie Street, Dallas, Texas 75207 Phone: (214) 748-0564.

Some large publishing concerns have offices in several major cities. With most companies, you may place your order by telephone. Often, they will have a stock of books on hand—especially if they are recent publications—and can send your order right out.

Abingdon Press, 201 Eighth Ave., S., Nashville, TN 37202

Addison-Wesley Publishing Co., Inc., Jacob Way, Reading, MA 01867

American Heritage Press (see McGraw-Hill)

Anchor (see Doubleday)

Appleton-Century-Crofts (see Prentice-Hall)

Atheneum Publishers, 122 E. 42nd St., New York, NY 10017

Aurora Publishers, Inc., 118 16th Ave. S., Nashville, TN 37203

Avon Books, 959 Eighth Ave., New York, NY 10019

Baker Book House, 1019 Wealthy St., S.E., Grand Rapids, MI 49506

Ballantine Books, Inc., Div. of Random House

Basic Books, Inc., 10 E. 53rd St., New York, NY 10022

Batsford, B. T. Ltd., 4 Fitzhardinge St., London W 1, England

Beacon Press, Inc., 25 Beacon St., Boston, MA 02108

Beginner Books, Div. of Random House

Bentley, Robert, Inc., 872 Massachusetts Ave., Cambridge, MA 02139

Bobbs-Merrill Company, Inc., Subs. of Howard W. Sams & Company, 4 W. 58th St., New York, NY 10019

Bowmar Publishing Co., 4563 Colorado Blvd., Los Angeles, CA 90039

Bradbury Press (dist. by E. P. Dutton)

Brunner/Mazel, Inc., 64 University Pl., New York, NY 10003

Burgess Publishing Co., 7108 Ohms Lane, Minneapolis, MN 55435 (dist. by J. A. Majors Co., P.O. Box 47552, Dallas, TX 75247)

Carolrhoda Books, Inc., 241 First Ave., N., Minneapolis, MN 55401

Child Evangelism Fellowship Press, Box 1156, Grand Rapids, MI 49501

Childrens Press, Inc., 1224 W. Van Buren St., Chicago, IL 60607

CLC Press, affiliated with John Knox Press, 341 Ponce de Leon Ave., N.E., Atlanta, GA 30308

Collier Books, Subs. of Macmillan

Collins, William, & World Publishing Co., Inc., 2080 W. 117th St., Cleveland, OH 44111

Concordia Publishing House, 3558 S. Jefferson Ave., St. Louis, MO 63118

Cook, David C., Publishing Co., 850 N. Grove Ave., Elgin, IL 60120

Coward, McCann & Geoghegan, Inc., (formerly McCann Coward, Coward-McCann, Inc., & Coward McCann), 200 Madison Ave., New York, NY 10016

Crowell, Thomas Y., Co., 666 Fifth Ave., New York, NY 10019

Crowell Collier & Macmillan (see Macmillan)

Dallas Public Library, 1954 Commerce St., Dallas, TX 75202

Day Care & Child Development Council of America, Inc., 1012 14th St., N.W., Suite 1104, Washington, DC 20005

Dean & Sons, 41/43 Ludgate Hill, London EC 4, England

Delacorte Press (dist. by Dial Press)

Dell Publishing Co., Inc., 1 Dag Hammarskjold Plaza, 245 E. 47th St., New York, NY 10017

Dial Press, 1 Dag Hammarskjold Plaza, 245 E. 47th St., New York, NY 10017

Discus Books (see Avon)

Doubleday & Co., Inc., 245 Park Ave., New York, NY 10017

Dutton, E.P., & Co., Inc., 201 Park Ave. S., New York, NY 10003

Farrar, Straus & Giroux, Inc., 19 Union Square W., New York, NY 10003

Fideler Co., 31 Ottawa Ave., N.W., Grand Rapids, MI 49502

Fides Publishers, Inc., P.O. Box F, Notre Dame, IN 46556

Four Winds Press (see Scholastic Book Services)

G/L Pubs. (see Gospel Light)

Gibson, C. R., Co., Knight St., Norwalk, CT 06856

Ginn & Co., a Xerox Education Co., 191 Spring St., Lexington, MA 02173

Golden Press (see Western)

Gospel Light Pubs., 110 W. Broadway, Glendale, CA 91204

Grosset & Dunlap, Inc., 51 Madison Ave., New York, NY 10010

Group for Environmental Education, 1214 Arch St., Philadelphia, PA 19107

Hale, E. M., & Co., 128 W. River St., Chippewa Falls, WI 54729

Harcourt Brace Jovanovich, Inc. (formerly Harcourt Brace

& World; Harcourt Brace & Co.), 757 Third Ave., New York, NY 10017

Harper & Row Publishers, Inc., 10 E. 53rd St., New York, NY 10022

Harper Brothers (see Harper & Row)

Hart Publishing Co., 15 W. 4th St., New York, NY 10012

Harvey House, Inc., Publishers (see E. M. Hale)

Hastings House Publishers, Inc., 10 E. 40th St., New York, NY 10016

Hawthorn Books, Inc., 260 Madison Ave., New York, NY 10016

Hill, Lawrence, & Co., Inc., 24 Burr Farms Rd., Westport, CT 06880

Hill & Wang, Inc., Div. of Farrar, Straus & Giroux

Holt, Rinehart & Winston, Inc., 383 Madison Ave., New York, NY 10017

Houghton Mifflin Co., 2 Park St., Boston, MA 02107; 551 Fifth Ave., New York, NY 10017

Intext Publishers Group, Subs. of International Textbook Co., 257 Park Ave. S., New York, NY 10010

John Day Co., Inc., 666 Fifth Ave., New York, NY 10019

Knopf, Alfred A., Inc., Subs. of Random House

Lane Publishing Co., Willow & Middlefield Rds., Menlo Park, CA 94025

Lerner Pubs. Co., 241 First Ave. N., Minneapolis, MN 55401

Lippincott, J. B., Co., E. Washington Sq., Philadelphia, PA 19105

Little, Brown & Co., 34 Beacon St., Boston, MA 02106

Logos International, 201 Church St., Plainfield, NJ 07060

Lothrop, Lee & Shepard Co., Div. of William Morrow

McCall Books (see E. P. Dutton)
McCall Publishing Co., (see E. P. Dutton)
Macdonald & Company, Ltd., St. Giles House, 49-50 Poland St., London W1, England
McGraw-Hill Book Co., 1221 Ave. of the Americas, New York, NY 10036
McKay, David, Co., Inc., 750 Third Ave., New York, NY 10017
Macmillan Publishing Co., Inc., 866 Third Ave., New York, NY 10022
Maranatha Evanglical Assn. of Calvary Chapel, P.O. Box 1498, Costa Mesa, CA 92626
Mentor Books (see New American Library)
Montessori Workshop, 501 Salem Dr., Ithaca, NY 14850
Moody Press, 820 N. LaSalle St., Chicago, IL 60610
Morrow, Williams, & Co., Inc., 105 Madison Ave., New York, NY 10016

Nash Publishing Corp., 1 Dupont St., Plainview, NY 11803
National Geographic Society, 17 "M" St., N.W., Washington, DC 20036
New American Library, 1301 Ave. of the Americas, New York, NY 10019

Orion Press (see Viking)

Palmco Investment Corporation, 4411 First National Bank Bldg., Dallas, TX 75202
Pantheon Books, Div. of Random House
Parents Magazine Press, 52 Vanderbilt Ave., New York, NY 10017
Penguin Books, Inc., 625 Madison Ave., New York, NY 10022

Platt & Munk Publishers, Div. of Questor Educational Products, 1055 Bronx River Ave., Bronx, NY 10472

Prentice-Hall, Inc., Englewood Cliffs, NJ 07632

Putnam's, G. P., Sons, 200 Madison Ave., New York, NY 10016

RCA (Radio Corp. of America), RCA Educational Programs, Rte. 38 E. of Haddonfield Rd., Bldg. 204-1, Cherry Hill, NJ 08108

Rand, McNally & Co., P.O. Box 7600, Chicago, IL 60680

Random House, Inc., 201 E. 50th St., New York, NY 10022

Regal Books, Div. of G/L Pubns., P.O. Box 1591, Glendale, CA 91209

Regnery, Henry, Co., 180 N. Michigan Ave., Chicago, IL 60601

Revell, Fleming H., Co., 184 Central Ave., Old Tappan, NJ 07675

Ritchie, Ward, Press, 474 S. Arroyo Pkwy., Pasadena, CA 91105

Ronald Press Co., 79 Madison Ave., New York, NY 10016

Running Press, 38 S. 19th St., Philadelphia, PA 19103

Salisbury, Gordon, Box 1075, Ventura, CA 93001

Schocken Books, Inc., 200 Madison Ave., New York, NY 10016

Scholastic Book Services, Div. of Scholastic Magazines, 50 W. 44th St., New York, NY 10036

Scott, Foresman & Co., 1900 E. Lake Ave., Glenview, IL 60025

Scott Publishing Co. (formerly William R. Scott, Inc.), 604 Fifth Ave., New York, NY 10020

Scribner's, Charles, Sons, 597 Fifth Ave., New York, NY 10017

Scripture Press, Pubs., Inc., 1825 College Ave., Wheaton,

IL 60187

Scroll Press, 129 E. 94th St., New York, NY 10028

Simon & Schuster, Inc., 630 Fifth Ave., New York, NY 10020

Standard Publishing Co., 8121 Hamilton Ave., Cincinnati, OH 45231

Sunset Books (see Lane)

Taylor Publishing Co., Newsfoto Education Div., Box 1392, San Angelo, TX 76901

Tyndale House Publishers, 336 Gundersen Dr., Wheaton, IL 60187

Van Nostrand Reinhold Co., Div. of Litton Educational Publishing, Inc., 450 W. 33rd St., New York, NY 10001

Vanguard Press, Inc., 424 Madison Ave., New York, NY 10017

Viking Press, Inc., 625 Madison Ave., New York, NY 10022

Walck, Henry Z., Inc., Div. of David McKay

Walker & Co., 720 Fifth Ave., New York, NY 10019

Watts, Franklin, Inc., Subs. of Grolier Inc., 845 Third Ave., New York, NY 10022

Weatherhill, John, Inc., 149 Madison Ave., New York, NY 10016

Western Publishing Co., Inc., 850 Third Ave., New York, NY 10022

Whitman, Albert, & Co., 560 W. Lake St., Chicago, IL 60606

Wilson, H. W., 950 University Ave., Bronx, NY 10452

Windmill Books, Inc., an Intext Publisher

Word Books, Inc., Publisher, 4800 W. Waco Dr., Waco, TX 76703

World Distributors (Manchester) Ltd., Box 111, 12 Lever

St., Manchester, M60 1TS England
World Publishing Company (see Collins, William, & World)

Young Scott Books (see Addison-Wesley)

Zondervan Publishing House, 1415 Lake Dr., S.E., Grand
Rapids, MI 49506

INDEX

307

310

313

314